C++ Database Development

2nd edition

Al Stevens

MIS:
PRESS

A Subsidiary of
Henry Holt and Co., Inc.

Second Edition—1994

```
Stevens, Al, 1940-
    C++ database development / Al Stevens. -- 2nd ed.
      p.  cm.
    Includes index.
    ISBN 1-55828-357-9
    1. C++ (Computer program language)   2. Database design.
  3. Object-oriented databases.   4. PARADY.   I. Title.
  QA76.73.C153S72    1995
  005.75--dc20                                        9436834
                                                         CIP
```

Printed in the United States of America.

10 9 8 7 6 5 4 3 2

Trademarks

Publisher: Brenda McLaughlin
Managing Editor: Cary Sullivan
Development Editor: Debra Williams Cauley
Copy/Tech Editor: Betsy Hardinger
Production Editor: Stephanie Doyle
Assoc. Production Editor: Joseph McPartland

To Katie Margaret Stevens and Jesse Collin Stevens

Contents

Chapter 3: A Brief History of Database Management 27

Chapter 4: C++ and Persistence 41

Chapter 5: Solving the Persistent Object 53

Chapter 6: The Object Database and the Relational Database 63

Chapter 7: Designing an Object Database 77

Chapter 8: PARODY 103

Chapter 9: Using a PARODY Database 135

Chapter 10: PARODY in Applications 157

Appendix A: Building the Software 187

Preface

In 1987, I wrote the first edition of *C Database Development*, a book that describes how to build database software applications with a subset of the relational data model implemented in the C language. That book included the C source code for a database management system and implemented a design approach in which the programmer uses the features of C to define an application's database. In the approach taken by that book, C serves the traditional functions of the data definition and data manipulation languages, which are usually implemented as separate languages in formal DBMSs.

In 1991, after the ANSI X3J11 committee completed the standard definition of C, I wrote a second edition of *C Database Development*, which used the same methods but with Standard C. Both editions of that book continue to be widely read, and programmers throughout the world have used the software in these books to develop many diverse applications. The principle is tried and proven.

The first edition of *C++ Database Development* in 1992 continued that tradition with the C++ programming language and the object-oriented data model—not with a *wrapper* around the old C function library, but instead with a completely new C++ class library called *PARODY* that uses the object-oriented features of C++ to implement what has come to be known as *persistent objects*.

This book is the second edition of *C++ Database Development*. It updates PARODY's source code to incorporate into PARODY II the latest features of C++ as they are being defined by the ANSI X3J16 committee. Those features include templates, exception handling, an improved casting mechanism, and run-time type identification. Although the first two features were defined in the *C++ Annotated Reference Manual* when I wrote the first edition, they were not implemented in the more popular compilers for the PC. The definition of templates has changed significantly since then, and several compilers now implement templates and exception handling. The Borland compilers for MS-DOS and OS/2 implement most of the new features, and, by the time this book reaches publication, so will others.

C++ is still evolving. I am writing this edition in the summer of 1994, and the X3J16 committee is still considering major additions to the language. Its procedures involve publication of a draft standard document to which the programming community at large reacts. The draft is due to be published late this year. The process of public reaction and committee response takes a long time, more so in this case because many C++ language changes have been proposed. Compiler vendors try to keep pace with the evolving draft standard, but this one is a constantly shifting target; the committee is innovating a lot of language changes. The language features that I used for PARODY II reflect the ones that were accepted by the committee in March of this year and that have been implemented by Borland in its MS-DOS and OS/2 compilers. Some of these features can and most likely will change. For example, the first edition of this book used a *String* class that I designed. Since then, the committee has accepted a *string* class that is substantially the same as mine but with some minor differences. Borland implemented the ANSI *string* class in its compilers, and I substituted its class for my own in PARODY II. Now X3J16 is considering a different *string* class that uses new template features and accommodates strings of various character widths. It is not clear how the whole issue will shake out. Eventually, when the newer features are available in compilers, there may be a third edition of *C++ Database Development*.

In addition to upgrading PARODY to use new C++ language features, I have made changes to how PARODY itself works and how you use it, reflecting reports and requests from readers. I have also added to the example applications to fill in some gaps that I perceived based on questions you asked.

By using the techniques presented in this book, you can define and build an object database in C++. The programs that you write use *abstraction* to define the database, *inheritance* to create persistent objects, and *polymorphism* to assist in their own persistence. In short, they are object-oriented database programs. This book contains the necessary C++ source code, a valuable tool for the development of applications. As you read the book and use the software, you will learn about persistent objects, object-oriented databases, and object-oriented programming.

Object-oriented programming languages have been in use since the 1970s. C++ saw its first light as the object-oriented extension to C about 15 years ago within AT&T. In recent years, C++ compilers for personal computers have proliferated, and C++ is rapidly replacing C as the programming language of choice for new development.

Database management technology dates back to the 1960s, when the first general-purpose file management utility packages were developed. Throughout its history the data processing industry has refined and improved the formal database models and the techniques and procedures that implement them, culminating in the object-oriented data model.

This book brings together C++ and the persistent object data model to provide all the tools—with source code—that you need to build persistent object databases.

Al Stevens
1994

Chapter 1

Introduction

She did not cease to wonder at the persistence of the unforeseen...

—Thomas Hardy

This book and its software deal with C++ persistent objects. The pervasive growth of object-oriented programming technology has made it the chosen technique for software development in the 1990s, and C++ has experienced similar growth, becoming the language of choice for writing object-oriented programs. Persistent objects are one facet of the many-faceted object-oriented programming paradigm, but one that is not and has never been supported by the C++ programming language. To have persistent objects in a C++ program, programmers must implement them, either by using a database management system or by writing the persistence code.

This book adds persistence to C++ programs by providing support for persistent object database management. This is not to imply that object-oriented programs have had to do without database management for all this time. To the contrary, traditional database management techniques still work as well as they always have, and you can integrate

1

them effectively into object-oriented programs. However, the traditional methods do not fully exploit the wealth of expression that object-oriented programming brings to a software development project. There are several available commercial object-oriented database management systems. You have more choices now than before. One of them—this book—brings the technology directly to the programmer in a well-documented class library with source code and discussions on the implementation of the persistent object database management system and its underlying principles.

C++ Database Development is, therefore, about building database software applications by using the features of the C++ programming language. By carefully reading the text, studying the source code, and running the software, you will learn how to design and implement a persistent object database application. You will use a persistent object system called PARODY II (Persistent, Almost Relational Object Database), which later chapters explain fully. The complete PARODY II source code is on the companion diskette included with this book.

Before proceeding into the depths of object-oriented design and database design, we should dispense with one anomaly in our industry's use of the English language. The word *hierarchy* refers to an organization of ranking in which each level is subordinate to the one above. The traditional language of database management defines a hierarchy as an organization in which a member has only one superior—a parent record—but may have multiple subordinates—child records—reflecting the ancient clerical use of the word. An ordering of rank in which a child has multiple parents is a *network*. That distinction defines boundaries between two different database models. Object-oriented design makes no such distinction, however. Class systems with single inheritance and those with multiple inheritance are called hierarchies. When we mix the technologies, though, the varying usages can confuse us. This book tries to keep the differences clear.

C++ and Databases

C++ is an object-oriented superset of the C language. By using C++'s object-oriented extensions, a programmer can define new data types and build a class architecture that orders data types into a well-formed hierarchy.

The concept of the database record format, which dates to the earliest days of data processing, is enhanced by the C++ facility that allows a programmer to build a new data type by defining a class. The class describes the database record. If your database records essential data about a company's departments, for example, then there is probably a *Department* class that describes the data that the application needs to support department records.

That approach is similar to traditional database definition but with this significant exception. Design approaches prior to object-oriented design defined only the data representation of a database record and none of its behavior. All processing of the data—which, in the object-oriented view, determines a data record's behavior—was defined in the application programs themselves. Different application programs were free to define different and contradictory behavior for the same data, which is a weakness of that classic approach. Separation of data representation and behavior produces a potential for data disintegrity and, what is more, does nothing to prevent it.

Object-oriented design defines data's behavior and representation in one encapsulated unit called a *class*. Application programs that are themselves outside the class's definition use, but do not specify or otherwise change, the class's behavior. You will learn what that concept means, how it works, and its consequences beginning in Chapter 2.

What C++ does not include as an intrinsic part of the language is the ability to automatically store and retrieve instances of classes—objects—onto and from persistent storage media. In other words, C++ does not have a built-in database management system for storing and retrieving records in files. That's not surprising. Neither does C. Applications written in C that require record storage and retrieval use either a general-purpose database management function library or custom file input/output functions. C++ applications could use similar techniques, and many of them do. They read and write the data values defined in the class definitions of the objects. There are, however, extensions to C++ classes that go beyond traditional C structure declaration, and these extensions create their own unique problems with respect to data storage and retrieval. Furthermore, the concepts of an object-oriented data store offer the potential to support requirements that are not particularly well supported by traditional database management techniques. So the evolution of object-oriented technology has spawned a new data model—the object database—with the C++ language as a sound vehicle for building and using the model.

The Organization of C++ Database Development

The chapters that follow teach you the concepts of persistent object database design and how to build your own object database by using the PARODY software.

Chapter 2 provides a brief introduction to object-oriented programming. This is not a comprehensive treatment of the subject, which would take a volume of its own. Instead, the chapter defines the terms common to object-oriented programming and relates them to the architecture of object-oriented computer programs. The discussion addresses object-oriented programming as it applies to C++. The C++ object-oriented extensions to C do not, strictly speaking, support so-called pure object-oriented programming as defined in other programming languages. Yet C++ is the leader among object-oriented programming languages, and its approach to the technology is the one most programmers are using and the one you will use with the concepts taught by this book.

Chapter 3 is a brief history of database technology. It discusses the traditional hierarchical, network, and relational data models and introduces the object database model. As you will learn, students of object-oriented technology often confuse the hierarchical parent-child relationships of data files and those of base and derived C++ classes, perhaps because the two kinds of relationships can look alike in design diagrams. You must keep these distinctions clear, however, and Chapter 3 helps you do that.

Chapter 4 is about C++ and persistence. The chapter discusses how C++ programs store data structures on disk and how those traditional techniques do not work with persistent objects in a class inheritance, object-oriented design.

Chapter 5 defines the objectives for persistent objects. The chapter offers alternative solutions to the problems posed by Chapter 4, and it identifies objectives for persistent object database management.

Chapter 6 discusses the object-oriented and relational database models, what they have in common, how they differ, and how traditional relational design methods can be valid for object-oriented design. The chapter also discusses when to use a relational database management system and when to use the object database model.

Chapter 7 describes a step-by-step approach for designing an object database to support the functions of an application. These steps involve more than designing and writing code. You must learn the functional application, derive the requirements for automating parts of it, and build each class that goes into the design.

Chapter 8 introduces PARODY II—the Persistent, Amost Relational Object Database management system—hereafter called simply PARODY. You will learn how PARODY works and how to use the features of C++ class design to define the schema for an application's database—the data description language (DDL) of traditional database management. You will learn to integrate the classes that describe your database with the PARODY base classes to add persistent behavior to your objects.

Chapter 9 describes how a C++ application interacts with the objects in a PARODY database—how to create the database, add new objects, retrieve existing objects, modify them, and delete them from the database. This chapter describes the application program interface (API), also called the data management language (DML) in the parlance of database management.

Chapter 10 presents examples of programs that use PARODY. The chapter includes some utility classes and several example applications that use the PARODY database management system. The examples include source code to define the respective databases and implement the example applications. You will use these applications as examples in the design and implementation of your own applications.

Appendix A contains the instructions for building the PARODY class library and the case study applications. The appendix includes makefiles and instructions for using contemporary C++ compiler products that run under MS-DOS and OS/2.

Appendix B is the PARODY reference, including with descriptions of each of the PARODY classes and their application program interfaces. The reference guide includes examples of each of the class methods.

Appendix C has the source listings for the PARODY database management system. These are provided for reference during the technical discussions that appear elsewhere in the book. You should not build PARODY by typing in the code; the book includes a diskette. You can download newer versions from CompuServe, as described below.

What You Should Already Know and Have

This book assumes that you have a rudimentary understanding of the C++ programming language. I recommend my book, *Teach Yourself C++*,

4th Edition, MIS Press, for C programmers who want to learn C++. You should have a good handle on C++ before you attempt an understanding of the techniques presented here. A reference list at the end of each chapter lists programming texts that apply to the subjects at hand.

To use the software, you need one of the compiler products discussed in Appendix A. These compilers build the software with the MS-DOS and OS/2 operating systems. You might use a different compiler and a different operating system. The software is independent of any particular platform, but your compiler must support templates, exception handling, run-time type information, and the new typecast mechanisms. Your best bet is to use a Borland C++ compiler. I developed this code with Borland C++ for OS/2, version 1.5. I tested it with Borland C++ 4.0 for MS-DOS. Until the specifications for new language features are published, reviewed, and approved, the likelihood is slim that any two compilers from different vendors have identical implementations.

As language features change and more compilers support them, I will upgrade PARODY II. See the discussion titled "The Latest Version of PARODY" later in this chapter to see how to get upgrades.

The example applications employ a generic user interface that uses the standard C++ *iostream* class. Chapter 10 describes the generic user interface. This interface is independent of any computer or operating system. Most C++ implementations support it.

PARODY and Windows?

Readers of *C Database Development* and the first edition of this book often ask when I plan to integrate the two database management systems into Windows or with the screen management software I published in other books. I have no such intentions. PARODY is independent of other systems software beyond the requirement for a standard C++ compiler. You can integrate it with the user interface of your choice. It is bound to no particular architecture, and there are no portability layers for you to rewrite. It manages the database and leaves the user interface to whatever applications framework you use.

I am often asked about implementing PARODY as a Windows or OS/2 dynamic link library (DLL). It is possible but would be cumbersome to implement. The database management software is implemented as a class library with interface member functions. Installing those functions into a DLL from a Windows application would require two class systems—one to provide the DLL calling convention layer and one to implement the database manager. Keeping those two class systems synchronized could prove to be difficult.

Record and File Locking?

Many readers have asked about record and file locking to support multi-user environments, multitasking, and concurrency. Although those are noble and worthy objectives and certainly achievable, I have never considered pursuing them. The problems that I solve with these tools tend to be concentrated in single-user environments. Adding concurrency to a database manager adds a level of complexity far greater than that which you can readily publish in a book.

How to Get Help

The best—and often the only—way to get in touch with me is through the CompuServe Information Service, a national on-line system with electronic mail and many topical forums where members share their knowledge and experience. I log onto CompuServe every day and will answer your questions about this book and its software. I am sorry, but I cannot promise to answer letters or return phone calls. Please do not send me samples of your source code or the output from compilers and makefiles unless I ask for them after we've discussed your problem.

In addition to giving you access to me, CompuServe is the official on-line support facility used by most software vendors, including the vendors of the compiler products discussed later in this book. All you need is a personal computer with a modem and communications program and a CompuServe account. Most bookstores can sell you a kit that has what you need to open a CompuServe account. Once you have an account, you can log on, go into the MAIL section, and post messages directly. My account number is 71101,1262.

You can find help on CompuServe from the experts on Borland C++, Microsoft C++, Windows, DOS, UNIX, GNU, OS/2, and almost any other development or operating environment that you might use. The technical support available on CompuServe far outstrips any such support you get from a vendor's toll-free support number. CompuServe is as important a tool to a programmer today as are a good editor and debugger.

Other electronic mail delivery systems such as INTERNET have gateways to CompuServe, and you can write to me through those gateways if you initiate the dialog and send me your E-mail address.

The Latest Version of PARODY

I maintain PARODY in a file you can download from CompuServe's DDJ Forum, which supports *Dr. Dobb's Journal* readers. Log onto that forum and search for files with the keyword PARODY.

Your Rights to the Software

The source code in this book is for use by anyone for the development of computer software applications. You can make as many copies of the source code as you need for yourself and the other programmers on the team. Those who use the code will, I hope, have their own copy of the book to help them along.

You may build and distribute applications by compiling and linking with the code that you get from this book. There are no royalties for its use, and I do not require you to acknowledge my contribution to your system. If the conditions under which you distribute your programs require you to include source code, buy a copy of this book for each of your customers.

You may not publish the source code in a book, article or other technical journal. If you are publishing an application that uses PARODY, please tell your readers where they can get the book and the code.

Chapter 2

An Introduction to Object-Oriented Programming

Knowledge is the conformity of the object and the intellect.
—Averroës

In the 1990s, object-oriented programming and C++ in particular have begun to dominate the software development industry. C++ has been available in UNIX installations for years, and now most of the C compilers sold for MS-DOS systems include a C++ compiler. Many other contemporary software development systems use the object-oriented paradigm as their basis. As pervasive as object-oriented programming has become, many programmers still do not understand it. This chapter presents to those programmers a brief introduction to object-oriented programming.

This book assumes that you have a working knowledge of C++. That experience alone has exposed you to the object-oriented paradigm. If you have built and used C++ classes, even in a tutorial or classroom exercise, then you have already written some object-oriented programs. There are, however, many terms that you should understand so that you can relate your code to the discussions around you. Simply writing a C++ program does not qualify a programmer as an expert on object-oriented technology. There are certain rules and procedures to follow, and there are certain benefits to be gained by understanding and following the discipline of object-oriented programming.

An author of traditional procedure-oriented programs does not intuitively understand object-oriented programming. The notations and approaches to design are different from what you have learned and used in the past. Furthermore, explanations such as the one in this chapter do not usually complete the understanding of object-oriented programming. You need reinforcement—both from experience and from feeling that there is something to be gained from a new and different approach. Programmers might understand the concept at the intellectual level and yet not accept it as a pragmatic approach to programming simply because they have been writing good programs for a while and see no compelling reason to tamper with that success. For this reason, it is difficult to teach object-oriented programming, although it is not difficult to learn. Learning object-oriented programming is a process of discovery. Teaching it, therefore, becomes the management of that process.

Many of the current generation of programmers have learned and accepted object-oriented programming as a better way to express software algorithms. Most of them started from the procedural paradigm, having programmed in traditional languages such as C. Those who make the switch become advocates of the object-oriented approach. Enough of them have done so that the rest of us cannot deny that there is something to it. You can take a lesson from the observation that once a programmer takes the plunge, he or she almost always becomes a convert. Therefore, the best way to learn object-oriented programming is to try it. Until recently, however, the tools were not widely available. Now, virtually every PC can have a C++ compiler, and virtually every programmer has access to the tools.

The Basics

The first understanding of object-oriented programming is to be found in this design guideline:

> *The expression of an algorithm should model the application domain that it supports.*

This concept reflects an older one that states that the solution to a problem should resemble the problem that it solves—a guideline that allows observers of a solution to recognize its purpose without necessarily knowing in advance about the problem. When you see a properly designed word processor, you intuitively understand that the problem being solved is one of capturing and manipulating text. When you see a properly designed inventory management system, you recognize that its purpose is to maintain a record of stock quantities and locations. You recognize those things because the designs resemble and therefore remind you of the problems that they solve.

Carrying this concept to a higher level of abstraction, you recognize that the purpose of a programming language is to express with algorithms the solution to a data processing problem. The techniques used in that expression determine how successfully the solution models its problem domain. Object-oriented programming is one of several different approaches to the expression of algorithms, and it is often misunderstood—primarily by those who do not use it.

Procedural Programming

In the classic approach to programming, a programmer designs a set of data structures followed by functions and procedures to process the data. This approach is called procedural programming because it starts with the procedures. We think of programming in this way because that is how programming has been done for 40 years.

Procedural programming, does not always deliver a solution that resembles the problem, however, because it emphasizes the functions rather than the data—the procedures rather than the objects. Furthermore, procedural programming does not encourage the programmer to separate and hide the procedures related to different data objects from one another. Programmers have long known that those practices are worthwhile, but most procedural programming languages do not encourage them.

Object-Oriented Programming

The world and its applications are not organized into values and procedures separate from one another. Problem solvers in other crafts do not perceive the world that way. They deal with their problem domains by concentrating on the objects and letting the characteristics of those objects determine the procedures to apply to them. To build a house, grow a tomato, or repair a carburetor, first you think about the object and its purpose and behavior. Then you select your tools and procedures. The solution fits the problem.

The world is, therefore, object-oriented, and the object-oriented programming paradigm expresses computer programs in ways that model how people perceive the world. Because programmers are people, it is only natural that our approach to the work of the world reflects our view of the world itself. We have not, however, universally learned how to do that. The crafts of carpentry, farming, and mechanics are centuries old and originated in cultures that lacked technology. The objects and objectives of those trades were understood long before the development of the technologies that support them. Computer programming is relatively new. We are still forming its disciplines, and the technologies are developing faster than we can adjust.

The Object-Oriented Program

An object-oriented program has four fundamental characteristics:

- ♦ Abstraction defines new data types.
- ♦ Encapsulation designs a data type's representation and its behavior in one encapsulated entity.
- ♦ Inheritance derives a new data type from an existing one.
- ♦ Polymorphism customizes the behavior of a derived data type.

Object-oriented programming uses a vocabulary of such terms in ways that are unfamiliar to the procedural programmer. You hear these terms used frequently in discussions of object-oriented programming. Here is a more comprehensive list of object-oriented terms:

abstract base class
abstract data type
abstraction
base class
class

> derived class
>
> encapsulation
>
> implementation and interface
>
> inheritance
>
> instantiate
>
> message
>
> method
>
> multiple inheritance
>
> object
>
> polymorphism
>
> subclass
>
> superclass

The program defines abstract data types in classes, each of which has its own implementation and interface. Inherited abstract data types are derived subclasses of base classes. The program instantiates an object and sends messages to the object by using the object's methods.

The object-oriented programming community uses these terms universally. Therefore, when object-oriented programmers say "encapsulate", for example, you know that their meaning is consistent with the way others use it. When programmers acknowledge that a program is object-oriented, you know that the program contains abstraction, encapsulation, inheritance, and polymorphism and that it defines abstract data types, instantiates objects, and sends messages to the object's methods. The discussion that follows draws on your experience with C++ to explain these terms.

The Object

The first question that programmers often ask is, "What are the objects in object-oriented programming?" What is it about object-oriented programming that sets it apart from traditional programming? Early writings on the subject effectively explained object-oriented programming to those who already understood it, but these explanations were sometimes too abstruse for the newcomers.

Simply stated, an object is an instance of a data type. The program in Figure 2.1 declares two objects. The first object is a simple integer; the second object is an abstract data type.

```
void d()
{
    int ndays; // an instance of an int
    Date cdt;  // an instance of an ADT
    // ...
}
```

FIGURE 2.1 *A program with two objects*

Abstraction

Abstraction is the definition of an abstract data type. The definition includes the data representation and the data type's behavior. An abstract data type is new. It is not one of the primitive data types that are built into the programming language. The *int, long,* and *float* data types are primitive C++ data types. Their data representations and behavior are known to the compiler. A primitive data type's format and response to arithmetic, assignment, and relational operators are defined as a part of the C++ language.

An *abstract data type,* however, is not known to the language; the programmer defines its format and behavior by defining a C++ *class.* For example, the calendar date could be an abstract data type. The compiler and the computer do not know about calendar dates. Programmers have always had to define the behavior of dates by designing structures and functions. The Standard C library has several such date definitions. When you define a C++ calendar date class such as the one in Figure 2.2, you express its format and behavior very much as you did in C. It has month, day, and year data members. It might even support some arithmetic and relational operations.

```
class Date  {
    int month, day, year;
public:
    Date(int mo, int da, int yr);
    int operator+(int n);
    // ...
};
```

FIGURE 2.2 *An abstract data type (ADT)*

You can then declare an object that has the type of the date class and add to the object, subtract from it, compare it with other objects, and assign values to it. A C++ program declares instances of abstract data types in the same way that it declares instances of primitive data types. Refer again to Figure 2.1. The declaration of the *cdt* object is an instance of an abstract data type.

The ANSI C++ standard will define a *string* class to implement a string abstract data type similar to the strings of the Basic programming language. Other abstract data types will be container classes for stacks, lists, trees, and queues, perhaps with ordered and random-access variants of such containers.

Instantiate means to declare an object. When an object-oriented program declares an instance of a data type, the program has instantiated an object, whether the data type is primitive or abstract. The program in Figure 2.1 instantiates the *ndays* and *cdt* objects.

Encapsulation

Encapsulation is the design of a C++ class. A programmer encapsulates the data representation and behavior of an abstract data type into a class definition, thereby giving it its own implementation and interface. Figure 2.3 is an example of an encapsulated class.

The *implementation* of a class, which consists of the data members and private member functions, is hidden from the using program. The *month*, *day*, and *year* data members in Figure 2.3 are the class's implementation. A user of the class does not care about the details of implementation—only that it works. The class designer could totally change the implementation—perhaps changing the date representation to a long integer count of days—and the using program would not be affected.

The *interface*, which is visible to the user of the class, consists of the public member functions. The class user reads and modifies values in the data representation by calling public member functions. The class interface in Figure 2.3 consists of the constructor, which contains initialization parameters, and an overloaded plus operator, which presumably allows the user of the class to add an integral number of days to the date.

```
class Date {
// --- the class implementation
private:
    int month, day, year;
public:
// --- the class interface
    Date(int mo, int da, int yr);
    Date operator+(int n);
    // ...
};
```

FIGURE 2.3 *Encapsulation*

To use the abstract data type defined in Figure 2.3, a programmer makes assumptions about the interface based on its appearance and the programmer's understanding of C++ syntax. If the programmer is not the class's author, those assumptions may be invalid. The author might not have designed an intuitive interface. In this case, most programmers would assume that the overloaded plus operator adds an integer to a *Date* object and returns another *Date* object with the result. Figure 2.4 illustrates how the class interface works if it is intuitive.

```
void f()
{
    Date dt(6,29,92);
    dt = dt + 30;   // should now be 7/29/92
}
```

FIGURE 2.4 *An intuitive class interface*

Designing an intuitive class interface is not automatic. The C++ language provides the tools for you to do a proper job, but nothing in the language enforces good design. The class author can use unnecessarily clever techniques that obscure the meaning of the interface. An object-oriented design is not necessarily a good design. Experienced C++ programmers generally agree on certain design standards for C++ classes. The data members are usually private and constitute most of the implementation. The interface consists only of member functions that restrict access to the data members. The interface is generic in that it is not bound to any particular implementation. The class author should be able to change the implementation without affecting the using programs. These apparent rules are only guidelines, however. Sometimes you need to step around them to achieve some purpose. The fewer times you do that, the stronger your design.

Methods and Messages

Method is another name for C++ public member functions. Methods may be constructors, destructors, procedures, and overloaded operators. They define the class interface. The constructor and overloaded plus operator in Figure 2.3 are methods.

A *message* is the invocation of a method, which, in C++, is the same thing as calling the public member function. The program sends a message to an object telling it to invoke the method and sometimes provides parameters for the method to use.

Different kinds of methods are characterized by how they support the class definition. There are *functional* methods, *data type* methods, and *implicit conversion* methods. Note that this delineation and these terms are coined here for convenience and are not part of the official object-oriented lexicon. They define different levels of support that C++ provides for class design.

Functional Methods

Figure 2.5 shows three methods added to the *Date* class. The three methods in Figure 2.5 illustrate three typical method variants. The first method tells the object to do something, in this case to display itself. The class's implementation knows how to display the object's data representation. The programmer who uses the class is unconcerned about the details of the implementation.

The second method tells the object to change itself, in this case to adjust its month data value up or down the number that is specified in the method's parameter. This method is an example of one that includes a parameter. Once again, the using programmer does not care how the object stores the month value or what algorithm adjusts the month—only that it works.

```
class Date {
    // ...
public:
    // ...
    void Display();            // display the date
    void AdjustMonth(int m);   // +/- m months
    int DayOfWeek();           // return 0-6 = Sun-Sat
};
```

FIGURE 2.5 *Functional methods*

The third method is one that returns a value—in this case the day of the week—represented by the object's current value.

The methods in Figure 2.5 define behavior related to the functional properties of the class. The class is a calendar date, and you want it to behave like a date.

Data Type Methods

Data type methods make a class act like a primitive data type by giving it the properties of a primitive data type. These properties are usually implemented as overloaded operators in the class interface. Figure 2.6 shows the methods to compare dates, assign them to one another, and do some arithmetic on them.

Implicit Conversion Methods

The C++ language handles implicit conversion of primitive data types. If you write an expression with an *int* where the compiler expects a *long*, the compiler knows how to make the conversion and does so quietly. If, however, you write an expression where the compiler expects an abstract data type and if you provide a different data type, primitive or abstract, the compiler does not know how to deal with that. Similarly, if the expression expects a primitive data type and you use an abstract data type, the compiler does not know what to do. In either case, unless you have provided implicit conversion methods, the compiler issues an error message and refuses to compile the program.

```
class Date  {
    // ...
public:
    // ...
    // ---- arithmetic operators
    Date operator+(int n);
    Date operator-(int n);
    int operator-(Date &dt);
    // ---- assignment operators
    Date& operator=(Date &dt);
    // ---- relational operators
    int operator==(Date &dt);
    int operator!=(Date &dt);
    int operator<(Date &dt);
    int operator>(Date &dt);
};
```

FIGURE 2.6 *Data type methods*

You can add implicit conversion methods to a class so that the compiler knows how to convert from one data type to another. The conversion constructor function converts a data type to an abstract data type, and the member conversion function converts an abstract data type to a primitive C++ data type. When you code an expression in which the compiler expects to see something other than what you provide as just described, the compiler executes one of your implicit conversion methods to convert the data type. This is an example of a method that you do not explicitly call (or send a message to) from within your program. It executes as the result of the implicit call inferred by the compiler during its interpretation of your expression. Your program implies a call to the method by the context in which it uses data types in an expression.

Figure 2.7 shows two implicit conversion methods added to the Date class. The first method converts an *int* data type to a *Date* object. The second method converts a *Date* data type to an *int* object. The conversions are not restricted to converting between abstract data types and primitive data types. You can convert between abstract data types in the same manner. For example, you might have a *Date* class and a *JulianDate* class, and the same principles apply.

```
class Date  {
    // ...
public:
    // ...
    Date(int n);    // conversion constructor
    operator int(); // member conversion function
};
```

FIGURE 2.7 *Implicit conversion methods*

Member Functions

Having just learned about methods and messages in detail, you soon find that the terms themselves are not used much in C++ circles. The terms come from the object-oriented lexicon and reflect the syntax of pure object-oriented programming languages such as Smalltalk. Most C++ programmers prefer to say that they call member functions rather than saying that they send messages through methods. Nonetheless, you should understand the analogy, because you will read and hear the object-oriented terms frequently. Beyond this chapter, however, this book uses the C++ conventions and refers to methods and their messages as class member functions.

Inheritance

A class can inherit the characteristics of another class. The original class is called the *base* class and the new class is called the *derived* class. These classes are also called the *superclass* and the *subclass*. The word *subclass* is also used as a verb to mean the act of inheriting. This book refers to base classes and derived classes exclusively.

The derived class inherits the data representation and behavior of the base class except where the derived class modifies the behavior by overloading member functions. The derived class adds behavior that is unique to its own purpose.

A program can instantiate objects of a base class as well as those of a derived class. If the base class is an *abstract base class*—one that exists only to be derived from—the program may not instantiate objects of the base class.

Inheritance is the foundation of most object-oriented designs, and it is often over-applied. Some programmers get carried away with the power of inheritance, and C++ can offer some surprises to the unwary designer. Many designs use inheritance to solve problems that would be better supported by a different approach, usually an object member of the base class in what is otherwise the derived class. Despite this warning, inheritance is a powerful feature which, properly used, offers a rich design capability to the object-oriented programmer.

Single Inheritance

The C++ inheritance mechanism lets you build an orderly hierarchy of classes. When several of your abstract data types have characteristics in common, you can design their commonalities into a single base class and separate their unique characteristics into unique derived classes. That is the purpose of inheritance.

For example, a personnel system maintains information about employees. Employees have common characteristics—name, address, date of birth, and so on—yet the system might record different kinds of employees. Managers, project workers, and support personnel might be recorded differently. Therefore, you could design a base class of employees that stores name, address, social security number, and date of birth and then derive separate classes for managers, project workers, and support personnel. Each of the derived classes would inherit the characteristics of the employee class and would have additional characteristics specific to themselves. For example, the manager class might include an annual salary-augmenting bonus data member that the other employee classes do not have. The project worker class could have a list of project assignments. The support personnel class could record overtime hours worked. Figure 2.8 illustrates such a class hierarchy.

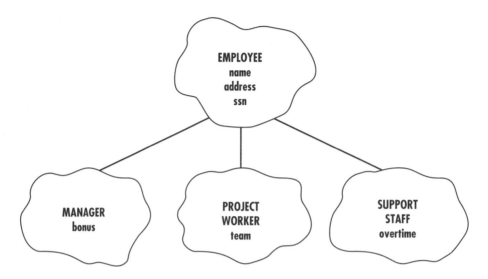

FIGURE 2.8 *An inherited class design*

Multiple Inheritance

A derived class can inherit the characteristics of more than one base class. This technique is called *multiple inheritance*. Not all object-oriented programming languages support multiple inheritance, and many experts assert that it is not a necessary design tool. Nonetheless, C++ does support multiple inheritance, and there are times when it is a good way to express class relationships.

Recall that the effectiveness of a programming language can be measured in its ability to model the problem domains that it supports. The objects in the world reflect membership in multiple-inheritance hierarchies, and programmers are called upon to write programs to model those objects. A sofa bed is a sofa and it is a bed, both of which are items of furniture. An amphibious airplane is a boat and an airplane, both of which are vehicles. A car phone is not a car and a telephone, however, and sometimes programmers get their designs confused by thinking that they need to inherit when they do not.

Suppose that the system supported by the class design in Figure 2.8 needed to record the support personnel class as union members. The support person class object is an employee, and now it is a union member, too. The other employees are not in the union, so their classes do not need to inherit the characteristics of the union member class.

Figure 2.9 shows how you would derive the support personnel class from the union member class as well as the employee class by using multiple inheritance.

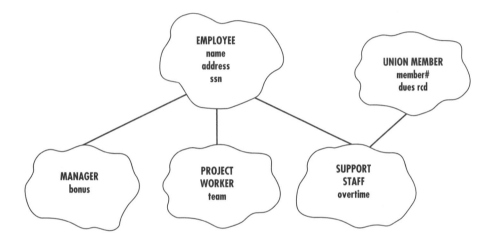

FIGURE 2.9 *Multiple inheritance*

Class Relationships

Object-oriented designers use the properties of class design to model the relationships between objects of different classes. There are three fundamental interclass relationships: *specialization*, *composition*, and *collaboration*.

Specialization

Inheritance models relationships in which a derived class represents objects that are a kind of the base class. A car is a kind of vehicle. An engineer is a kind of employee, which is a kind of person. This specialization relationship is also called the IS-A relationship. The derived class is a specialized version of the base class.

Composition

Inheritance is inappropriate for composition relationships in which one class embeds an object of another. An employee has a date of birth. A department has a manager. The owning class is composed of other class objects. This relationship is also called the HAS-A relationship. Instead of using inheritance, the class that has an object of another class embeds the object—or a reference or pointer to it—as a data member.

Collaboration

When objects of one class use the services of objects of other classes, a relationship of collaboration exists. This relationship is also called the USES-A relationship. It can be represented in class design in several ways, and in each of these ways the objects exchange messages. A class's member functions can communicate with other objects through global instances, references, or pointers. The reference or pointer can be a data member of the sending class, an idiom that resembles the composition relationship but exists for a different purpose. A member function of one class can instantiate an object of another class and send messages to the object.

Management

A fourth class relationship, one that has not been named by the establishment, exists when one class manages instances of another. For example, container classes manage generic types within defined data structures. The particulars of the type are unrelated to its containment, and the particulars of the containment are unrelated to the types that it contains.

In the past, this relationship was usually implemented with inheritance. A specialized class was built that derived from the class being contained and the container class. This gave rise to confusion because the relationship looked like specialization but did not model reality. Template classes in C++ solved that problem. The template implements the container, the type class implements the object being contained, and the two implementations are independent.

Polymorphism

In polymorphism, a derived class customizes the behavior of the base class to meet the requirements of the derived class. A C++ base class uses the *virtual* member function to specify that overriding member functions in derived classes have polymorphic behavior with respect to their methods.

If a derived class overrides a base class method and if the base class method is not a virtual function, then the overriding behavior is effective only when the compiler is dereferencing a pointer, reference, or object of the derived class itself. If the object's pointer or reference refers to the base class, then the base class method has precedence. Such behavior is not polymorphic. However, if the base class method is virtual, then the compiler selects the overriding derived class method regardless of the type being dereferenced by the compiler.

Suppose, for example, that the support staff class from Figure 2.8 was further decomposed into derived classes that represented the various kinds of support personnel. You could have typists, corporate pilots, chauffeurs, maintenance personnel, instructors, and so on. The system measures skill levels differently for each of these disciplines, but there is a requirement for a general-purpose skill index for the base support class. Each derived class exhibits different behavior for data entry and retrieval of the skill index, but some parts of the system invoke the skill method without knowing which kind of support personnel object is involved. The polymorphic skill method would modify the class's behavior at run-time based on the type of the derived class. Figure 2.10 shows how you might design such a class.

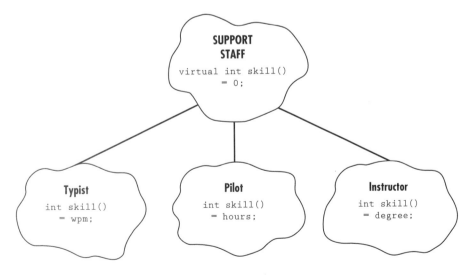

FIGURE 2.10 *Polymorphism*

Summary

The object-oriented programming paradigm is a rich environment for the expression of data formats and functions for an application. It is not necessary, however, for C++ programmers to immerse themselves in the object-oriented passion. The availability of improved design and programming methods does not automatically outdate all the traditional approaches. C++ has the facility to support the basics of object-oriented programming while permitting the programmer to use traditional procedural programming where it seems appropriate. C++, in fact, encourages that approach. By supporting traditional C flow control of nested functions, C++ allows you to leverage your existing investment in mature and useful C function libraries. Furthermore, C++ does not force a pure object-oriented hierarchical data structure in which every data type descends from one generic root base object. Instead, C++ allows you to build a number of class hierarchies representing the different problem domains that your application might deal with. There can be classes that define the data structures of the application's functional purpose; there can be classes that supply general-purpose data structures such as strings, lists, queues, and so on; there can be classes that integrate your application with a particular user interface. All these classes can coexist independently of one another in a system of hierarchies integrated by you into an application.

References

Objects in Action, Paul Harmon and David A. Taylor, 1993, Addison-Wesley

Object Oriented Design with Applications, Grady Booch, 1991, The Benjamin/Cummings Publishing Company, Inc.

The C++ Programming Language Second Edition, Bjarne Stroustrup, 1991, Addison-Wesley

Chapter 3

A Brief History of Database Management

Why is not all nature in confusion, instead of the species being, as we see them, well defined?

—Charles Darwin

This chapter discusses the progress of database management technology from the earliest ad hoc, hierarchical, and network data models, through the enduring relational model and into the newest model, the object database, which is the subject of this book. We discuss the earlier models for their contribution to the historical perspective and to prepare you for what you are about to learn. We must understand our past to manage our present and face our future. You are encouraged to learn more about the earlier database models by reading the references cited at the end of the chapter.

The history of database management traces the history of data processing itself. Ever since we have had information-processing machines, programmers have designed ways to organize data into formats that machines can process. Although today we are primarily concerned with files organized into direct-access mass storage, the field of database man-

27

agement began with information recorded in more primitive media, such as punched cards and paper tape. The common characteristic shared by all database management approaches, from the earliest to the most recent, is reflected in this concept:

> *An entity of data must take a form that the computer can recognize and deal with.*

An atomic entity of data, from the point of view of the database, is a *data element*. Aggregate entities of data are *records*. Collections of like records are *files*. To manage files of records, a database management system applies this rule:

> *All like records assume a common form.*

Given a file of records that adhere to a common form and a description of those records, a database management system adds records to the file, retrieves records from the file, changes records in the file, and deletes records from the file.

Records consist of data elements, which are singular entities with values that have functional meaning to the record. Data elements can be names, addresses, dollar amounts, hat sizes, batting averages, dates of birth, and so on. A data element may consist of one or more *data types* in a structure. For example, a calendar date consists of the integers day, month, and year.

A collection of files that support a particular application is a *database*. The information resource of an organization might consist of a number of independent databases. Some databases interface with others. For example, the payroll database might contribute transactions to the general ledger database.

The software system that manages a database is called, appropriately, a *database management system*.

The Database Management System

The purpose of a database management system is to store, maintain, and retrieve database records in files. A file contains records of the same format that serve a common purpose. A payroll system might have a file of employee records, for example, with one record for each employee.

Through the database management system, the program adds new employees when the company hires them, deletes records when employees resign, changes a record when an employee gets a raise, and retrieves each employee's record once every pay period to calculate paychecks.

A database management system can be custom code or general-purpose systems software. Programmers discovered long ago that common database design and programming considerations apply to most applications and that general-purpose database management systems can support these common requirements. The advantage of a general-purpose system is that developers do not have to rebuild database management software for each new application. The development team designs an application around the capabilities of the database management system.

Use of general-purpose database management systems mandates the application of *data models*. These models have evolved over time, reflecting their applicability to a wide range of applications and the inherent stability of databases that use them.

General-purpose database management systems use four language interfaces between the application programming language and the database manager: the data definition language, the data manipulation language, the query language, and the report writer language. Depending on the database management system, these interfaces are built into the programming language, a separate language processed by a separate language processor, or some combination of the two.

The Data Definition Language

The *data definition language* (DDL) defines the format—or *schema*—of the database. It identifies files, record formats, and the relationships between files. The DDL is usually an external file of statements used first to establish an initial empty copy of a new database and subsequently to specify the format of the files and records to data manipulation and query languages.

The Data Manipulation Language

The *data manipulation language* (DML) is the application program interface to the database management system. It provides the program interface to open and close a database, find records in files, navigate among the various file records, add new records, and change or delete existing records.

The Query Language

The *query language* describes criteria for searches of the database. Some query languages are processed by utility programs, and others are implemented as embedded extensions to the application's programming language. A query typically returns a temporary subset of records that match the search criteria. Often the subset has its own format independent of those in the formal database definition. Sometimes the subset consists of records formed from logical combinations of related database records.

The Report Writer Language

The *report writer language* defines reports formed from a query's output. The format specifies the sequence and presentation of data values on the report, typically with tables of rows and columns, headers, footers, and control breaks for totals and subtotals.

Database Models

Early database models were ad hoc. An application used whatever data files the designers came up with. If there was a database management system, it was usually a set of custom subroutines developed for the application itself. The disadvantages of this practice are apparent, and they were observed and recorded early on. In fact, they led to the development of the first general-purpose database management systems. Nonetheless, many systems were—and still are—developed this way for a lot of reasons.

Proprietary Data Models

Most spreadsheets, word processors, and other horizontal applications use proprietary database formats for three reasons: First, their purveyors prefer closed architectures that competitors cannot exploit. Second, general-purpose database management systems impose costs and performance implications over and above those of the application. The costs often involve run-time modules that users must have to run the application. Third, many implementations of the three traditional database models—discussed next—do not support certain data structures (variable-length data elements, lists, queues, and so on) that applications require.

The Hierarchical Data Model

The hierarchical data model was the first one identified and recognized. Programmers observed that many databases consisted of files with hierarchical relationships. An organizational database would have files of companies, divisions within each company, and departments within each division, for example. Figure 3.1 illustrates the hierarchical relationships of such a database.

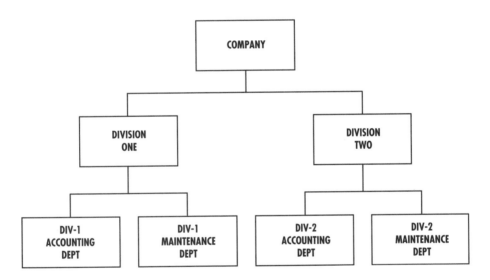

FIGURE 3.1 *A hierarchical database*

A file higher in the hierarchy is a *parent* file to the ones below it. Subordinate files contain *child* records. A child record may have children of its own; it can be a child to one level and a parent to another. In the hierarchical data model, a child record type may have only one parent record type, and each child record instance may have only one parent record instance.

Each department in Figure 3.1 might have its own independent hierarchical database as well. The maintenance department would have a file of equipment maintenance schedules. The accounting department would have files for the general ledger, accounts receivable, accounts payable, and payroll.

The natural hierarchical organization of such files indicates that a common system of software could support all of them if it knew their formats and interfile relationships. Systems of file descriptions, called the schema, evolved. Programmers defined the database files in the schema language and built their applications programs by linking with a general-purpose database management system.

Hierarchical database management systems support interfile relationships by embedding record pointers in the data records. The company record would have the address of the first division record assigned to the company. Each division record would have the address of its parent company as well as the address of the next division that belonged to that company. The record addresses were invisible to the applications programs, which would ask the database manager to retrieve the first and subsequent divisions for a particular company. From a particular division record, the program could ask for the first and subsequent department records, and so on.

The Network Data Model

The hierarchical data model does not support child records having more than one parent. If the organization supported by the design in Figure 3.1 reorganizes so that one accounting department supports several divisions, the hierarchical data model breaks down. The network data model evolved to support such requirements. Figure 3.2 shows the organization's database reorganized into a network.

Network databases are typically implemented with record address pointers like those of the hierarchical data model except that more than one parent record can point to a particular child record, and the child record points to a list of its parents.

In 1969, the Conference on Data Systems Languages (CODASYL) formalized the definition of network databases with the development of a standard for a data description language. A database management system that uses the CODASYL standard is said to implement a CODASYL database. The language itself resembles the data division statements of the COBOL programming language, and it organizes records into named sets that consist of owner records and member records. A set resembles a hierarchy in that a parent can have many children, and each child can have only one parent. Sets can overlap with respect to the records included in them, however, and a child record can have multiple parents if the parents are in different sets.

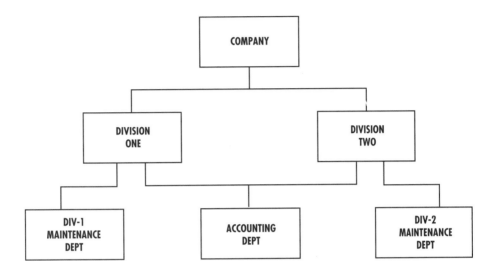

FIGURE 3.2 *A network database*

The Relational Data Model

The *relational* data model evolved in response to concern that, due to hidden pointers in the data records, the hierarchical and network models were vulnerable to the compromise of data integrity and, therefore, inherently unstable. System errors could damage record address chains. Functional relationships between records were compromised by broken physical relationships.

The solution to this concern was the relational data model, wherein the relationships between files are represented by data values rather than record addresses. This does not fully solve the problems of data disintegrity. It is possible for a system error to cause an employee record to point to a nonexisting department, for example. However, the process of error identification and correction is simpler when user-viewable data values are involved rather than system-managed hidden pointers.

Files in a relational database consist of fixed-length, fixed-format records, which form tables of rows and columns. Each file record has a *primary key* data element to uniquely identify the record. This requirement models the way systems traditionally identify things. People have Social Security numbers or employee numbers. Spare parts have part numbers and stock numbers. Virtually every object has at least one piece of information that sets it apart from other objects of the same type.

A record in a relational database file is *flat* in that it has no arrays—lists of common data elements—especially none with a variable number of entries.

File relationships in the relational model are maintained by data item values. For example, a department record contains the division number of the division that it belongs to. The division number in the division record is its primary key. In the department record, the division number is a *secondary key*, which means that the application can retrieve a set of all department records that have a given division number. Figure 3.3 shows a typical relational database.

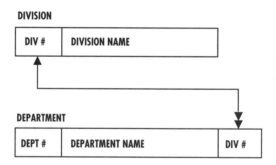

FIGURE 3.3 *A relational database*

The arrow icon that links the two record definitions in Figure 3.3 is not a physical pointer. Instead, it represents the relationship implied by the division number in the department record. Inasmuch as the division number is also the primary key of the division record, several department records can be related to a single division record, and only one division record can be related to any department record. This is called a *one-to-many* relationship and is indicated by the single and double arrowheads at the two ends of the arrow icon in Figure 3.3.

The one-to-many relationship between divisions and departments does not support the problem in which one department can be assigned to multiple divisions, however. The relational data model uses a connector file such as the one shown in Figure 3.4 to support the *many-to-many* relationship between data files.

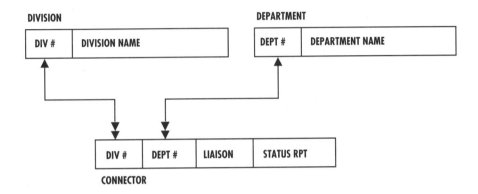

FIGURE 3.4 *The many-to-many relationship*

The concatenated division and department number data elements form the primary key to the connector file in Figure 3.4. Either number by itself also forms a secondary key. The application can thus find all the division records related to a given department record and all the department records related to a given division record. It might even identify data items that are unique to the connection itself and put them into the connector record as well. For example, the connector record might store the employee number of the division's liaison in the department and the date of the department's next scheduled status report to the division.

It has been shown that any interfile data relationships that you can represent with the hierarchical or the network model can be represented by the relational model through a process called *normalization*. This process examines a database's file relationships and reorganizes the data elements in several steps designed to eliminate redundancy, internal file pointers, and repeating groups (lists) of data elements in the records. Proponents of the relational model assert that the resulting gain in data stability far outweighs any overhead that the approach might add to the database.

The relational model has become the standard method for representing data in a database. The reasons are the inherent strength and stability of the model, the fact that the entire data file format is visible to the user, and the relative ease with which a general-purpose relational database management system can be designed and developed when compared to the effort required to build, for example, a CODASYL database manager.

The Object Data Model

The *object* data model is in a state of flux. Members of the object-oriented programming and database management industries are working on standard definitions, and that work is still in progress.

In 1993, the Object Database Management Group published its ODMG-93 draft standard for object databases, which includes an object model, an object definition language, an object query language, and bindings for C++ and Smalltalk. The group has formally proposed changes to C++ to support its work, and those proposals are under consideration by the ANSI X3J16 committee. To date, no database product fully complies with ODMG-93 as it has been proposed, but the group has among its members several prominent object database management system vendors, and implementations eventually will be available.

Object-oriented programming does not, by itself, change the traditional requirements for database management. A developer still identifies data elements and organizes them into files for retrieval and maintenance. Object-oriented programming adds to the culture ways to represent user-defined and class library data types with abstraction, inheritance, and polymorphism. The object-oriented designer searches for database management tools that circumscribe object-oriented class design.

An object-oriented program can use traditional database management techniques. To build or modify a database record, the program can collect an object's data members into a structure and write the structure to the database. To rebuild an object, the application can retrieve the structure from the database management system and distribute its data members into the data members of an object instantiated to receive the data.

Before committing to such a strategy, however, it is proper to consider what there is about an object-oriented design that lures the designer away from traditional relational databases.

DATA TYPES

The relational data model uses flat files of fixed-length, fixed-format records. There are no variable-length data items, no repeating groups, and no user-defined data types within the record's definition.

These restrictions move us to look for an alternative to the relational database, but the last one—the absence of user-defined data types—is particularly compelling. Data abstraction is the strength of object-oriented programming. An object-oriented application applies user-defined data types because they solve problems of the domain. If the database management system does not support user-defined data types, the programmer has to intercede between the parts of the design that define classes and the parts that manage the database.

If a relational database management system does not support variable-length objects and lists, applications suffer. Many applications use variable sizes and numbers of objects. CAD/CAM programs store digital renderings of engineering drawings. Cartographic systems store variable-length lists of geographic coordinates, feature renditions, and free-form map legends. Imagery systems store the compressed raster scans of digitized images. Multimedia audio and video data streams have widely varying lengths. Word processors use data streams to record documents, macros, style sheets, and graphics. Electronic mail systems store variable-length files of text and attachments. Simulations can consist of anything at all. The relational database has limited applicability in these applications; it was never intended for them. Until the object model was developed, such data types were not supported by general-purpose database management systems, and programmers turned to custom, ad hoc solutions.

Class and Database Design Notation

A natural tendency exists to confuse the hierarchical relationships among database files with those among classes in an object-oriented design. This tendency is reinforced by the organizational similarities of the two. In the database, the employee is subordinate to the department. In the class design, the engineer is derived from the employee. The difference is subtle and can be obscured by the way that we represent the relationships in our design notation.

Think of the differences this way: an engineer *is* an employee. The class that defines the engineer inherits all the characteristics of the employee class and adds some unique ones of its own. The employee, however, *is not* a department. The department *employs* the employee instead, and the employee does not inherit any of the department's behavior.

When you design a class to be a data record, you design the data file's record format. The format includes all the data elements in the class *including the data elements that it inherits from its base class.*

When you design a child record, you design the relationship between the record and its parent. The two records might have only one data element—the primary key of the parent record—in common.

To distinguish these two kinds of relationships, this book uses two distinct design notations, as shown in Figure 3.5.

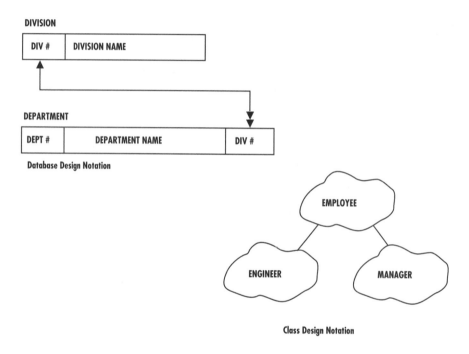

FIGURE 3.5 *Class and database design notations*

Object-oriented design texts often use a common symbol to represent classes, and they use different pointer notation to distinguish between IS-A (an engineer *is an* employee), HAS-A (an employee *has a* department), and USES-A (a payroll paycheck *uses a* name from an employee). These texts usually address the design of object-oriented applications and do not encounter the collisions that occur between the notation of class design and that of a database design.

There are interclass relationships beyond the simple IS-A and HAS-A types, and the succinct object-oriented design notations of other texts provide for them. The examples in this book do not use complex class design, however, being primarily aimed at presenting and explaining the PARODY database manager and its use. For purposes of clarity, therefore, this book adopts the more visually distinct notation shown in Figure 3.5.

Summary

This chapter discussed the evolution of database management technology and presented an overview of what an object database is. Implementing such a database, particularly as a general-purpose class library to support the persistence of as-yet-undefined class designs, is no trivial task. Chapter 4 compares the traditional techniques for storing C structures to those for storing C++ classes and describes some of the problems of a common, general-purpose object database manager.

References

The Object Database Standard: ODMG-93, R.G.G. Cattrell, 1994, Morgan Kaufmann Publishers

A Guide to the SQL Standard, C.J. Date, 1987, Addison-Wesley

An Introduction to Database Systems, Second Edition, C.J. Date, 1977, Addison-Wesley

Computer Data-Base Organization, Second Edition, James Martin, 1977, Prentice-Hall

Chapter *4*

C++ and Persistence

...persistence covers every thing from writing an object out to disk and getting it back to having a full-blown distributed object-oriented database system with concurrency control, transaction logging, etc., for multiple users.

—Bjarne Stroustrup

This chapter discusses how C++ programs store data structures on disk and how those traditional techniques do not always work with C++ objects in an object-oriented design. The problems cause programmers to rethink file and database management. Ultimately those problems influence any design in which object persistence is a concern, and they are the primary motivation for developing object database managers such as PARODY.

File Input/Output in C

Reading and writing data records in C is a relatively simple matter. You define a structure, put some data into it, and write the structure to a disk file. A generic file input/output function can read and write the structure by using the *sizeof* operator. This method adjusts to modifications that change the structure. If you need features beyond simple record input/output, you can use a database management system, but, either way, you use flat record structures. The C solution looks like Figure 4.1.

```
struct Employee    {
    /* ... */
} Employee empl;
fread(&empl, sizeof(struct Employee), 1, dp);
```

FIGURE 4.1 *Persistence in C*

The C solution is not perfect. If the structure contains a pointer, the generic file input/output function becomes somewhat less generic. It has to know what the pointer points to, the length of that object, whether the pointer points to a single object or an array, and, if the pointer points to array, the size of each element and how many there are. If the pointer points to another pointer, the problem is compounded. Except for these restrictions, file input/output in C is a straightforward procedure.

File Input/Output in C++

Does the absence of consequential problems mean that C is a better language for database management than C++? No, it does not, because C's ability to support straightforward record input/output reflects its limitations in the expression of data records. You can read and write in C what you can express in C.

C++ is a richer environment for expressing user-defined data types. Its breadth has consequences that influence how you store and retrieve objects. C++ introduces a new set of problems related to what you can put in a class.

The features of C++ suggest a solution to the problems they pose. Inheritance is a likely mechanism for adding a persistent property to an object. Consider a *Persistent* base class that manages object input and output for derived classes. With such a base class, you could derive a class from it in the manner shown in Figure 4.2.

```
class Employee : public Persistent  {
    EmployeeNo emplno;
    string *name;
    Department& dept;
    int promotion_ctr;
    Date *promotions;
public:
    virtual int SalaryReviewPeriod();
};
```

FIGURE 4.2 *A derived Persistent class*

The would-be persistent *Employee* class in Figure 4.2 has several data members:

 ♦ an embedded instance of another class, known to the application.

 ♦ a pointer to an object of the standard string class.

 ♦ a reference to an object of one of the application's classes.

 ♦ a count of the number of members in an array.

 ♦ a pointer to the first member of an array.

To complicate matters, the class has a virtual function, which means that there is a *vptr* (virtual function table pointer) somewhere among the other data members. Furthermore, you do not know whether the embedded objects themselves have *vptr*s.

The Problem with C++ Persistent Objects

How would you design a *Persistent* base class that would know how to find all the pertinent data members and write them to disk? How would the class know how to construct those data members properly to read them back in? How would it know the size and location of the data members? How could it possibly understand the application-dependent relationship between the *promotion_ctr* member and the *promotions* member? How would it know to get around the one or more *vptr*s in the class?

The answer is, it would not, and you could not design such a *Persistent* base class. The following paragraphs examine each of these problems in detail.

The Size of the Object

Assuming that the object's format is a flat structure of data members with none of the attendant problem members such as pointers, references, and so on, you might consider a *Persistent* base class that begins like the one in Figure 4.3.

```
class Persistent   {
    fstream objfile;
public:
    Persistent()
        { objfile.read(this, sizeof(*this)); }
    virtual ~Persistent()
        { objfile.write(this, sizeof(*this)); }
};
class Employee : public Persistent  {
    // ...
};
```

FIGURE 4.3 *A flawed Persistent base class*

In theory, a class that wants to be persistent would derive itself from the *Persistent* base class, as shown in Figure 4.3. The base constructor and destructor functions would read and write the object.

Can you see the flaws in this scheme?

The constructor for a base class executes before the constructor for the derived class. Therefore, when the base constructor executes, no *Employee* object yet exists, except for the part that the *Employee* class inherits from the *Persistent* class. None of the derived class's members has been initialized. None of what its constructor contributes to its construction has been done. Assuming that the object would eventually somehow identify itself well enough for the *Persistent* class to find its disk record address, none of that work is done yet.

Conversely, a base destructor does not execute until the derived destructor has completed. The *Persistent* destructor executes after the *Employee* object's destructor has destroyed the *Employee* data members. There might be nothing left to save to disk. The data values may or may not have survived in the object's allocated memory. Everything would depend on what the derived destructor does.

The solution shown in Figure 4.3 will rarely work, if it works at all. The program must wait until the object is fully constructed before it can read the data members, and it has to write them before they are destroyed. Figure 4.3 is a failed design. The base class in Figure 4.4 attempts to correct these flaws.

```
class Persistent   {
    fstream objfile;
public:
    void Read()
        { objfile.read(this, sizeof(*this)); }
    void Write()
        { objfile.write(this, sizeof(*this)); }
};
```

FIGURE 4.4 *Improved but flawed Persistent base class*

The *Persistent* base class in Figure 4.4 adds *Read* and *Write* member functions that can be called after the object is constructed and before it is destroyed. Apparently, the derived class and/or its user must participate in the object's persistence. Merely inheriting the behavior of a *Persistent* base class is not enough. This is an important discovery. It figures prominently in later chapters.

Whether the derived class calls *Read* and *Write* from its own constructor and destructor or the using program calls them while the object is in scope is irrelevant. The base class still does not work. Can you see why?

The base class is using the *sizeof* operator to specify the size of the object. The *sizeof* operator is not polymorphic. When you apply *sizeof* to a base class, it returns the size of an object of the base class, whether or not the object is a derived class. To solve that problem, the *Persistent* class levies another responsibility on the derived class—the derived class must supply its own size. Figure 4.5 shows that modification in place.

```
class Persistent   {
    fstream objfile;
    int size;
protected:
    Persistent(int sz) : size(sz)
        { objfile.open("DB",ios::in|ios::out|ios::binary); }
    void Read()
        { objfile.read((char *)this, size); }
    void Write()
        { objfile.write((char *)this, size); }
    virtual ~Persistent()
        { objfile.close(); }
};
class Employee : public Persistent   {
    // ...
public:
    Employee() : Persistent(sizeof(*this))
        { Read(); }
    ~Employee()
        { Write(); }
};
```

FIGURE 4.5 *A Persistent base class that almost works*

The *Persistent* base class in Figure 4.5 almost works. The constructor for the *Employee* class provides the size of its own object in the call to the constructor to the *Persistent* class. From that value, the *Persistent* class now knows the size of the object, and it can read and write the correct size. If you can assume that the problems yet to be discussed cannot occur or that they are not allowed in a derived class, then the base class is capable of reading and writing the data members of objects of the derived class. There are two small bugs, however. Can you find them?

> **Note:** This discussion has avoided—for now—how to position the file's pointers to the object's location. It also defers any discussion about how to handle objects whose sizes change while they are in scope and how to delete objects. These are valid concerns, but their solutions involve no obstacle more serious than the

selection of an appropriate approach. The book addresses these matters after identifying and resolving more serious problems.

Non-Persistent Members

The issue of object size is resolved, but the other problems are still ahead. Figure 4.5 hints at the next two problems. By reading and writing the entire size of the object beginning at its address, the program reads over the *objfile* data member that defines the *fstream* object and the *vptr* variable that points at the hidden *vtbl* for the class. More about that later. These bugs will surely cause the system to fail.

You could define the *objfile* object as *static* and get it out of the object's data space. That would solve that particular problem if all *Persistent* objects used the same file, but the bug is an indication of ones that your derived classes could have as well.

Many derived classes would have objects that should not be read and written. Some data variables deal with the run-time context. There could be state variables such as input/output handles or user interface window handles that depend on run-time conditions and that must not or should not persist beyond a specific instance of the data type. The *Persistent* base class cannot know about these data members in the derived class and therefore cannot, without cooperation from the derived class, do anything to get around them.

Pointers in the Object

Refer to Figure 4.2. The hypothetical derived class has pointers. A *Persistent* base class cannot know anything about those pointers. It has no way of knowing the data types the pointers point to. Even though you, the programmer, can look straight at that class definition and see clearly what the pointers are, the base class cannot—particularly at run-time. C++ is not that kind of object-oriented language. Such languages might exist, but C++ is not one of them.

Clearly, the base class cannot write and read the pointer values to and from the database. The value from one instance of the object is not likely to persist for a subsequent instance. The pointer would point into unknown territory. The object that it points to might not even have been constructed for the subsequent instance. Moreover, the base class cannot tell that the data member is a pointer because the base class cannot know anything at all about the contents of the derived class.

Clearly, something other than the *Persistent* class has to decide which data members to read and write and which ones to skip.

References in the Object

The class in Figure 4.2 has a reference to another object. When you see a reference to an object within another object, you know that the data members for the referenced object are somewhere else. Chances are, the referenced object has not been constructed at the time the referencing object gets read in. The problems are similar to those of the pointer but with one more wrinkle—a reference in an object *must* be initialized by the object's constructor declarator block. To instantiate an object that has a reference in it, you must already have the referenced object in scope. A *Persistent* base class cannot know how to do that. Only the derived class or the application that uses it can know where the referenced object is.

Format-Defining Related Objects

You can probably assume that the *promotions* pointer in the class definition in Figure 4.2 points to an array of objects and that the *promotion_ctr* integer is a count of the number of objects in that array. You can make that assumption because the members' identifiers and their proximity to one another suggest that to be the case. A *Persistent* class could not infer such relationships among the members in the derived class and could not, therefore, do anything appropriate with them.

Embedded Objects

An object that is embedded in the would-be persistent object repeats all the same problems of the *Persistent* object except that they are not as obvious at first glance. You have to go to the class design for the embedded object. If you designed the embedded object for your application, then you have some control over how much and how well it participates in its own persistence. Nonetheless, you still have to address all the same problems of persistence that the original class has.

Remember, too, that embedded objects can themselves contain embedded objects.

Objects from Class Libraries

If the persistent class embeds, references, or points to objects from class libraries, the format and design of those classes are probably beyond your control. You can do little to recruit those classes for participation in their own persistence, particularly if you have no source code for the class members. Even if you have the code, the classes might be under rigid project management that forbids their modification. (You could contrive persistent specializations of those classes through multiple inheritance, but the resulting design could become too complex to comprehend.)

It would be a shame to have to adopt a persistent object strategy that does not permit you to use other class libraries in your design. A reason for choosing C++ in the first place is the vast resource of class libraries that support specific problem domains. You should not have to forsake such a resource just to include persistence.

Virtual Functions

The class in Figure 4.2 includes a virtual function. When a class has virtual functions, the compiler builds a table of pointers to the functions to accompany the class. Usually, only one table exists in memory for the class, and each object of the class has a pointer to the table. These conventions might vary between compilers, but the mechanics, and therefore the attendant problems, are similar to those described here. The pointer in the object is called the *vptr*, and the table is called the *vtbl*. When the class has derived classes and when those derived classes override the virtual functions, the compiler puts the overriding function addresses in the *vtbl*. The C++ language supports polymorphism by calling virtual functions through these tables.

The presence of a hidden *vptr* presents another problem for the *Persistent* base class and is another reason that the base class shown in Figure 4.5 cannot work some of the time. If the program writes the full contents of the object to a disk file, the image includes the *vptr*. If another program instantiates the object and if the base class reads its image from the database, the image writes an old, incorrect value over the new program's *vptr* for the object. When the program tries to execute one of the virtual functions, the system probably crashes.

There is no way around the *vptr* problem. You cannot eliminate virtual functions. The *Persistent* base class must have a virtual destructor so that the derived destructors are executed in cases when destruction occurs through a reference or pointer to the base class.

Copies of Objects

A persistent object can exist in two places: in the database and in the memory of the computer when a program instantiates it. While the object is in memory, the memory copy represents the object. Any changes that the program makes to the object reflect the current state of that object, and the disk copy is—at least for the moment—out of date and potentially unstable. When the object goes out of scope, the persistent database manager returns the memory copy to the disk, and everything returns to a stable condition.

What happens when the program makes two copies of the object? There are several ways that this can happen: The program can instantiate more than one copy and have both of them in scope at the same time; the program can pass an object by value to another function; the program can assign the object to another object of the same class.

To C++, these multiple copies are different objects, but to the application, they are the same. Employee 123 is Bobby Pickwood, regardless of how many copies of Bobby's employee record are in the computer. Now suppose that the program changes the two copies in different ways. Whichever copy of the object goes out of scope last is the one that prevails, and that is not necessarily the desired effect.

The situation just described represents a less-than-perfect program design, but sometimes it can happen to the unwary. Should the persistent database manager worry about this problem, or should there simply be a rule stating that you do not write code that duplicates objects? These issues are addressed in later chapters.

Summary

This chapter discussed the problems associated with storing and retrieving objects in a persistent object database. The process is not as easy as it might appear at first glance, and this chapter explained why. Chapter 5 discusses some alternative solutions to those problems and identifies the objectives of a persistent object database.

References

The Annotated C++ Reference Manual, Ellis and Stroustrup, 1990, Addison-Wesley

Chapter 5

Solving the Persistent Object

> *Persistence is the property of an object through which its existence transcends time (i.e. the object continues to exist after its creator ceases to exist) and/or space (i.e. the object's location moves from the address space in which it was created).*

> —Grady Booch

Chapter 4 posed several problems related to supporting persistent objects in a higher-level C++ base class that assumes most of the burden for persistence. This chapter looks at alternative solutions to those problems and identifies the objectives of a proposed solution.

Alternative Solutions

How can you solve the problems posed in Chapter 4? There are a number of ways to approach the solution. Some of them solve parts of the problem, and some solve other parts. Some solutions are less than no solution at all. Among the alternatives are:

- Use custom file input/output methods.
- Extend the C++ language.
- Write a C++ preprocessor.
- Limit the scope of a persistent class.
- Use a relational database management system.
- Let the persistent class participate in its own persistence.

The most frequently used solution, described next, is one of the least desirable.

Custom File Input/Output Methods

This first alternative is nothing more than what many C++ programmers have been using all along. They forgo the idea of a *Persistent* base class because of the difficulties. Instead, they write custom file storage and retrieval methods for the persistent classes in their design. This approach, although widely used, betrays everything that programmers have learned about database management in the last 30 years.

A long time ago, programmers discovered the inherent similarities in the requirements for database management across applications. From that discovery grew disciplined data models and database management software systems that implemented them. These were important discoveries and developments. Many large-scale software systems exist today only because database management tools existed to make them possible. It is unthinkable that the software industry would not have hit upon what is now obvious—that the processes of organizing, storing, and retrieving data records should be managed by reusable, general-purpose systems software.

The apparent persistence-contrary nature of the C++ class definition described in Chapter 4 is the result of its power. You can design a class with all the things that are difficult for a database manager to pin down.

You want those things in your classes even though they get in the way of an easy persistence strategy. But that doesn't mean you should abandon the effort—only that it is going to take some thought and work.

Extend the C++ Language

The second alternative is to change the syntax of C++ to include persistence. You can't do that on your own, though. C++ is a formal language undergoing formal definition by the ANSI X3J16 C++ standardization committee. You might propose to X3J16 that it add the persistent attribute to the language and that it figure out how to make it work. Perhaps you could develop the syntax and implementation details. Assuming that you propose a workable design, it is doubtful that you could persuade the committee's Extensions Group (chaired by Bjarne Stroustrup) to adopt it. The committee has charted a course that standardizes the language in ways that conform with the *Annotated Reference Manual* with a few extensions, and many influential experts rightly assert that persistence is not a language issue. The nature of persistence tends to draw the solution closer to the target operating environment. C++ is a portable language, as portable as C if not more so. One of the features of both languages is that their compilers are written in the languages themselves. If you add input/output primitives to the language, the portability of the compiler and of the language is compromised.

There are language features that the X3J16 committee can add to C++, however, that enhance object database management systems. One such feature is run-time type information (RTTI). When I wrote the first edition of this book, RTTI was under consideration but not yet defined or approved. Now, RTTI is officially a part of the language, and software systems such as PARODY can use it.

The Object Database Management Group has, as part of its ODMG-93 standard, maintained an interest in proposals to the ANSI X3J16 committee for extensions to the C++ language that would support object database management. Two of these proposals (ANSI document X3J16/92-0048) are:

- ◆ Permit overloading the dot (.) operator so that dynamic logical views of object retrievals can be supported.
- ◆ Distinguish between *rvalue* and *lvalue* usage of overloaded dot (.) and subscript ([]) operators so that an object database

manager can automatically sense when a program has written a change to a memory-resident persistent object and automatically write the object to disk.

Write a Preprocessor

You can extend C++ without getting involved with X3J16 by writing a preprocessor program that translates an extended C++ language into correct C++ code. This approach is consistent with the tradition of C++; the original C++ implementation from AT&T translates C++ code into C. Depending on the extent of your translator's support for persistence, the preprocessor might need to search all the header files included in your program down to the deepest nested level. This search would ferret out the formats of embedded classes to see how to save and retrieve their data members. The preprocessor approach does not solve problems discussed in Chapter 4, such as the relationship between the array element counter and the array pointer, but it is a step closer. Some object-oriented database management systems use preprocessors.

Limit the Scope of a Persistent Class

You can probably get around all the problems mentioned in Chapter 4 by laying down ground rules for users of your persistent object database system. You can specify that to derive from the *Persistent* class, an object may not use any of the C++ features that cause those problems. If your application can get by without the features, then such an approach might work. However, if limiting a persistent object class to what is easy to implement suits you, then you might as well use one of the relational DBMSs that are already available.

Use a Relational DBMS

You can build an object database manager by putting a C++ wrapper around an existing C library that implements a relational DBMS. That is a viable approach, and there are times when it is the appropriate one. Some so-called persistent object database management systems are simply wrapper classes. Chapters 6 and 10 discuss some of the considerations for making this decision.

The Persistent Class Participates in Its Own Persistence

This alternative is the one used by the software in this book. Every problem identified in Chapter 4 points to one undeniable conclusion. The intelligence that identifies what can and should be persistent in a class is contained in the class itself. The class must cooperate with the persistent object database management system. That conclusion is the basis for the PARODY database management software described later in this book. The rest of this chapter is about the objectives for PARODY, the Persistent, Almost Relational Object Database manager in which a class cooperates in its own persistence.

Objectives of a Persistent Object Database

The first objective is for an effective method to describe the persistence cooperation of the using class. It must be easy for programmers to use. The database manager must have a simple, intuitive, and consistent interface. There should be a minimum number of member functions in the interface, and they should use C++ language features in an intuitive manner. This objective permeates the PARODY project. Following are specific objectives for how the persistent object database system must work.

Object Identity

When a program creates an object, the object's identity is (if nothing else) its location in the program's memory–that is, its address. Certainly the program knows where it is. When the program is finished with the object, the database manager stores the object in a database, and the program has no further need to identify the object. Subsequently, when the program or another program reuses the object, the program provides identifying information to the database manager to retrieve the object. The original object's memory address is without meaning then. There must be something about the object known to the program that the database manager can use to retrieve the object from the database.

There are two ways to access objects in a database—navigational and associative access—and support for both is an objective of a persistent object database manager.

NAVIGATIONAL ACCESS

Navigational access assigns object identifications—usually related to the object's logical address in the database—as the object's identity. The application remembers these addresses in order to retrieve the objects at a later time. Objects related to other objects of other classes use object identities to point to their relatives.

When a program creates a persistent object, the object database manager reports the object's identity to the program. The application decides how to use the identity to retrieve the object and relate it to other objects of the same and other classes.

ASSOCIATIVE ACCESS

Associative access uses key data members to associate objects with their position in the database. The application retrieves objects by providing primary key data member values to search. It relates objects by storing primary key data members as secondary keys in other classes.

The persistent object database manager maintains index files that associate navigational object identities with key member values. When a program creates an object with a primary key value, the database manager updates the index. When a subsequent program instantiates an object of the same class and specifies the same key value, the database manager retrieves the associated object. The database manager maintains secondary indexes, too, so that programs can retrieve specific objects on the basis of data values other than the primary key.

Maintenance of Objects

The persistent object database manager includes methods to add, retrieve, change, and delete objects in the database. The database is not merely a repository or cache of stray objects. The application creates objects and specifies that they are to be persistent. The application retrieves specific persistent objects that were created earlier, changes their data values, and returns the updated objects to the database. The application deletes specific objects from the database. These capabilities have implications with respect to the application-specific integrity of the relationships between objects.

Object Integrity

Maintaining object integrity means that the database does not store ambiguous objects and that it does not retrieve objects that have not previously been stored. Ensuring object integrity in an associative access database is one of the objectives. The persistent object database manager indicates when a requested object is not in the database, and it refuses to add objects when the addition would collide with—have the same identity as—an existing object.

If the application instantiates an object with a primary key value that the database does not recognize, the database manager so indicates.

If the application tries to add an object when one already exists with the same primary key value, the database manager refuses to add the object and returns a negative response to the add request.

Maintaining object integrity keeps the database in a stable condition with respect to the requirements of the application. There should not be two department records with the same department number. A program should not behave as if it has retrieved an employee object when no employee record exists with the requested employee number.

Navigational Class Relationships

In a navigational access database, classes are related to one another by data members in the class design that emulate C++ reference objects but that extend the reference to the database. If a class maintains a persistent reference to an object, the program instantiates both objects and assigns the reference. Both objects must be instances of persistent classes. When the referencing object is written to the database, the reference information is written along with it. The technique uses navigational object identity—which is hidden from the class user—to form the reference. When the program reinstantiates the referencing object, the database manager automatically instantiates the referenced object, reads it from the database, and forms the reference through the persistent reference data member in the referencing class. The referencing object can access the referenced object through its persistent reference data member.

Associative Class Relationships

In an associative access database, classes are related to one another in ways that the application manages. The relationship is important to the application. Objects of the employee class are related to objects of the department class where the employees work. In a strictly object-oriented program, classes can be related by references or pointers in one class to other classes. This method works as long as the objects are memory-bound. The references and pointers refer to memory addresses. When the objects are in the database, such addresses are not usable. When other programs retrieve the objects, the addresses are meaningless. Some object-oriented database managers assign logical addresses to the persistent objects and an index of those addresses to the physical disk addresses. For those addresses to have meaning to an application, the application must relate them to data values that identify the object.

The persistent object database specified in this chapter maintains relationships between associative access classes on the basis of key data values rather than on the basis of pointers, and it maintains the integrity of those relationships. If a class includes another class's primary key as a secondary key, the classes have an implied relationship. The persistent object database does not delete an object if other objects that are related to it remain, and it does not attempt to relate an object to one that does not exist.

If the application retrieves an employee object and changes its department identification—perhaps because of a user's input—to an invalid department, the database manager does not allow the object to be returned to the database. What is more, the database manager notifies the application that the replacement was not allowed. Without these controls, a database would have the potential to become chaotic, with records implying relationships that could not exist. The database would have lost track of the employee's department assignment. A subsequent application program might depend on the presence of department information for every employee, and that program would fail when it processed the errant object.

If the application deletes a department object while there are employee objects related to it, the same kind of integrity violation occurs. Therefore, the object database manager does not allow an application to delete an object if other objects are related to it. You cannot shut down (delete) the department while employees are still working there. You must transfer (change) or terminate (delete) the employees so that none of them are assigned to the department that you want to delete. The data model reflects the problem domain that it supports.

Copies of Objects

If a program declares multiple memory copies of an object—whether through assignment, copy construction, or multiple instances—the database manager must know about it. There are several ways to deal with that situation. One solution marks all subsequent copies as being read-only. The application can change only the original copy. Another solution simply ignores the problem and treats it as a policy matter. Programs should not make copies of objects in this approach. A third solution, which the software in this book uses, is to apply a C++ idiom called *reference counting*, in which all such copies are actually references to the original. Chapter 8 describes how that works.

Summary

This chapter discussed several alternative solutions to the problems presented in Chapter 4. Then it chose one of them as the basis for the PARODY system and developed the objectives for that system. Chapter 6 compares the object database with the relational data model, shows how the object model benefits from the lessons of relational technology, and discusses when you should choose each one.

References

The Design and Evolution of C++, Bjarne Stroustrup, 1994, Addison-Wesley

The Object Database Standard: ODMG-93, R.G.G. Cattrell, 1994, Morgan Kaufmann Publishers

The Annotated C++ Reference Manual, Ellis and Stroustrup, 1990, Addison-Wesley

Chapter 6

The Object Database and the Relational Database

The compass and square produce perfect circles and squares. By the sages, the human relations are perfectly exhibited.

—Mencius

The object database is a relatively new concept. There are not nearly as many implementations as there are of the traditional relational database, although that situation is changing.

Some persistent object implementations emulate the in-memory nature of object relationships in a program by writing a disk image that contains all of memory. Others put C++ wrapper classes around existing relational database management systems. Still others use *Extern "C"* linkage specifications to link with database management function libraries. There is still no consensus about what constitutes a genuine *object-oriented database*. The work of the Object Database Management Group will eventually provide that definition, but the technology is young. We are still learning about its implications, complications, and consequences.

The relational database is, on the other hand, a time-worn and proven concept. Relational technology evolved in the 1970s to solve the problems associated with traditional hierarchical and network databases. The relational data model eliminated hidden pointers by forming file relationships with data values, and it improved the user's perception of data representations by making the schema visible to the user and functionally relevant to the application.

There are restrictions in the relational data model that discourage its use in an object-oriented design. Conversely, it has benefits that encourage its use. This chapter compares the requirements for an object database to the advantages of the relational data model for two purposes: first, to identify the items you should consider when deciding whether to use the object or relational models; second, to identify and justify those features of the relational model to adopt for the PARODY object model.

The Object Database Model

If the object model—the basis for object-oriented design—applies the principles of abstraction, encapsulation, inheritance, and polymorphism, then the object database model must extend the object model into the realm of database management. Objects, therefore, may be stored in and retrieved from an object storage medium that survives after the object's creator expires. An object stored in such an object database is a *persistent object*.

Each persistent object possesses a unique identity. Except for that, the object database model imposes no requirements or restrictions on the content or format of the persistent object. Therefore, if you can define and instantiate an object of a user-defined data type, you can store that object in an object database and retrieve it at a later time.

Until recently there has been no formal definition of how the object database model should be implemented. Its internal format and architecture are still not defined. Its interface with a using program is being studied and developed now. The work is not yet complete. The PARODY object database implementation in this book does not comply with any standard, de facto or otherwise, because so far no such standard exists.

To understand why this is so, you must consider the relationships between traditional programming paradigms and database models. There is no *relational* programming paradigm. There is no *structured* database model. Programmers adopted structured programming because it was superior to the ways they had been using to express procedural algorithms. Database designers adopted the relational database model because it was superior to the ways with which they had been designing databases. The two came together only coincidentally. A structured program could always use a nonrelational data model. A nonstructured program was in no way prevented from using the relational data model. But because procedural programming does not encapsulate the design of data representation and data behavior, the two then-superior approaches to software design were never necessarily bound.

The object model is the first attempt to marry a programming model with a database model. Why? Object-oriented design expresses data abstraction in ways that no traditional data model does. Object-oriented design needs its own database model.

Inasmuch as there are no restrictions on the format and content of a persistent object, the object data model is able to represent any kind of data. There are applications that use streams of data that traditional database management systems do not manage well. Usually, these data streams represent long, variable-length, formless bit packages which are sometimes in arrays of variable dimensions.

CAD/CAM systems deal with such objects. They store digital representations of engineering designs that consist of wire-frame and solid models. The models record the properties of their composition to facilitate finite-element analysis of their reactions to stress, temperature, vibration, and motion. Imagery systems store raster scanned images. Cartography and meteorological systems store points, vectors, and references to cataloged features. Multimedia systems store bit streams of audio and video recordings. Text-processing systems store streams of text with embedded formatting control fields.

Objects such as the ones just described appear formless to the casual observer, and so they are not particularly suitable for a database model that imposes rigid form. You would have to reform the objects to make them fit the database.

The Relational Database Model

The relational model is the result of the work of E.F. Codd in the 1960s. He described a data model in which entities of data are represented by *relations*, which resemble tables of *rows* and *columns*. Most programmers view these relations as files in a database. The rows are the individual file records, and the columns are the fields within the records. Codd does not define the model to that level, however, leaving the details of how to form the relations to the implementor. Codd calls the rows by another name—*tuples*.

Figure 6.1 shows a typical, simple relational database with two relations.

DEPARTMENTS	
DEPT_NO	DEPT_NAME
00020	SALES
00030	ACCOUNTING
00040	ENGINEERING
00050	MANUFACTURING

EMPLOYEES				
EMPL_NO	EMPL_NAME	DATE_HIRED	SALARY	DEPT_NO
00001	JONES	05/06/84	22000	00030
00002	SMITH	02/04/83	22000	00020
00003	BROWN	09/21/82	21000	00030
00004	GREEN	07/12/80	18000	00040
00005	WHITE	11/11/85	25000	00020

FIGURE 6.1 *A relational database*

Any discussion of the relational model is incomplete without consideration of Codd's 12 rules. Without enumerating them here or presenting them in their original sequence, this discussion addresses the essence of the rules to the extent necessary to compare the features with the object model.

As shown in Figure 6.1, all the rows in a relation have the same columns. The data value for a particular row/column may be *null*, which means that no value has been assigned.

There are no repeating groups—arrays—in a relation. There are no variable-length columns.

Each relation has a column or aggregate of columns that is its primary key data element. Each row must have a unique value in that key to distinguish the row from the other rows in the relation. The EMPL_NO column is the key data element for the EMPLOYEES relation in Figure 6.1. The DEPT_NO column is the key data element for the DEPART-MENTS relation. A program may not add an EMPLOYEE relation with an EMPL_NO column value of 00002, for example, because one already exists.

The application program may retrieve any element of data in the database by specifying the relation, the column name, and the value of the relation's key column, which might not be the same column as the one being retrieved. Many implementations simply allow the application to retrieve the full record by providing a buffer that holds it and the key value.

The relational database describes its own schema in a file called the *catalog*. This catalog allows general-purpose query and report writer languages to interact with the user and the database.

The user can create *views* of the database from queries. The views look like relations but are the result of specifying a different configuration of columns with the PROJECT operator, combining the contents of multiple relations with the JOIN operator, and using a subset of the possible rows with the SELECT operator. These views are not, theoretically, new relations. If a data value in the database changes, any views that the data element participates in reflect the change. The user can change a view only when the change would not damage the integrity of other views or of the database itself.

The database manager enforces the integrity of the relationships that exist between relations as specified by rules in the catalog. With the database shown in Figure 6.1, a program cannot delete the DEPARTMENT row that has the 00020 DEPT_NO column value because employees are still assigned. Similarly, a program cannot assign an employee to a department that does not exist.

Database administration does not affect the users' operations. If the administrator reorganizes the physical or logical organization of the database, the users are unaffected.

Choosing a Database Model

When should you use a relational database and when should you use an object database? The answer depends on several considerations. Is your problem domain already supported by a mature database and database management system? If so, you might not want to risk the change. Pioneers, although heroes in history, did not reap the rewards of their explorations. Those who followed after the way was made safe found profit and success. The same is true in software design. If your design can leverage earlier successful efforts, it stands a better chance for success of its own.

If you are not building on earlier work, then the answer lies in an analysis of the mutually exclusive strengths and weaknesses of the two data models and the requirements of your application. The relational data model has advantages that the object data model cannot support. Among these are:

♦ The relational schema is stored in the database catalog.

♦ General-purpose query programs can use the catalog.

♦ The SELECT, PROJECT, and JOIN operators can build new database views at run-time.

♦ The database is compatible with other applications that use the same DBMS.

Conversely, the object data model supports data representations that the rules for the relational data model prohibit:

♦ Variable-length data members can support such applications as imagery, multimedia, geographic data, and weather.

♦ Abstract data types support user-defined data abstractions.

♦ Arrays permit repeating groups.

♦ Encapsulation of data formats with methods binds data representation and behavior.

♦ Polymorphism customizes the behavior of derived data types.

Clearly, the strength of the object data model is that it supports an object-oriented design. A designer must decide which way to go by weighing the benefits of both approaches. If you decide that you need those relational features not available in the object model, then use a relational database manager. If your database is organized into well-defined tables of rows of fixed-length columns, the relational database is the clear winner. You will find, however, that the object model can emulate some of the behavior of the relational model, and if the parts it omits are expendable, then the object model is a better choice for the C++ program.

Adapting the Relational Model to Objects

Having chosen the object model, one must decide how to implement it. Chapter 5 identified the objectives for the PARODY system of object database management. There are advantages to the relational model that the object model can adopt in support of those objectives. The most prominent one is the ability to support associative access, and a secondary one is the maintenance of relational integrity among objects. The discussion that follows describes in narrative how PARODY emulates some of the features of a relational database. Later chapters describe the PARODY interface in detail.

The Database Schema

The relational model includes a data definition language (DDL) in its catalog that defines the format of records in the database files and the relationships of files to one another. The DDL is said to define the database schema. The PARADY DDL is C++ itself. You design a database by designing classes that define the file formats and their key data members. Figure 6.2 illustrates such a design.

```
// -------- department class
class Department : public Persistent   {
    Key<int> deptno;        // primary key
    string *name;
    // ...
};
// -------- Employee class
class Employee : public Persistent      {
    Key<int> emplno;     // primary key
    Key<int> deptno;     // secondary key
    string *name;
    Date date_hired;
    Currency salary;
public:
    // ...
};
```

FIGURE 6.2 *A database schema*

The *Employee* and *Department* classes in Figure 6.2 are derived from the *Persistent* class, which is how they acquire the persistent attribute. You will learn how the *Persistent* class works in later chapters. You will learn, too, that classes derived from the *Persistent* class do specific tasks in their constructors and destructors and provide a few additional members to support their persistence.

Three data members in the two classes in Figure 6.2 use the *Key* template class. This is how you specify primary and secondary key data members. Later chapters explain how *Key* classes support the PARODY indexing mechanism. The *Employee* class has two *Key* members: the *emplno* and *deptno* objects. The first *Key* object is the class's primary key. All subsequent *Key* objects are secondary keys. There can be only one primary key member in a class, because the primary key value identifies the object. Multiple objects of the same class can however, share secondary key values. The *Department* class in Figure 6.2, for example, has a *deptno* member as its primary key, so there may be only one *Department* object with a department number of 123. The Employee class has a *deptno* member as a secondary key. There can be several employees assigned to department number 123. This relationship is an implied one based on the presence of those *Key* data members. You will learn in Chapter 8 how PARODY enforces implied relationships. The design implies the relationship, so the persistent object database can maintain it. You are not allowed to write an *Employee* object with a non-null *deptno* value unless there is a corresponding *Department* object with the same key value. You are not allowed to delete a *Department* object if any *Employee* objects include the matching *deptno* key value.

Retrieving Objects

A program retrieves a persistent object by declaring an instance of it with its primary key member value as an initializer. The program then asks the instantiated object whether it does, in fact, exist in the PARODY database. Figure 6.3 is an example of that.

```
Employee empl(123);
if (empl.ObjectExists())   {
    // --- the object exists
    // ...
}
```

FIGURE 6.3 *Retrieving a persistent object*

We will revisit this and subsequent examples in Chapter 9, which has more detail about using the PARODY *Persistent* class member functions.

Adding Objects

A program adds an object to the PARODY database by declaring one that does not exist, providing whatever data member values it needs, and telling the object to write itself to the database. Figure 6.4 is an example.

```
Employee empl(123);
if (!empl.ObjectExists())   {
    // --- the object does not exist
    // ...
    empl.AddObject();
}
```

FIGURE 6.4 *Adding a persistent object*

Changing an Object

A program changes an object on the PARODY database by declaring one that exists, changing the object's data members, and telling the object to rewrite itself to the database. Figure 6.5 is an example.

```
Employee empl(123);
if (empl.ObjectExists())   {
    // --- the object exists
    // ... (change the data members) ...
    empl.ChangeObject();
}
```

FIGURE 6.5 *Changing a persistent object*

Deleting Objects

A program deletes an object from the PARODY database by declaring one that exists and telling the object to delete itself from the database. Figure 6.6 is an example.

```
Employee empl(123);
if (empl.ObjectExists())   {
    // --- the object exists
    // ...
    empl.DeleteObject();
}
```

FIGURE 6.6 *Deleting a persistent object*

Maintaining Object Integrity

The database imposes limits on when a program is allowed to add, change, or delete an object. The program may not add an object that already exists. It may not add an object or change one if the new or changed object is related to another object that does not exist in the database. It may not delete an object if other objects are related to it. The application program needs to test for these conditions. PARODY reports the exceptions when the program tries to add, change, or delete objects in ways that violate integrity. The errors might result from user input errors, for example, and the program would need to issue an error message to the user. The *AddObject*, *ChangeObject*, and *DeleteObject* functions return a true value if they permit the action and a false value if they do not. Figure 6.7 shows how these functions work.

```
if (!empl.AddObject())
    // --- add was rejected
if (!empl.ChangeObject())
    // --- change was rejected
if (!empl.DeleteObject())
    // --- delete was rejected
```

FIGURE 6.7 *Maintaining object integrity*

Navigating a Class

A program locates an object by constructing it from the value of its primary key. A program can also find an object in the persistent database by specifying a value for one of its secondary keys. First, it instantiates an empty object, which the database does not search for. Then it initializes the secondary key value and uses the *FindObject* function to find the first object of that class in the database that has the secondary key value. Figure 6.8, which assumes that the *Employee* class has *SetDeptNo* and *DeptKey* member functions, shows how that works.

```
Employee empl;
empl.SetDeptNo(1); // initialize the dept#
empl.FindObject(empl.DeptKey());
if (empl.ObjectExists()) {
    // --- at least one object exists
    // ...
}
```

FIGURE 6.8 *Finding an object with a secondary key*

The program can retrieve the first and last persistent objects of a class in the sequence of the key value by using the *FirstObject* and *LastObject* functions, as shown in Figure 6.9.

```
Employee empl;
empl.FirstObject(empl.DeptKey());
if (empl.ObjectExists())  {
    // --- the object exists
    // ...
}
// ....
empl.LastObject(empl.DeptKey());
if (empl.ObjectExists())  {
    // --- the object exists
    // ...
}
```

FIGURE 6.9 *Finding the first and last objects of a class*

Following a *FindObject*, *FirstObject*, or *LastObject* function call, a program can navigate the persistent objects in a class in the sequence of the keys by using the *NextObject* and *PreviousObject* functions, as shown in Figure 6.10.

```
// ----- navigate forward
Employee empl;
empl.FirstObject(empl.DeptKey());
while (empl.ObjectExists())  {
    // --- process the object
    empl.DeptKey().NextObject();
    // ...
}
// ----- navigate backward
empl.LastObject(empl.DeptKey());
while (empl.ObjectExists())  {
    // --- process the object
    empl.DeptKey().PreviousObject();
    // ...
}
```

FIGURE 6.10 *Navigating a class*

Navigating Among Classes

To navigate class relationships, the program declares an object of a class that has, as a secondary key, the primary key class of another persistent class. It uses the secondary key value to declare an object of the other class. Then it processes that object and the following objects as shown in Figure 6.11, which assumes that the *Department* class has *DeptNo* and *DeptKey* member functions.

```
Department dept(321);
if (dept.ObjectExists())  {
    Employee empl;
    empl.SetDeptNo(321);
    empl.FindObject(empl.DeptKey());
    while (empl.ObjectExists() &&
             empl.DeptNo() == dept.DeptNo())  {
        // ...
        empl.NextObject(empl.DeptKey());
    }
}
```

FIGURE 6.11 *Navigating among classes*

Summary

This chapter compared the relational and object data models and offered ways to decide which you should use. Then it identified the features of the relational model that the PARODY system incorporates into the object model. Chapter 7 digresses to discuss the design process for an application's object database.

References

Database Modeling in the PC Environment, Bradley D. Kliewer, 1992, Bantam Books

An Introduction to Database Systems Second Edition, C.J. Date, 1977, Addison-Wesley

Computer Data-Base Organization Second Edition, James Martin, 1977, Prentice-Hall

## Chapter 7

Designing an Object Database

Nothing is particularly hard if you divide it into small jobs.

—Henry Ford

Object-oriented design is a big topic, one that a single chapter in a book cannot do justice to. Designing a full object-oriented software system—particularly a large, complex one—is a major undertaking that should include the counsel and participation of experienced designers. One facet of an object-oriented design is its database. Most texts about object-oriented design concentrate on in-memory object hierarchies rather than databases, teaching you to visualize classes and build accurate and meaningful class relationships. If they get into database design at all, they usually retreat to traditional relational methods, which is understandable; few object-oriented programming languages support a persistent object database. There are no systems to provide examples for a book.

This chapter explores the basics of object database design. You will learn that any programmer can design a workable database by using intuition and common sense and without applying or even understanding the mysteries of database administration. I contend that if you are smart enough to write a computer program, you are smart enough to design a database. I took the same position in *C Database Development*, asserting that database design is inherently easy, requiring only a few intuitive procedures to ensure a sound design. Thousands of programmers used the book and proved it. But that position could have been a potential target for harsh criticism by the practiced experts of relational technology. It flies in the face of tradition and threatens the sanctity of their priesthood. Taking the same position with an object database is safer. Few experts exist who can criticize it; the technology is too new.

Readers who used the earlier book will see few differences in this approach because the procedures for identifying and decomposing traditional and object database requirements are similar.

This chapter avoids the arcane disciplines usually advanced as proper database design techniques. You won't need special forms, templates, rigid rules, or disciplined procedures for design review and refinement. This chapter does not promote a formal methodology. Those tools and procedures have their place; they are for the big development project with a big system, a big staff, a big problem to solve, and structured management watching every move.

General Design Guidelines

Develop a clear understanding of the problem you are trying to solve, the solutions you might consider, and the ways to translate the solutions into a database design. Be willing to modify the solution as it evolves.

Design an object database in small increments. Learn to isolate the functionally independent parts. Build individual components that have single points of interface. Deal with each component as if it were its own database. Then integrate them as loosely as you can so that modifications to one component do not interfere with the operations of the others. If you build an *Employee* class and a *Department* class, build them separately. Except for the appearance of a department number in the employee's class and the maintenance of that relationship, the two classes should be independent. When an object of one class needs data from an object of the other or when one needs to update data in the other, add to the class interfaces—the public member functions.

The 10 Steps of Object Database Design

The design of an object database involves 10 steps taken, for the most part, in succession:

1. Identify the basis for the database requirements.
2. Define the database's functional and performance requirements.
3. Identify the data items.
4. Separate the data members from the persistent classes.
5. Build a data member dictionary.
6. Gather data members into persistent classes.
7. Identify the key data members of each class.
8. Identify the relationships between classes.
9. Identify the class methods.
10. Add the inheritance and member functions to make the classes persistent.

There is always an 11th step, which is to reiterate the first 10. Let the solution to the problem modify the problem, and let each successive solution enhance your understanding of the problem. As it does, retrace your steps through the design process, stay loose, and change your results. Don't be afraid to throw out old work and start over. This 11th step, called *refinement*, is often left out.

Identify the Basis

If you are about to design a database, you must have a mission and a purpose. Someone has asked you to automate something. Who made that request and how? How much did they know about the problem when they asked for a solution? Is the problem solved now? Is the present solution automated or not? Has anyone ever solved a similar problem in a different environment? You need to define the functional and performance requirements for the database, and the definition of these requirements should proceed from an understanding of the functions to be supported. You start by identifying the basis of that understanding.

The basis for a database specifies the problem that is to be solved, what resources can be used in the solution, and some likely approaches to the solution. The problem specification can be as simple as a one-line statement of objectives, or it can be a multiple-volume report. Consider a personnel database. A problem specification for this database could be as simple as the one shown here.

> **Problem:** Keep track of the employees within the departments where they work, including their salaries and the dates they were hired. Record the status of projects assigned to departments. Record the employees who are working on projects. Distinguish managers from project workers. Distinguish department managers from project managers.

The list of available resources includes such information as existing source documents (employee time cards, for example), interfaces to other databases, people who understand the function, and so on. Where appropriate, include examples in the list. The resources list for the personnel database could resemble the following:

Company Personnel Action Form
Project Work Order
Employee Time Card

Next, you need to analyze the possible approaches to the problem. Be as creative and unconventional as you want, but be careful. Make it clear to everyone, including yourself, that these designs are preliminary. Don't make an emotional investment in a premature design, and don't get caught in a situation where someone can hold you to one particular approach.

To define the basis, start with the present solution. If there is no present solution, start from scratch.

Starting from an Existing Solution

If the user is already using a computer to solve the problem, then you have a good place to start. The existing system provides insight into the requirements for the database. The user has experience with an automated solution and is able to tell you where the new solution can improve on the old. An existing system is a good basis for a database design.

If the user works with a manual system, start there. Collect the functions that the system supports and turn them into functional and performance requirements. A manual system probably contains enough information to guide you in automating it. As such, it is a good basis for your design. Usually the purpose of automation is to improve the system's performance, functionality, or both, in which case you can extend the basis to include the improvements.

Starting from Scratch

It is hard to imagine designing a database from scratch with no prior procedure to use for a model. Almost everything has either been automated or set up as a manual procedure. If a user asks you to initiate a completely new procedure and solve a brand new problem, you should look for an existing solution to a similar problem. Chances are, someone has already developed one. If you do not find one, you must start from scratch. The best approach is to develop manual procedures, use them for a while, and allow them to influence the basis for a new database. If you cannot do that, you must work with the user to develop an initial basis. Be advised that your design and implementation will no doubt change several times as the database takes form and is used. You rarely see the best solution the first time.

Write Down the Basis

Once you have the basis for your database, write it down. Make it clear enough that anyone who understands the application can understand the basis. Keep the written basis handy while you design and develop the system, and make updates to it as design changes occur. The basis is your foundation for the requirements analysis.

Define the Requirements

This step enumerates the requirements for the database, addressing functional requirements and performance requirements separately. A database requirement should be clear and unambiguous. It should address itself to one specific aspect of the functions or performance of the system. Each statement should stand alone, and each statement should completely define the requirement. Word it so that users and programmers alike can understand it. The requirements list is the planning document for the database. Anyone who has it and understands it should know what to expect from the system. Without it, you never know when you are finished.

Functional Requirements

Functional requirements specify the kind of data that the database contains and the system's output. Document everything you know about the functions that are supported. Write about the problem but not the solution. Say what, not how. Be specific in identifying pieces of information the database must know about. Here is an example of a list of requirements for the personnel database.

1. The system will record and report the departments in the organization by department number and name.

2. The system will record and report the organization's employees by employee number. Each employee's record will include the employee's name, salary, and date hired.

3. The system will record and report the organization's projects by project number. Each project's record will include its name and schedule, which will be represented by the start and completion dates and the number of labor hours budgeted to and expended against the project.

4. The system will record the assignment of employees to departments. An employee is assigned to one department at a time, but a department may have many employees.

5. The system will record the assignment of projects to departments. A project is assigned to one department, and a department may be responsible for many projects.

6. The system will record the assignment of employees to projects. An employee may work on several projects, including projects assigned to departments other than the department to which the employee is assigned. A project may have multiple employees assigned to it.

7. The system will record the hours worked by each employee on each project.

8. The system will record the assignment of an employee as department manager.

9. The system will record the assignment of an employee as manager of a specific project.

This list is a beginning. You would also develop requirements for specific queries and reports, perhaps with accompanying screen or report layouts. Identify cyclic processes such as transaction posting cycles. Identify archiving requirements. Such requirements can influence a database design.

Performance Requirements

Performance requirements specify frequencies, speeds, quantities, and sizes—how often, how fast, how many, and how big—that the database must support. Some of the personnel system's performance requirements might look like this list:

1. The system will support as many as 10 departments.
2. The system will support as many as 100 employees.
3. The system will support as many as 20 projects.
4. The system will support unlimited employee-to-project assignments—all the employees can be assigned to all the projects.
5. Retrieval of data recorded about an employee, project, or department will be on-line and will be in response to the user's entry of the employee, project, or department number. The system will deliver the related data within three seconds of entry of the associated control number.

This list, too, is only a beginning. The completed list would include performance criteria about backups, restart/recovery, scheduled maintenance downtime, and database administration. In a multiuser environment, it would specify access privileges and record and file locking requirements. This analysis must take growth into consideration. Make those numbers reflect the requirements for the future as well as for today.

Identify the Data Items

Having identified the requirements for the database, you can translate those requirements into identifiable elements of data. First, you identify data items. Later, those items will become classes and data members.

Delay that definition; it begins to define the solution, and, for now, you are seeking a clear and unambiguous expression of the problem.

Organize the data items that you identify. Use 3x5 cards, an on-line notepad on your computer, or some other technique that allows you to itemize, sort, and shuffle.

Rummage around in the work you have already done, looking for potential data items. From your basis and your requirements, extract references to things that look like data items. Start by pulling out the nouns. Each noun is a potential data item. Write the name of each onto a 3x5 card. Add to the card, everything else you know about the item highlighting the verbs. You'll use the verbs later when you identify the class methods.

The personnel system basis and requirements list delivers a collection of nouns as shown in Figure 7.1.

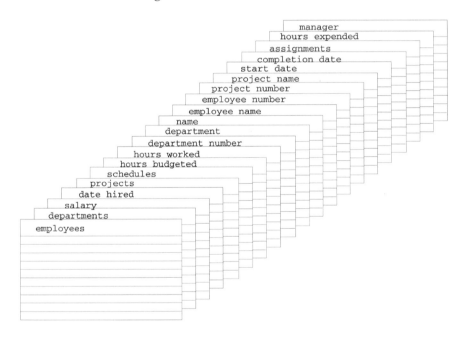

FIGURE 7.1 *Basis and requirements nouns*

You can use this list as an initial collection of the items to be recorded in and reported from the database. As your work proceeds, you can change the list.

Separate the Data Members from the Classes

You now have a collection of data items. Some of them take the form of data aggregates that represent persistent classes, or files, in the database. Others are data members within those classes. This step distinguishes the two.

Unlike similar parts of traditional database design, this step does not clearly separate the aggregates from the data elements. In an object-oriented design, some of the so-called data elements are themselves abstract data types, or classes. Your task is to recognize which of the data items are to be persistent classes and which are to be data members of persistent classes.

This is where you apply judgment, intuition, and guesswork. Look at the data items you have collected. Which of these items seem to be individual data members, and which seem more like logically organized aggregates of data members? Shuffle them up, sort them out, and move them around. The 3x5 card method works well here. It should become obvious which items are members and which are not. A date, for example, is clearly a data member even though it is likely to be an instance of an abstract data type, perhaps taken from a class library. It is not as obvious that an assignment is not a data member. Can you see how a department number is a data member whereas a department is an aggregate represented by a number of data members, including the department number?

The objective of this exercise is to separate the data members from the persistent classes so that you can take the next two steps. The data member nouns from the list above are in this subset of the list:

- ♦ salary
- ♦ date hired
- ♦ hours budgeted
- ♦ hours worked
- ♦ department number
- ♦ department name
- ♦ employee name
- ♦ employee number

- project number
- project name
- start date
- completion date
- hours expended
- manager

Build the Data Member Dictionary

Now you begin to formulate the solution. Once you have identified what the data members are and have a list like the one above, build the data member dictionary, which enumerates the various data members in the database. It is important to itemize these members separately so that later you can identify the redundancies and interclass relationships.

The nouns in the list of data items are the ones that are not going to be persistent classes; they are going to be members of persistent classes. Some of them are abstract data types. The salary is probably an instance of a currency class. The dates are no doubt instances of a date class. The names are instances of a string class.

The data types for several data items are not apparent from this list. The employee number, department number, and project number could be something other than simple integer types, depending on how the application defines them. The hours data items might be primitive integer types, or they might be abstract integer types with defined ranges. The format of the manager data item is unclear at this time. The requirement is to record department and project managers. You will address that one later.

You must collect everything that is known or that can be determined about each data member. At the very least, you need to know the data type. If you are basing the design on an existing system, the documentation—if any—can contribute to your dictionary. If the documentation is inadequate but the source code is available, you can reverse-engineer the data member characteristics by seeing how the existing software uses them. If you are automating a manual system, you can look at the entry forms (time cards, posting ledgers, and so on) to see how the manual system uses the data members. Sometimes these forms have accompanying procedures. You can use these procedures to find the descriptions of the manual entries and extrapolate the requirements for the data members.

Describing dates, Social Security numbers, telephone numbers, ZIP codes, or shoe sizes is easy: These data members have known ranges, formats, and/or enumerated values, and there may be library classes that you can use. But other data members are not so well defined by common usage. Quantities and amounts may have limits—how high can they get? Can they be negative? How many decimal places? And so on. Account numbers, vendor numbers, client numbers, employee numbers, part numbers, stock numbers, customer numbers, and untold numbers of other numbers are not universally defined. Many so-called numbers consist of letters and punctuation as well as digits.

It is important that you clearly define the physical properties of all the data members in the database. You must complete as much of this definition as possible before you proceed with the design. When a data member has a clearly defined format and behavior, you should build a class to implement the member as an abstract data type.

Gather the Data Members into Classes

When you separate data members from aggregates, the aggregates are left over. You must deal with those aggregates, and chances are they are going to be persistent classes. The following data items did not make it into the data member dictionary:

- ◆ employees
- ◆ departments
- ◆ projects
- ◆ schedules
- ◆ assignments

Look at your requirements now to see which of those items should be persistent classes. None of the requirements calls for the permanent retention of specific schedule records. The information that might be used to report a schedule condition is information that would be recorded about a project (the dates, the budget) or an assignment (the hours worked). So you can drop schedules from the list. Those that remain are potentially—but not absolutely—the persistent classes.

Now you can define the data representation of the persistent classes. To define a class, start with its data members. Use your trusty 3x5 cards.

Fan out the cards and pull out everything related to an employee. This is not as simple as it sounds. It is obvious that the department name is not related to the employee and that the employee name is. But is the data member that records the hours worked by an employee on a project specifically related to the employee? It is not, at least not immediately. You cannot put that data member into the employee's class because there could be multiple values for that member for the same employee—the employee can work on more than one project. The department name is not related to the employee, but is the department number? Yes. An employee is assigned to one and only one department, and the departments are identified by department number, so the department number can be a part of the employee record.

By examining each data member and viewing it in the light of its relevance to an employee, you can build a stack of 3x5 cards that are the data members for the *Employee* class. This stack contains the cards for the employee number, employee name, date hired, salary, and department number. Assuming that the abstract data types for dates, money, and strings already exist, and that the employee, project, and department numbers can be integers, you can make a first cut at the data representation of the *Employee* class design. Figure 7.2 shows how that might look.

> **Note:** Observe the use of *typedef*s to define types for controlling data elements. By defining these type synonyms, you isolate their definitions in one location. If you decide later that the employee number should be another type, perhaps even a class, you can make the change in one place and recompile the program.

```
typedef int EmployeeNumber;
typedef int DepartmentNumber;
class Employee {
    EmployeeNumber emplno;
    string name;
    Date date_hired;
    Money salary;
    DepartmentNumber deptno;
};
```

FIGURE 7.2 *The Employee class*

Next, you design the other persistent classes. Remember that you are never finished. Always be willing to change what you have done before. Do not allow your current design to be constrained by the ones that preceded it. If you cannot get something designed correctly because of an earlier design, then retreat and review that earlier design. Figure 7.3 shows a first cut at the *Department* and *Project* classes, which assume that data members such as *hours_budgeted* are unbounded integer types.

```
class Department  {
    DepartmentNumber deptno;
    string name;
};
typedef int ProjectNumber;
class Project  {
    ProjectNumber projno;
    string name;
    int hours_budgeted;
    Date start_date;
    Date completion_date;
};
```

FIGURE 7.3 *The Department and Project classes*

The design has not yet considered the *Assignment* class, the requirement to record employee hours expended on a project, or the requirement to record department and project managers. You have some design decisions to make about these items. It's been easy until now because the design is producing nice flat files. You'd almost think you were designing a relational database.

There are several things to consider about the *Assignment* class. The requirements state that an employee can work on several projects and that a project can have several employees working on it. The system has to record the hours expended by each employee on each project. You have three alternatives for this design. The relational database designer has only one. The alternatives are:

- ◆ Build an *Assignment* class that records the employee-project assignment and records the hours expended by the employee against the project.

♦ Put an array in the *Employee* class that contains an entry for each project that the employee works on along with the hours expended.

♦ Put an array in the *Project* class that contains an entry for each employee working on the project and the hours expended by that employee.

The relational database designer has the first alternative only. Which alternative do you choose for the object database? Your decision should consider the implications of each alternative. Consider the second alternative. There can be 100 employees and only 20 projects. The project array could have, at most, 20 elements for any employee object. That seems more efficient than using the third alternative, in which a project record might need an array of 100 employees.

Suppose you choose the second alternative and one of the requirements is to retrieve all the employees that work on a project. The retrieval would involve reading the entire employee file and scanning the project array of each to pick out the employees assigned to the project.

Given that requirement, you choose the third alternative instead of the second. But suppose another requirement is to retrieve all the projects that a selected employee works on. You have the same problem in reverse.

That's not so bad, you say, because you do not have those requirements. Well, what if the functional requirements change after the system is running? Suppose those requirements are added to the basis. Moreover, it looks as if you do have one of those requirements. The requirement to report hours expended against a project implies that the system needs to deliver the sum of the hours expended as recorded in whichever array you chose. More about that later.

Not so bad, you say again, because the small number of employees and projects does not represent a serious performance penalty when you scan those files. Suppose, then, that the performance requirements change after the system is running. Suppose the company grows to 1000 employees and 200 projects. Suppose that the requirements expand to include more data about each assignment, such as expense items, duty location, task identification, and deadlines. What happens to performance then?

Why did the founders of relational technology eliminate repeating groups such as these two arrays from the data model in the first place? The object model supports arrays, and there are valid uses for them: An array of points can define a graphic rendering; an array of coordinates can define a map; an array of dots can define a screen; an array of notes can define a concerto. The example of employee-project assignments is not, however, a good application for an array. By looking ahead, you can forestall problems by learning from the relational tradition and normalizing the design. Remember that the design of a database is influenced more by what you must get out of it and how than by what you must store in it.

Figure 7.4 is the first cut at the *Assignment* class.

```
class Assignment  {
    EmployeeNumber emplno;
    ProjectNumber projno;
    int hours_expended;
};
```

FIGURE 7.4 *The Assignment class*

The design is beginning to take form. But there is a problem. The system maintains the hours expended against a project as the sum of those hours for each employee. Suppose the employee leaves the project. What do you do with the hours expended when you delete the *Assignment* object that associates the employee with the project?

Suppose the employee leaves the company. According to the rules of interclass integrity, you could not delete the employee object as long as another object was related to it—in this case, the object that associates employees and projects. Once again, what do you do with those hours? Clearly, the *Projects* class needs to maintain an independent sum of hours expended, so you must add that data member to its design. Furthermore, that sum cannot be expected to reconcile with the totals for the project from the *Assignment* objects for the project because some employees may have left.

The requirement to record department and project managers is still unresolved. A review of the requirements reveals that they are unclear as to whether a department or employee can have more than one manager. Furthermore, they do not specify whether the manager of a department must be assigned as an employee of that department or whether the manager of a project must be assigned to work on that project. Here is a situation in which you reiterate the design process, revisit the requirements, and make some modifications.

Assume that a department and a project can have only one manager each, that the department manager must be an employee of the department, and that the project manager cannot charge labor hours to the project (and, therefore, may not be assigned as a worker on the project). How do you represent all that in the database?

There are some data interdependencies that a general-purpose database management system cannot enforce, and these appear to fall into that category. By adding a department manager employee number data element to the department class and a project manager employee number to the project class, the database can reflect the required management positions. Figure 7.5 shows the two classes with their manager data items in place.

```
class Department {
    DepartmentNumber deptno;
    string name;
    EmployeeNumber manager;  // department manager
};
class Project {
    ProjectNumber projno;
    string name;
    int hours_budgeted;
    Date start_date;
    Date completion_date;
    EmployeeNumber manager;  // project manager
};
```

FIGURE 7.5 *Managers added to departments and projects*

The *manager* employee numbers in both classes satisfy the requirement to record managers, but they introduce the potential for data disintegrity.

You now have an *Employee* object that points to a *Department* object, which points to an *Employee* object. According to the requirements, the department manager must be an employee of her own department. If the two objects do not point to each other, the database is out of synchronization.

Conversely, you have a *Projects* object that points to its manager's *Employee* object, which might point to an *Assignment* object—assuming that the manager can work on projects other than his own—which points to a *Projects* object. According to the requirements, the project manager must not be a worker on his own project. If the chain of objects is completed so that the project manager is assigned to his own project, the database is out of sync again.

Maintenance of complex relationships such as these involves the application of a rule-based inference engine that is way beyond the scope of most general-purpose database management systems. The relational data model does not solve the problem any better than the object model can. The responsibility for such database integrity remains with the application. Failure to take this responsibility does not create the same kind of chaos caused by objects being related to nonexisting objects, a forbidden condition that the data model can enforce. At worst, the database reflects relationships that the application prefers not to permit, and so the responsibility is placed at the correct doorstep.

Identify the Key Members

A class that supports associative access must have a primary key data member and can have several secondary key data members. The primary key identifies objects of the class. The secondary keys identify alternative ways that you can find an object.

If the work you have done up to now includes a would-be persistent class that has no uniquely identifying data member or combination of data members, then either the design is incomplete, the class cannot be persistent, or navigational access is called for. If you cannot identify an object, you cannot retrieve it.

This rule is consistent with relational theory, but some object-oriented database systems do not support it. In those systems, an object acquires an identity when it becomes persistent. The database manager assigns the identity and returns it to the program that created the object. The application must associate the system-defined identity with the object at a later time.

To be useful in a data-processing context, an object needs to be unique, so it follows that there is something about every useful object that sets it apart from others of its class. Otherwise, there is no point to its persistence. Whatever sets the object apart is its real identity, and an arbitrary one assigned by a database manager is just a handle. Associating true object identity with an internal handle should be in the province of the database manager and not something the application needs to be concerned with.

If your persistent class lacks a primary key, perhaps you should redesign your persistent class. As you will learn later, there are valid persistent object designs that do not use key data elements. Most database designs of any consequence—object-oriented or not—do, however, use some method to index the objects.

The employee number is the primary key for the *Employee* class. Every *Employee* object has a unique employee number. The department number is a secondary key for the *Employee* class. Every *Employee* object has a department number, and multiple employees can have the same department number.

The next step in the object database design is the identification of the primary and secondary keys.

Primary Keys

The four persistent classes are defined. Now you can identify the data member that, as the primary key, uniquely defines objects in each one. The *Employee*, *Department*, and *Project* classes are easy. The employee number, department number, and project number serve that purpose. Figure 7.6 shows the class designs with primary key data elements identified.

The design in Figure 7.6 shows that keys are implemented with a template class. You add keys to the class by declaring parameterized *Key* types with instances in the class design.

What about the *Assignment* class? What is its primary key? It has employee number and project number data members. Can either of them be the key? Because an employee can work on several projects, there are multiple *Assignment* objects with the same employee number. The employee number cannot be the primary key. Because a project can have many employees working on it, there are multiple *Assignment* objects with the same project number. The project number cannot be the primary key. What's left?

```
class Employee {
    Key<EmployeeNumber> emplno;    // primary employee key
    string name;
    Date date_hired;
    Money salary;
    DepartmentNumber deptno;
};
class Department  {
```

FIGURE 7.6 *Primary keys identified*

```
    Key<DepartmentNumber> deptno; // primary department key
    string name;
    EmployeeNumber manager;
};
class Project  {
    Key<ProjectNumber> projno;      // primary project key
    string name;
    int hours_budgeted;
    Date start_date;
    Date completion_date;
    EmployeeNumber manager;
};
```

FIGURE 7.6 *Continued*

Remember from Chapter 2 that a many-to-many relationship such as the one that exists between employees and projects is represented in a relational database by a connector file that has as its primary key the concatenated primary keys of the related files. The *Assignment* class is the object database equivalent of a relational connector file. Therefore, its primary key is the concatenation of the employee number and the department number. That combination of data members uniquely identifies each *Assignment* object. Figure 7.7 shows the addition of the concatenated primary key to the *Assignment* class.

```
class Assignment  {
    CatKey<EmployeeNumber,ProjectNumber> assignment;
    int hours_expended;
};
```

FIGURE 7.7 *Concatenated primary keys*

Concatenated keys are also implemented with a template. In this case, the two data members—*emplno* and *projno*—are replaced with one instance of a *CatKey* parameterized type consisting of the employee and project numbers and given the name *assignment*.

Secondary Keys

Secondary keys are the ones that provide alternative access to the objects of a persistent class. In theory, you can retrieve any subset of objects by serially retrieving all the objects in a class and testing them against your search criteria. Many times, this is appropriate. A monthly or yearly report does not need its own index to support its unique sort requirements. Other requirements are for on-line access, and they can use secondary keys. If you frequently retrieve all the employee objects of employees who work for a selected department, then the department number in the *Employee* class should be a secondary key. If the receptionist looks up the telephone extensions of employees based on their names, then the employee name should be a secondary key in the *Employee* object. Figure 7.8 shows the *Employee* class with the department number changed to a secondary key.

```
class Employee {
    Key<EmployeeNumber> emplno;   // primary key
    string name;
    Date date_hired;
    Money salary;
    Key<DepartmentNumber> deptno; // secondary key
};
```

FIGURE 7.8 *Secondary keys*

Secondary keys support class relationships, which are discussed in the next section. When a secondary key is the same data item as the primary key of another class, an implied relationship exists between the classes. To maintain those implied relationships, you would probably turn the *manager* data members in the *Department* and *Project* classes into secondary keys.

In a connector class such as the *Assignment* class, the primary key is the concatenation of two key members, which are primary keys of the two classes being associated in a many-to-many relationship. Each of the two key members in the *Assignment* class must be half of the primary key, and the two keys must also be secondary keys. This permits the system to locate the first instance of an object with a specified value for either half and to navigate the connector objects, retrieving the connections for the specified connected object. The *CatKey* template provides that the concatenation of the two types is a primary key and that the two types are themselves secondary keys.

Identify the Class Relationships

In an object database, persistent classes are related when they contain a common data member and when that data member is the primary key in one of the classes. The *Employee* class in Figure 7.8 is related to the Department class because the employee record includes the department number data member as a secondary key, and the department number is the primary key to the *Department* class.

Because of this relationship, you can view the *Department* class from two perspectives based upon the two purposes it serves. First, it is the system's record of everything related to a department. All by itself, it could be a *Department* database rather than a class in a larger database. Except to identify its manager, it needs nothing from the *Employee* class to fulfill its purpose. Second, the *Department* class is the table of information about the department in which an employee works. It validates the department number being stored in an employee's record and provides the department name when you retrieve the employee.

For the implied relationship to work, it must have integrity. If an *Employee* object contains a department number, there should be a matching *Department* object.

In your design, you evaluate each potential relationship to see whether it is real. Sometimes a control number is included in a class as information only. Users do not care whether the corresponding object still exists; it may have been retired. For this reason, database management systems do not usually automatically infer a relationship simply on the basis of shared key data members. The database designer must explicitly declare the relationship so that the database manager knows whether to enforce it or ignore it.

More often, the relationships are real and must be protected. In one-to-one and one-to-many relationships, the software must preserve data integrity. In the case of the many-to-many relationship, the connector class supports the relationship, and it must always be synchronized with the two classes it connects.

The relationships between classes can describe potential retrieval paths for multiple-class retrievals. Sometimes, the apparent paths are incorrect. Observe the relationships between the *Employee*, *Department*, and *Project* classes. If you designed a retrieval that began by retrieving a department object, each project for the department, and then each employee who is assigned to each project, you might not have the answer you are looking for. If the purpose of the retrieval is to list the employees who are working on projects assigned to the department, the response is correct. But if the retrieval is supposed to deliver a list of employees who work in the department, then the response is incorrect. In this case, you have chosen a retrieval path based on interclass dependencies that don't work. Remember from the requirements that an employee in one department can work on a project that is assigned to a different department. The database design supports these relationships, but, as seen in this example, the potential exists for you to describe paths that deliver incorrect results. This is not a flaw in the database design. The design is correct. The problem lies in the description of a retrieval path. You must develop these paths carefully to ensure that the answer is the one you are looking for.

Identify the Methods

An object database consists of objects of persistent classes. A C++ class contains its data representation and its behavior. There is often a misunderstanding about what this means. Some object-oriented programmers believe that an object-oriented database stores the methods along with the data. This is not practical for a C++ program. The methods are the public member functions—compiled by the compiler, cataloged in relocatable libraries, linked by the linker to your application programs, and stored with them in executable binaries. Those executable files are where the methods are kept. The compiler associates them with the persistent objects by virtue of the class definitions. There is no magic involved.

Nonetheless, you must identify the methods for your persistent classes. This part of the design is exactly the same as for the design of any other C++ program. Recall that when you built those 3x5 cards, you made notes on them about the data items. Return to the ones that refer to data items that became persistent classes. Look at the verbs in your notes. Those verbs are the first step toward defining the application-dependent behavior of the persistent classes.

When you identify how the application processes the data members, you reveal requirements for member functions that let the application read and change the data members. Does the system need a value that it computes from among the data members of a class? Do you need the hourly rate for an employee to compute charges against a project? Add a member function to the *Employee* class to do the computation. Figure 7.9, which assumes a work year of 2080 hours, shows how that would work.

```
const int hours_year = 2080;
class Employee {
    // ...
    Money salary;
public:
    virtual Money Rate()
        { return salary / hours_year; }
};
```

FIGURE 7.9 *A persistent class method*

The example in Figure 7.9 is a small one, but it makes this point: Add object-oriented methods to your persistent classes the same way you do in any other C++ program design. The so-called persistent method is bound to the persistent object, not because some unknown operating-system/database-system magic wand stores the method in the persistent object database, but because the program that retrieves the object uses the same class definition and class library used by the program that created the object.

Make the Class Persistent

The last step—except for continuing to iterate—is to integrate the persistent object class design into the persistent object database management system. You need to add attributes to the key data members and to the persistent classes so that they can participate in their own persistence.

The nature of those attributes depends on the database management system that you use. With the PARODY software contained in this book, those attributes consist of implementing inheritance, calling some base class functions at the correct times, and adding some special member functions to the persistent class that the base class calls. Figure 7.10 shows the beginnings of that design.

```
typedef int EmployeeNumber;
typedef int DepartmentNumber;
typedef int ProjectNumber;
class Employee : public Persistent {
    Key<EmployeeNumber> emplno;
    string name;
    Date date_hired;
    Money salary;
    Key<DepartmentNumber> deptno;
};
class Department : public Persistent {
    Key<DepartmentNumber> deptno;
    string name;
    Key<EmployeeNumber> manager;
};
class Project : public Persistent {
    Key<ProjectNumber> projno;
    string name;
    int hours_budgeted;
    Date start_date;
    Date completion_date;
    Key<EmployeeNumber> manager;
};
class Assignment : public Persistent {
    CatKey<EmployeeNumber,ProjectNumber> assignment;
    int hours_expended;
};
```

FIGURE 7.10 *The start of a persistent object database*

Returning to the design notation from Chapter 3 (Figure 3.5), we can represent the persistent object database as shown in Figure 7.11.

We will complete this design in Chapter 10 when we discuss this and several other example object-oriented database applications.

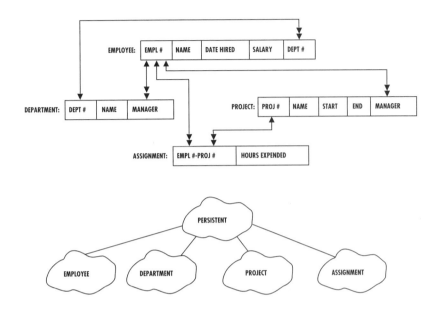

FIGURE 7.11 *A personnel database*

Summary

Now you know what constitutes an object database and how to design one. A database design needs a software system to process it. You've done some of that already. The member functions of the classes you designed are a large part of your database application. Database software consists of two parts: those applications programs that process the objects—from within and outside the object—and the general-purpose software that manages database organization, storage, and retrieval. This software is called the database management system. Chapter 8 introduces PARODY, the database management system.

References

C Database Development, Second Edition, Al Stevens, 1991, MIS:Press

PARODY

> *Parodies and caricatures are the most penetrating of*
> *criticisms.*
>
> —Aldous Huxley

PARODY is the Persistent, Almost Relational Object Database management system implemented in this book as a C++ class library. PARODY
achieves the objectives identified in Chapter 5. It implements a persistent
object database with a relatively simple interface to its classes. Its data
model resembles the relational model in some respects and assumes the
properties of C++ objects in others—a parody of sorts. This chapter and
the next introduce PARODY and show you how it works. This chapter
describes how to define the classes in a PARODY database and how
PARODY and the classes coordinate the persistence of objects of their
own type. Chapter 9 discusses how an application program declares and
uses the persistent objects.

PARODY Class Hierarchy

Figure 8.1 shows the class hierarchy that PARODY uses to implement
persistent objects. You are primarily concerned with the four classes at

the lowest level of this hierarchy. The *Key<T>* and *CatKey<T1,T2>* template classes encapsulate the operations of index key data elements. The *PersistentObject<T>* template is one that you can use to manage the persistence of flatly structured class definitions without keys. Persistent objects with complex class structures and primary and secondary keys are derived from the *Persistent* class.

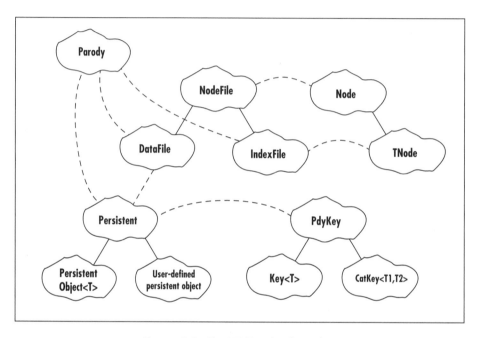

FIGURE 8.1   *The PARODY class hierarchy*

The classes above the bottom level in Figure 8.1 are mostly internal to PARODY. The *Parody* class encapsulates the database. You instantiate an object of this class to open and process the database. It contains *DataFile* and *IndexFile* objects to manage the persistent storage of data objects and the indexes into them. It maintains a list of currently instantiated persistent objects. The *DataFile* and *IndexFile* classes are derived from the *NodeFile* class, which manages disk input and output of *Node* objects—disk records. The *TNode* class is a specialization of the *Node* class to add the behavior of the index B-Tree mechanism. The *PdyKey* class is the base class for the *Key<T>* and *CatKey<T1,T2>* template classes. The *Persistent* class is the base class for all persistent objects. It maintains a list of the object's keys and other data members associated with the object's storage and retrieval.

Defining a PARODY Database

Defining a set of related persistent classes is equivalent to building a database schema that describes the contents of the files. Most traditional database management systems use a data definition language to describe the database schema. PARODY uses the C++ class definition into which you encapsulate not only a description of the data members in each class but also the integration of the class with the PARODY database manager.

You define a database by designing classes that represent the persistent objects and by designating the key data members of those classes. The persistent object and key member classes derive from abstract base classes defined in the PARODY class library. Objects of the persistent class type cooperate in their own persistence by calling PARODY member functions at specific times and by providing member functions that PARODY can call to perform tasks that require knowledge of the content and format of the persistent object.

Declaring the PARODY Database

To use persistent objects, a program must first declare the persistent object database first. PARODY includes a class named *Parody*. You must declare an object of this class for each database. The object must be in scope for as long as your program creates and retrieves persistent objects. The address of the object must be available to the constructors of your persistent classes. Figure 8.2 is an example of how a program declares a *Parody* database object.

```
Parody *personnel;
void main()
{
    personnel = new Parody("PERSONEL");
    Employee empl(123);
    Department dept(5);
    // ...
    delete personnel;
}
```

FIGURE 8.2 *Declaring a PARODY database*

The "PERSONNEL" initializer in the *Parody* declaration is the name of the database. PARODY uses it to name two files—one for the objects and one for the index. These files are discussed later in this chapter. The initializer is in the format of a file name without a file extension. In MS-DOS systems, for example, the initializer must be a valid one-to-eight-character DOS file name. PARODY adds the file extensions ".DAT" and ".NDX" to the two file names.

If you declare a *Parody* database and none exists with the name of the initializer, PARODY builds a new database with that name, and you can begin using it by creating persistent objects for it.

Defining the Persistent Object Class

A PARODY object is an instance of a class. You define the class, giving it attributes that make it persistent in the *Parody* object. PARODY provides the base classes and the interface that make it possible. Your class manages its own persistence with the help of the behavior it inherits from PARODY.

CLASS DEFINITION

A persistent class derives from the *Persistent* abstract base class, which is defined by PARODY. The persistent class usually includes a primary key data member. It must contain a constructor, a destructor, and two private member functions named *Read* and *Write*. Figure 8.3 is a *Department* class, which represents the minimum persistent class along with a *name* data member and member functions in the class interface to set and read the department name. This class and the other example classes in this chapter figure prominently in the case studies of Chapter 10.

The *Department* class in Figure 8.3 acquires the persistent attribute by deriving from the *Persistent* class. Except for the base class specification, the only visible things that distinguish the *Department* class from a non-persistent class are the *Read* and *Write* member functions. The constructor and destructor also have a role to play in the class's persistence. The following sections address the four basic cooperating member functions.

PERSISTENT OBJECT CONSTRUCTOR

The constructor has three responsibilities in a persistent class. First, it initializes the base *Persistent* constructor with a reference to the *Parody* database object. Second, it initializes the persistent object's primary key data member to identify the object. Then, after any custom construction of its own, the constructor calls the *LoadObject* member function in the *Persistent* base class. Figure 8.4 is an example of a persistent class constructor function.

```
typedef DepartmentNumber int;
class Department : public Persistent   {
    Key<DepartmentNumber> deptno;
    string name;
    void Read();
    void Write();
public:
    Department(int dn = 0);
    ~Department();
    string &Name()
        { return name; }
    void SetName(string& nm)
        { name = nm; }
};
```

FIGURE 8.3 *A persistent object*

```
Department::Department(DepartmentNumber dn) :
        Persistent(*personnel), // identify database
        deptno(dn)              // initialize primary key
{
    // ...
    LoadObject();
}
```

FIGURE 8.4 *The persistent object constructor*

Usually, the constructor's custom construction consists of setting the data members to null values in case the specified object is not in the database. If other data members need special construction, such as allocating memory from the free store, the constructor does it before calling *LoadObject*. If construction of a data member depends on its representation in the database, such as the number of elements in an array, the persistent object's *Read* member function can do it.

The constructor should call the *LoadObject* function even if the key data member value is null. PARODY uses the first call to *LoadObject* from a class in a program's execution to capture the class's key data member configuration.

You can omit the second step—that of identifying the database—if the persistent object is stored in the most recently declared *Parody* object database. PARODY automatically associates the object with the most recently declared *Parody* object that is still active—in scope and not destroyed. When you use that option, the database reference does not have to be global. The *personnel* pointer in Figure 8.2 can be declared within the *main* function, for example. Figure 8.5 illustrates this usage.

```
Department::Department(DepartmentNumber dn) : deptno(dn)
{
    // ...
}
void main()
{
    Parody *personnel = new Parody("PERSONEL");
    // ...
    delete personnel;
}
```

FIGURE 8.5 *Using the default open database*

PERSISTENT OBJECT DESTRUCTOR

The persistent class destructor has one responsibility. It calls the *SaveObject* member function in the *Persistent* base class before completing its own destruction. Figure 8.6 is an example of a persistent class destructor function.

Often, the *SaveObject* function call is all the destruction that the destructor needs. If any data members need further destruction, such as deleting allocated free store memory, the destructor does it after *SaveObject* returns.

```
Department::~Department()
{
    SaveObject();
    // ...
}
```

FIGURE 8.6 *The persistent object destructor*

Read MEMBER FUNCTION

The persistent object's class constructor calls the *Persistent* base class's *LoadObject* function to locate and read an object from the PARODY database. That function in turn calls the derived class's *Read* function. *Read* is defined in the *Persistent* base class as a pure virtual function, so all derived classes must include one.

The *Read* function reads the data members into the persistent object by calling the base class's *ReadObject* function for each data member. Figure 8.7 is an example of a persistent class's *Read* function.

```
void Department::Read()
{
    DepartmentNumber dpno;
    ReadObject(dpno);
    deptno.SetKeyValue(dpno);
    ReadObject(name);
}
```

FIGURE 8.7 *The Read member function*

The *Read* function calls the base class's *ReadObject* function once for each data member in the object. The *ReadObject* function accepts a reference to the data member and does the physical input operation into the data member. The *ReadObject* function has overloaded versions for all the intrinsic C++ types, and it understands certain generic abstract data types, such as *string* and *Date*, but it does not understand specific ones such as the *Key<DepartmentNumber> deptno* object. For that reason, the program reads the data into a local variable and then assigns the local variable to the *deptno* object's data member. *SetKeyValue* is a member function of the *Key* template class. The function takes an object of the parameterized type and assigns it to the key data member.

It might seem odd that the persistent derived and base classes bounce back and forth in this series of function calls. The derived class's constructor calls the base *LoadObject* function, which calls the derived *Read* function, which calls the base *ReadObject* function. Later in this chapter you'll learn why. The same pattern applies to the *Write* function, discussed next.

If the object contains variable-length fields such as arrays, lists, or data items in dynamic free store allocations, the *Read* function constructs them. To know how many array or list elements to construct or how much free store to allocate—and, therefore, how many data items to read—the *Read* function first calls *ReadObject* to get an integer value that represents the dimension of the array or the buffer size. The *Write* function will have written that value when the object became persistent, as you'll see next.

Write MEMBER FUNCTION

The persistent object's class destructor calls the *Persistent* base class's *SaveObject* function to save new or changed objects in the PARODY database. That function in turn calls the derived class's *Write* function. *Write* is defined in the *Persistent* base class as a pure virtual function, so all derived classes must include one.

The *Write* function writes the data members from the persistent object by calling the base class's *WriteObject* function for each data member. Figure 8.8 is an example of a persistent class's *Write* function, which is the reciprocal of the *Read* function.

```
void Department::Write()
{
    WriteObject(deptno.KeyValue());
    WriteObject(name);
}
```

FIGURE 8.8 *The Write member function*

The *Write* function calls the base class's *WriteObject* function once for each data member in the object. *WriteObject* understands the format of certain generic abstract data types the same way that *ReadObject* does. *KeyValue* is a member function of the *Key* template class. It returns the parameterized type object that represents the key's value.

If the object contains variable-length fields such as arrays, lists, or data items in dynamic free store allocations, the *Write* function should not destroy them after it writes them. The destructor should do that. To tell the PARODY copy of the object how many array or list elements or how much free store it contains for a particular data member, the *Write* function first calls *WriteObject* to write an integer value that represents the dimension. The *Read* function uses that value to read the object into memory when the object is instantiated at some later time.

The reason that you do not destroy the memory in *Write*—even though you might have allocated it in *Read*—is that programs can call *SaveObject* from elsewhere than in the destructor simply to refresh the database with current changes to the object.

Defining Keys

Figure 8.3 shows a persistent class definition in which the first data member is a *Key<DepartmentNumber>* object. The *Key* template gives the data item the behavior of a key and registers the key with the *Persistent* class currently being constructed.

A key is one of the data members of a persistent class. Its data value can be an object of any fixed-length type, but it must be a parameterized type within the *Key* template class.

A key's fixed-length property is critical to its operation. This requirement is levied by the B-tree algorithm, PARODY's indexing mechanism, which works with fixed-length key values. Appendix B explains the B-tree algorithm at some length.

The *Key* template class determines the length of a key from the size of the object that it parameterizes. If the object's type is a C++ intrinsic type or a user-defined type represented by a flat structure (no pointers, references, virtual functions, arrays, or variable-length fields), then all that is needed to establish the key is its declaration within the persistent object in the same way that Figure 8.3 declares the *deptno* variable. If the key is not a flat structure or a *string* object, you must provide specialized *Key<T>* member functions as described in the next section.

Specialized Keys

Most applications can use the *Key<T>* template class as is. Occasionally, however, you need to support an indexing type more complex than the intrinsic C++ types. In that case, you must provide specialized member functions for the *Key<T>* template. Figure 8.9 is an example of a specialized key that uses a user-defined type named *MyClass*, which is assumed to have two data members of unspecified types named *datamember1* and *datamember2*. The example provides a few details and serves as a model for you to use when you build your own specialized keys.

```cpp
// ==================================================
// specialized Key<MyClass> template member functions
// ==================================================
// --- construct a key from an object of the type
Key<MyClass>::Key(const MyClass& key) : ky(key)
{
    keylength = sizeof datamember1 + sizeof datamember2;
    // etc....
}
void Key<MyClass>::ReadKey(IndexFile& ndx)
{
    // --- one of these for each data member
    ndx.ReadData(&datamember1, sizeof datamember1);
    ndx.ReadData(&datamember2, sizeof datamember2);
}
void Key<MyClass>::WriteKey(IndexFile& ndx)
{
    // --- one of these for each data member
    ndx.WriteData(&datamember1, sizeof datamember1);
    ndx.WriteData(&datamember2, sizeof datamember2);
}
PdyKey *Key<MyClass>::MakeKey() const
{
    Key<MyClass> *newkey = new Key<MyClass>; // null key
    newkey->SetKeyLength(keylength);
    newkey->ky.datamember1 = 0;
```

FIGURE 8.9 *A specialized key*

```
        newkey->ky.datamember2 = 0;
        return static_cast<PdyKey*>(newkey);
}
bool Key<MyClass>::isNullValue() const
{
    // --- return true if the key is null
    return datamember1 == 0 && datamember2 == 0;
}
int Key<MyClass>::operator>(const PdyKey& key) const
{
    Key<MyClass>& ky = dynamic_cast<Key<MyClass>&>(key);
    if (datamember1 == ky.datamember2)
        return datamember2 > ky.datamember2;
    return datamember1 > ky.datamember1;
}
int Key<MyClass>::operator==(const PdyKey& key) const
{
    Key<MyClass>& ky = dynamic_cast<Key<MyClass>&>(key);
    return datamember1 == ky.datamember1 &&
           datamember2 == ky.datamember2;
}
PdyKey& Key<MyClass>::operator=(const PdyKey& key)
{
    Key<MyClass>& ky = dynamic_cast<Key<MyClass>&>(key);
    datamember1 = ky.datamember1;
    datamember2 = ky.datamember2;
}
```

FIGURE 8.9 *Continued*

OVERLOADED RELATIONAL OPERATORS

The overloaded greater than (>) and equal to (==) operator functions logically compare the values in two key objects. These functions permit the PARODY indexing algorithm to order and locate keys in the B-tree. If your application does similar comparisons, you need to include additional overloaded relational operator functions in the public class interface.

OVERLOADED ASSIGNMENT OPERATOR

The overloaded assignment operator assigns the contents of a *Key<T>* object to another one of the same class. If your application also assigns key objects, you might include an overloaded assignment operator in the key class's public interface that uses the derived class type. Do not use your overloaded operator to assign new key objects to the key objects in the persistent class. The ones in the class have internal control values that must not be disturbed. It's better to simply work with the key's data values and ignore its *Key* properties outside the class.

ReadKey AND *WriteKey* MEMBER FUNCTIONS

The *ReadKey* and *WriteKey* member functions read and write the key's data values from and to a specified *IndexFile* object. These functions must always read and write the same number of characters for a particular key.

Do not assume that because you have these functions you do not need to read and write the key data members from within the persistent class. These functions are to support the B-tree index files only. Because the application does not normally have visibility into the index files, you should include the index data values in the *ReadObject* and *WriteObject* calls in the derived persistent class's *Read* and *Write* functions.

THE *MakeKey* FUNCTION

Every key must provide a *MakeKey* function. It constructs a null object of the derived key type with the C++ *new* operator and returns its address. The *Key<T>* class does not *delete* this construction. PARODY calls the *MakeKey* function for two purposes. First, it builds empty buffers of the correct size into which it reads keys. Second, it identifies the key class with respect to the class identification of the objects it indexes and the relative position of the key object within the persistent class. The callers of the *MakeKey* function handle the *delete*. Your program should never need to call the *MakeKey* function; nonetheless, if you are specializing a *Key<T>* you must provide it.

THE *isNullValue* FUNCTION

The *isNullValue* function tells PARODY whether a key value is null. The meaning of *null* depends on the data members that constitute the key itself, so the persistent class's keys must provide the information. PARODY does not attempt to verify class relationships when the relating key value is null. This allows you to add objects to the database when two classes are mutually related.

For example, the *Employee* class is related to the *Department* class; an employee is assigned to a department. The *Department* class is related to the *Employee* class; each department object has an employee assigned as the manager. You must be able to add objects with null relating keys, because the database is empty to start, and you must be able to add either employees without department numbers or departments without manager employee numbers as a first step.

String Keys

When a key is an object of the standard *string* class, PARODY supplies the specialized *Key<string>* member functions. The only thing that you must do is specify the key's fixed length in the constructor. Figure 8.10 shows two ways to do that.

```
const int keylen = 25;
// --- set key length in default constructor parameter
class Person : public Persistent  {
    Key<string> name;
    void Read();
    void Write();
    // ...
public:
    Person(const string& nm = string('\0', keylen));
};
// --- set key length with Key<string>::SetKeyLength()
class Place : public Persistent  {
    Key<string> name;
    // ...
public:
    Place(const string& nm = string()) : name(nm)
        { name.SetKeyLength(keylen); LoadObject(); }
};
```

FIGURE 8.10 *Setting the length of a Key<string> object*

The first technique, used by the *Person* class in Figure 8.10, uses a default constructor parameter with the key length specified in the construction of the *Key<string>* argument. In the second technique, the constructor calls the *Key<string>::SetKeyLength()* function before calling *LoadObject*.

Once a key is established with its length in the database, you should use the same length when performing operations that use the key. If you try to change an established key length, PARODY throws an exception.

The *Read* and *Write* functions for the *Persistent* derived class read and write the string values from and to the database, as shown in Figure 8.11.

```
void Person::Read()
{
    string nm;
    ReadObject(nm);
    name.SetKeyValue(nm);
    // ...
}
void Person::Write()
{
    WriteObject(name.KeyValue());
    // ...
}
```

FIGURE 8.11 *Read and Write key values*

Secondary Keys

The first *Key<T>* object that the persistent class declares is its primary key. All other *Key<T>* objects are secondary keys. The position of the key data members, therefore, determines which one is the primary key. All except the first one are secondary.

PARODY treats primary and secondary keys differently. A class in the database may have only one object with a particular primary key value. There may be only one project with project number 123, for example, but several projects may have the same manager.

Concatenated Keys

When a database design calls for the relational equivalent of a connector file, the derived *Persistent* class includes a concatenated key as its primary key. A concatenated key contains two other key objects as its data values. Each of them is a primary key to another class and is treated as a secondary key to the connector class. The application program can retrieve objects based on either key value or the combination of the two.

For example, to represent the many-to-many relationship in which employees can work on many projects and each project can have many employees working on it, Figure 8.12 expands on the *Assignment* class from Chapter 7.

```
class Assignment  {
    CatKey<EmployeeNumber,ProjectNumber> assignment;
    int hours_expended;
    // ...
public:
    Assignment(EmployeeNumber en = 0, DepartmentNumber pn = 0):
                                    assignment(en, pn)
        { hours_expended = 0; LoadObject(); }
    ~Assignment()
        { SaveObject(); }
    // ...
};
```

FIGURE 8.12 *A class with a concatenated key*

The program instantiates an *Assignment* object by specifying the *EmployeeNumber* and *DepartmentNumber* values. The constructor initialization list initializes the *assignment* concatenated key object with those values.

Relating Classes

Objects in one class can be implicitly related to objects in another class by reference. If a class has a secondary key of the same *Key<T>* type as the primary key of another class, an implicit relationship exists. You may or may not elect to let PARODY enforce that relationship. For example, it might be acceptable to retain assignments information long after an employee has left or the project has closed down. On the other hand, it might not be acceptable to delete an employee who is still on record as the manager of a department. The degree to which the system enforces the relationships is a function of the application itself. Therefore, PARODY requires that you identify the relationships that you want it to enforce. Figure 8.13 shows how a class specifies a relationship by calling the *Persistent* base class's *Relate* member function from within the constructor.

```
class Project : public Persistent {
    Key<ProjectNumber> projno;    // primary key
    Key<EmployeeNunmber> manager; // secondary key
    // ...
public:
    Project(ProjectNumber pn = 0);
    // ...
};
Project::Project(ProjectNumber proj) : projno(proj),manager(0)
{
    manager.Relate(&typeid(Employee));
    hours_expended = 0;
    LoadObject();
}
```

FIGURE 8.13 *Relating classes*

The *Relate* function call in Figure 8.13 tells PARODY that the *Project* class and the *Employee* class are related. PARODY does not allow you to add or change a project object in which the *manager* data item is non-null and represents an *Employee* object that is not in the database. The *Relate* function call is all that you need to enforce that relationship.

Conversely, PARODY does not allow you to delete an *Employee* object if any related *Project* objects still exist. However, you might need to take one more step to ensure this enforcement. PARODY builds a table in memory of classes and their relationships as you declare objects. It does not know about the relationships between classes until a constructor calls the *Relate* function. Therefore, if a program deletes an *Employee* object but that program has never declared a *Project* object *during the current execution of the program*, PARODY does not know about the relationship because no *Project* object has called the *Relate* function to record it. Lacking knowledge of the relationship, PARODY deletes the *Employee* object regardless of whether any *Project* objects exist in the database that refer to the employee being deleted.

To ensure that PARODY enforces all relationships, instantiate an empty object of each class that calls *Relate* from its constructor. Do this at the beginning of the program. You can let the empty objects go out of scope right away. Simply having them declared once is enough to record the relationships for the duration of the program's execution. Figure 8.14 shows how a program handles that.

```
int main()
{
    Parody *personnel = new Parody("PERSONEL");
    {
        // ---- empty objects to declare relationships
        Employee empl;
        Department dept;
        Project proj;
        Assignment assgn;
    }
    // ...
    delete personnel;
    return 0;
}
```

FIGURE 8.14 *Ensuring relationships*

Observe that the program in Figure 8.14 declares the four empty objects from within a brace-surrounded block. This form allows them to go immediately out of scope so that they do not occupy stack space for the balance of the program's execution.

Multiple-Copy Objects

None of the persistent class examples in this chapter has copy constructors or overloaded assignment operators. This is not an oversight. As a rule, you do not want to make in-memory copies of objects. Making copies of a persistent object has its perils. PARODY would not know which copy to save on the database when the object goes out of scope.

Therefore, PARODY must ensure that there is only one copy of any particular persistent object in memory at a time.

There are several ways that a C++ program copies objects. The copy constructor and assignment are two. In a third way, the program declares another instance of the same object. Rather than allow these processes to make copies of an object, the *Persistent* class must take measures to prevent it.

When a persistent object is constructed, PARODY adds a reference to a list of currently instantiated persistent objects. If the program attempts to instantiate a copy of an instantiated object, PARODY throws an exception. If the application program does not catch the exception, the program aborts.

The exception thrown is a pointer to type *Persistent*, and the value of the thrown pointer is the address of the first instantiation of the object. When PARODY throws the pointer, a reference counter in the *Persistent* part of the object is incremented. PARODY includes a pseudo *delete* operator named *Destroy*, which deletes the copied object only when there is only one copy remaining.

There are valid cases in which a program instantiates an object that is in use elsewhere in the program. In these circumstances, always instantiate the object with the *new* operator, do it from a *try* block, and provide a *catch* handler that catches the *Persistent** exception. Use the *Destroy* function to delete the object. Figure 8.15 is an example.

```
void ProcessEmployee(EmployeeNumber en)
{
    Employee *ep;
    try    {
        // --- instantiate the Employee
        ep = new Employee(en);
    }
    catch(Persistent *obj)  {
        // --- the Employee is already instantiated
        // --- use the existing copy
        ep = obj;
    }
    // process employee through ep
    // ...
    Persistent::Destroy(ep); // pseudo delete
}
```

Figure 8.15 *Processing multiple copies*

Consider a function that processes two projects. The caller passes the project numbers, and there are times when those two project numbers could be the same. Figure 8.16 shows how you would use the *Persistent** exception to handle this condition.

```
void DoProjects(ProjectNumber pn1, ProjectNumber pn2)
{
    Project *proj1 = 0, *proj2 = 0;
    try
    {
        proj1 = new Project(pn1);  // values of pn1 and
        proj2 = new Project(pn2);  // pn2 might be the same
    }
    catch(Persistent *obj)
    {
        // --- processing the same object twice
        proj2 = static_cast<Project*>(obj);
    }

    // process the two Project objects ...
    // delete the two instances of Project objects
    Persistent::Destroy(proj1); // use Destroy instead of
    Persistent::Destroy(proj2); // delete if multi copies
}
```

FIGURE 8.16 *Processing multiple object copies*

The *Destroy* function works whether the two pointers point to the same or to different objects. Unlike the conditions illustrated in Figure 8.15, the two pointers in Figure 8.16 are in close proximity, and you could use the idiom shown in Figure 8.17 instead of calling *Destroy*.

```
    delete prog1;
    if (prog2 != prog1)
        delete prog2;
```

FIGURE 8.17 *Deleting multiple copies*

The only problem with either approach occurs when the program declares an instance of the object before calling the *DoProjects* function. In that case, the catch handler executes before either pointer gets an address. Only *proj2* would point to an object to process. The code that processes the two objects would need to recognize that condition and behave accordingly.

At first glance, it would appear that an overloaded *delete* operator for the *Persistent* class could manage the reference counter and selective deletion. This does not work, however, because the *delete* operator does not execute until all the object's destructors have executed. The object would be effectively destroyed on the first call.

The *Destroy* function is a *static* member function of the *Persistent* base class rather than a regular member function. It would seem that it could have been a regular member function and that you could call it like this:

```
ep->Destroy();
```

This usage puts the *Destroy* function in the position of having to perform this dubious operation:

```
delete this;
```

Most C++ programmers consider the statement just shown to be a dangerous practice. Therefore, *Destroy* is a *static* member function that takes as an argument the address of the object to be destroyed.

Persistent References to Persistent Objects

Sometimes a persistent object needs a perpetual reference to another persistent object. For example, if you have a *Task* class that gets much of its meaning from the *Project* class with which it is associated, you might find that your application instantiates the parent *Project* object every time it declares a *Task* object. Rather than doing this every time yourself, you can define the classes so that the *Project* object is a persistent reference in the *Task* class. Whenever you declare a *Task* object, the associated *Project* object is automatically declared, too. Figure 8.18 shows the *Task* class.

```
typedef int TaskNumber;
class Task : public Persistent  {
    Key<TaskNumber> taskno;  // the primary key
    string name;
    Reference<Project> proj; // referenced object
    void Read();
    void Write();
    // ...
public:
    Task(int tno);
    ~Task();
    void SetProject(Project& pr)
        { proj = pr; }
    // ...
};
```

FIGURE 8.18 *A referenced object*

The *Reference* template class manages an object's reference to another object. Its declaration in the referencing class establishes the reference. Figure 8.19 shows how the referencing class's *Read* and *Write* member functions call *ReadObject* and *WriteObject* for the referenced object. Those calls take a different form than the others. The functions are called through the referenced object rather than through the referencing object for which the *Read* and *Write* functions are running.

Until you do something to the contrary, the persistent reference is null—no referenced object is instantiated when you instantiate the referencing object. To assign another object to the persistent reference, you use a simple assignment statement. The *Task::SetProject* member function in Figure 8.18 assigns the *Project* object argument to the *proj* persistent reference. The argument must have been constructed with the *new* operator, and you must delete it with the *Persistent::Destroy* function. Subsequent instantiations of the same object of the *Task* class automatically instantiate the referenced *Project* object. You do not need to delete that object. The referencing *Task* object does it for you.

The application can use the referenced object as shown in Figure 8.20.

```
void Task::Read()
{
    TaskNumber tno;
    ReadObject(tno);
    taskno.SetKeyValue(tno);
    ReadObject(name);
    proj.ReadObject();   // instantiate a referenced object
}
void Task::Write()
{
    WriteObject(taskno.KeyValue());
    WriteObject(name);
    proj.WriteObject(); // store reference to the object
}
```

FIGURE 8.19 *Reading and writing object references*

```
Task tsk(123);
Project& prj = *tsk.proj.obj;  // referenced object
cout << "Hours expended on project = ";
cout << prj.Hours();
```

FIGURE 8.20 *Dereferencing a persistent reference*

The *Reference<T>* class has a public non-*const* pointer named *obj* that points to the persistent object being referenced. You can use that pointer for any access to the referenced object that its class permits. If you change it and if you want the changes to be recorded in the database when the referencing object goes out of scope, be certain to call the *ChangeObject* function, discussed later. You can even delete the referenced object from the database by calling the *DeleteObject* function (also discussed later), but if you do, you should remove its reference in the referencing object. Figure 8.21 shows how you use the *Reference<T>::RemoveReference* function to do this.

```
    Task tsk(123);
    tsk.proj.obj->DeleteObject(); // delete ref'd obj
    tsk.proj.RemoveReference();   // remove reference
```

FIGURE 8.21 *Deleting and removing a persistent reference*

There is one more requirement for using *Reference<T>* objects in a derived *Persistent* class. The class being referenced must provide a conversion constructor with an *ObjAddress* parameter, as shown in Figure 8.22.

```
class Project : public Persistent  {
// ...
public:
    Project(ProjectNumber pn = 0);
    // --- constructor used by Reference<T> class
    Project(ObjAddr oa)
        { LoadObject(oa); }
    // ...
};
```

FIGURE 8.22 *ObjAddr conversion constructor*

The *ObjAddr* type is used by PARODY to store the logical database address of each object. This is the value that is stored in the referencing object to point to the referenced object. You must provide this constructor so that PARODY can construct a persistent referenced object when the referencing object is instantiated.

Keep in mind that PARODY makes no relational integrity checks on persistent references. If you delete a referenced object without removing its references in any other objects, PARODY still attempts to instantiate the referenced object. The results are unpredictable.

Using the PersistentObject<T> Class

PARODY includes the *PersistentObject<T>* template. It parameterizes persistent objects and provides all the things that you normally provide when you derive a persistent object from the *Persistent* base class. You can use it when your persistent object is a flat structure—no keys, pointers, references, arrays, or virtual functions. Your application is responsible for recording the *ObjAddr* values for these *PersistentObject<T>* objects. Figure 8.23 shows how you can use the template.

```
// --- a simple structure
struct PayrollRcd   {
    char name[NameLength+1]; // Employee name
    float wage;             // Hourly wage
};
int main()
{
    // --- an instance of a flat structure
    PayrollRcd pr = { "Jones", 9.50 };
    // --- a persistent copy of that instance
    PersistentObject<PayrollRcd> ppr(pr);
    // --- use the persistent copy
    ppr.Obj.wage = 6.50;
    // --- add the persistent object to the database
    ObjAddr oa = ppr.AddObject();
    // ...
    // --- retrieve it some other time
    PersistentObject<PayrollRcd> opr(oa);
    // ...
    return 0;
}
```

FIGURE 8.23 *Using the PersistentObject<T> template*

How PARODY Brings It Together

With *Key<T>* and derived *Persistent* classes defined, the next thing to do is write a program that builds a database and declares and uses persistent objects. This section is an overview of how PARODY works with your classes to make the objects persistent. You will revisit some of the procedures that this chapter has already discussed, this time from the viewpoint of how PARODY uses the procedures.

Opening the PARODY Database

The first thing your program does is declare the *Parody* object just as the example in Figure 8.14 does. This declaration opens the database if it exists and creates one if it does not. The database is identified by the file name that you provide in the *Parody* declaration.

Constructing a Persistent Object

When you declare a persistent object, the sequence of constructors is important to how PARODY works. Consider a derived *Persistent* class such as the *Project* class in Figure 8.24.

```
class Project : public Persistent  {
    Key<ProjectNumber> projno;    // primary key
    Key<EmployeeNumber> manager;  // secondary key
    // ...
public:
    Project(ProjectNumber pn = 0);
    ~Project();
    // ...
};
```

FIGURE 8.24 *A persistent class*

THE *Persistent* BASE CLASS

When you declare an object of the *Project* class in Figure 8.24, the first constructor that executes is the one for the base *Persistent* class. That constructor initializes the base member variables, and it initializes a static global *Persistent* type pointer named *Persistent::objconstructed* to point to the object being constructed.

THE KEYS

Next comes the *PdyKey* base class constructor for the *projno* object followed by the derived *Key<ProjectNumber>* constructor. The *PdyKey* constructor uses the *Persistent::objconstructed* pointer to add its key object to a list of keys associated with the persistent object.

The constructors for the *manager* key object execute next in turn, and the manager key appends itself to the list. This sequence is what establishes the *projno* object as the primary key. Its constructor executes first, so it is first on the list.

THE DERIVED *Persistent* CLASS

After all the keys are constructed, the constructor for the derived *Persistent* class executes. Figure 8.25 is an example of that constructor.

```
Project::Project(ProjectNumber proj) : projno(proj)
{
    // ...
    LoadObject();
}
```

FIGURE 8.25 *Constructor for a derived Persistent class*

At a minimum, the derived persistent class constructor initializes the primary key with a search value and the other data members with null values. Then it calls the *Persistent::LoadObject* member function to load the specified object from the database into the data members in memory.

THE *Persistent::LoadObject* FUNCTION

The first thing that *Persistent::LoadObject* does is clear the *Persistent::objconstructed* pointer so that any further construction of *key* objects does not try to associate the keys with the object in the primary/secondary ranks. This measure is important because the indexing algorithms make copies of keys for different reasons throughout the life of the object, and the key constructors need to know the difference.

LoadObject looks to see whether the program has already instantiated a copy of the object. If it has, the function throws the *Persistent** exception with the address of the existing object in the pointer that it throws.

If no copy of the object has been declared, *LoadObject* searches for the object in the database using the primary key value that the object's constructor initialized.

If the object exists in the database, *LoadObject* positions the PARODY file system to where the object is stored. *LoadObject* does not know enough about the object to load it. This is where the cooperation of the derived persistent class comes in. *LoadObject* calls the derived class's *Read* function so that it can specify the size of each data member and the address into which to read it.

If the object does not exist in the database, *LoadObject* records that condition in the object and returns, assuming that the calling constructor has properly initialized the data members to null values.

THE *Persistent::Read* FUNCTION

The derived class's *Read* function calls the base class's *ReadObject* function for each of the data members. Figure 8.26 is an example of a persistent class's *Read* function.

```
void Project::Read()
{
    ProjectNumber prno;
    ReadObject(prno);             // read the proj #
    projno.SetKeyValue(prno);     // put proj # in obj
    ReadObject(name);             // read the name
    EmployeeNumber mgr;
    ReadObject(mgr);              // read the mgr's #
    manager.SetKeyValue(mgr);     // put mgr in obj
    ReadObject(hours_expended);   // read hours
}
```

FIGURE 8.26 *A persistent class's Read function*

Following the last *ReadObject* call, the *Read* function returns to the *LoadObject* function, which finishes up and returns to the object's constructor.

THE *Persistent::ReadObject* FUNCTION

There are several overloaded *Persistent::ReadObject* functions, one for each of several data types. All of them reduce to a common function that has as its parameters an address and a character count. That function uses the PARODY file input/output system to read the correct number of characters into the specified address. The function assumes that the PARODY file system has already been positioned to the correct address. The read operation is not direct, however. A PARODY database is organized into fixed-length nodes. Each object occupies one or more nodes in a linked thread, depending on the object's length. The *ReadObject* function reads data characters by following the object's thread in the file. Appendix B describes PARODY's input/output system of nodes.

Destroying a Persistent Object

When you destroy a persistent object, the sequence of destructors is as important as the sequence of constructors was to the object's declaration. Consider the destruction of the *Project* class in Figure 8.24.

Destroying the Derived *Persistent* Class

The first destructor executed is the derived class destructor. Figure 8.27 is the destructor for the *Project* class.

```
Project::~Project()
{
    SaveObject();
    // ...
}
```

Figure 8.27 *Destructor for a derived persistent class*

When the destructor begins to execute, nothing in the memory copy of the object has been destroyed yet. All the data members are intact. The database copy of the object, if one existed, has the same state it had when the program instantiated the object in memory. The destructor calls the *Persistent::SaveObject* function before it does anything else.

The *Persistent::SaveObject* Function

If the object did not exist on the database when the program instantiated it and if the program has specified that the object is to be added to the database—a procedure that Chapter 9 addresses—the object must be written to the database. Likewise, if the object did exist and the program specified that the data members had changed, the object needs to be written.

The *Persistent::SaveObject* function assigns a database address to a new object and adds its key values to the class's indexes. If the object is changed, the *SaveObject* function positions PARODY's file system to the object's address and updates any changed key values in the existing indexes. In either case, the *SaveObject* function then calls the derived class's *Write* function to write the data members.

If the object existed and the program specified that the object was to be deleted, the *SaveObject* function releases the database file space owned by the object, deletes the key values from the class's indexes, and does not call the *Write* function.

THE *Persistent::Write* FUNCTION

The derived class's *Write* function calls the base class's *WriteObject* function for each of the object's data members. The sequence of calls must exactly mimic the sequence of *ReadObject* calls in the *Read* function. Figure 8.28 is an example of a persistent class's *Write* function.

```
void Project::Write()
{
    WriteObject(projno.KeyValue());  // write proj #
    WriteObject(name);               // write name
    WriteObject(manager.KeyValue()); // write mgr's #
    WriteObject(hours_expended);     // write hours
}
```

FIGURE 8.28 *A persistent class's Write function*

Following the last *WriteObject* call, the *Write* function returns to the *SaveObject* function, which pads and writes the last node owned by the object, finishes up, and returns to the object's destructor.

THE *Persistent::WriteObject* FUNCTION

There are several overloaded *Persistent::WriteObject* functions, one for each of several data types. All of them reduce to a common function that has as its parameters an address and a character count. That function uses the PARODY file input/output system to write the correct number of characters from the specified address. The function assumes that the PARODY file system has already been positioned to the correct address. The *WriteObject* function writes data characters by following the object's node thread, growing new nodes if necessary.

DESTROYING THE KEYS

Destructors for the *Key<T>* objects execute after the derived persistent class's destructor, with the derived *Key<T>* destructor executing ahead of its base *PdyKey* class destructor.

DESTROYING THE *Persistent* BASE CLASS

The base *Persistent* class destructor executes last. It cleans up some tables built by the base class and returns. The object is now destroyed from within the program and is properly restored to or deleted from the database as appropriate.

Object Input/Output: An Overview

Figure 8.29 summarizes the flow of function calls to load and save an object.

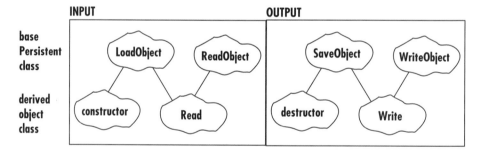

FIGURE 8.29 *Object persistence flow*

To load an object, the derived class's constructor calls the *LoadObject* function in the base *Persistent* class, which calls the *Read* function in the derived class, which in turn makes several calls to the *ReadObject* function in the base class.

To save an object, the derived class's destructor calls *SaveObject* in the base class, which calls *Write* in the derived class, which in turn makes several calls to *WriteObject* in the base class.

Your responsibilities in persistent class design are to provide the derived class's constructor and destructor and its *Read* and *Write* functions. None of these functions needs to understand the complexities of the database file structures. Their responsibilities are focused on the format of the object itself.

Integrity Checks

Chapter 9 describes how the using program calls the *AddObject*, *ChangeObject*, and *DeleteObject* functions to tell the *Persistent* base class how to handle the object in the *SaveObject* process. When those functions are called, they decide whether the object, as it is configured at that time, maintains or violates class relationship integrity.

The *AddObject* and *ChangeObject* functions test each of the secondary keys in the object. If the key is related to another persistent class, the functions search the related class in the database for an object that matches the value of the key. If no match is found, the functions refuse to set the flags that tell the *SaveObject* function to write the object to the database when it is being destroyed.

The *DeleteObject* function tests to see whether any other classes are related to the class of the object being deleted. If they are, the function searches those classes to see whether other objects are related to the one being deleted. If they are, the function refuses to set the flag that tells *SaveObject* to delete the object.

In all three cases, when the functions refuse to do what the program has requested, the functions return a false value that the calling program can test.

It is important to understand the timing of these integrity checks. Suppose that you call one of the three functions, which approves the add, change, or delete. Then you modify the object or the database so that the action would not have been approved. The action occurs anyway.

Summary

This chapter described PARODY and how you define a PARODY database. It discussed how PARODY implements your database in cooperation with the classes you design. Chapter 9 is about how an application uses a PARODY database to create, modify, and delete objects. You will also learn in Chapter 9 an alternative to PARODY's almost-relational data model. In that model, you can retrieve objects by their logical address rather than by key values—navigational rather than associative access.

References

Advanced C++ Programming Styles and Idioms, James O. Coplien, 1992, Addison-Wesley

Chapter 9

Using a PARODY Database

An object in possession seldom retains the same charm that it had in pursuit.

—Pliny the Younger

This chapter is about how programs use the object database. Chapter 8 described how you define the database by designing properly inherited classes. In this chapter you will learn how to declare persistent objects, manipulate them, and tell PARODY what it should do about them.

Building a Database

You build a new PARODY database the first time you declare an object of the *Parody* type. The *string* name that you give the database becomes the file name for the object data and index files. PARODY adds the file extensions ".dat" and ".ndx" when it creates the files.

Declaring the *Parody* object opens the database for use by your program. The database remains open as long as the *Parody* object is in scope.

You can have more than one database open at the same time. If you are using objects from multiple databases, the derived *Persistent* constructors must specify in their member initialization list which database an object is stored in. You need to make the address of the *Parody* object known globally so that the constructors can associate themselves with the correct database. If an application uses only one database, the constructors may omit the reference to the database, and the database object does not need to be global.

Managing Persistent Objects

With an open PARODY database you can add persistent objects, retrieve them, change them, and delete them. PARODY maintains the integrity of the interclass relationships, and you can monitor its actions in this regard. You can navigate among the objects of a class and among related objects of different classes. The examples that follow assume that you are using the *Employee* class shown in Figure 9.1.

```
typedef int EmployeeNumber;
typedef int DepartmentNumber;
class Employee : public Persistent     {
    Key<EmployeeNumber> empno;
    Key<DepartmentNumber> deptno;
    // ...
public:
    Employee(EmployeeNumber en = 0);
    ~Employee();
    Key<DepartmentNumber> *DeptKey()
        { return &deptno; }
    SetDeptNo(DepartmentNumber dn)
        { deptno.KeyValue() = dn; }
    DepartmentNumber DeptNo() const
        { return deptno.KeyValue(); }
    // ...
};
```

FIGURE 9.1 *An example persistent class*

Working with Keys

The class in Figure 9.1 has two keys. By default, the first key is the primary key for objects of the class, and all others are secondary keys. The keys are parameterized types of the *Key<T>* template class, which builds single-element keys. Concatenated keys are built with the *CatKey<T1,T2>* template class.

Single-Element Keys

A program needs to assign values to keys and read those values back. You have seen some of that in the discussion on the persistent object's *Read* and *Write* functions. Figure 9.2 shows how the persistent class's constructor places initial values in the keys.

```
Employee::Employee(EmployeeNumber en) : emplno(en), deptno(0)
{
    // ...
}
```

FIGURE 9.2 *Initializing key values*

The constructor in Figure 9.2 initializes the *emplno* key with the *EmployeeNumber* parameter and the *deptno* key with zero. Programs can subsequently assign values to keys with the *SetKeyValue* function as shown in Figure 9.3.

```
deptno.SetKeyValue(101);
```

FIGURE 9.3 *The SetKeyValue function*

The example in Figure 9.3 shows how a member function of the persistent class would change the key value. Inasmuch as the key is a private data member, the *Employee* class includes the public *SetDeptNo* function to allow a user to set the class's department number key value.

The program retrieves a key's value by calling its *KeyValue* function as shown in Figure 9.4.

```
DepartmentNumber dn = deptno.KeyValue();
```

FIGURE 9.4 *The KeyValue function*

The example in Figure 9.4 shows how a member function of the persistent class would retrieve the key value. Inasmuch as the key is a private data member, the *Employee* class includes the public *DeptNo* function to allow a user to retrieve the class's department number key value.

CONCATENATED KEYS

Concatenated keys consist of two key values and use the *CatKey<T1,T2>* template. Figure 9.5 shows this usage.

```
class Assignment : public Persistent    {
    CatKey<EmployeeNumber,DepartmentNumber> assignment;
    // ...
public:
    Assignment(EmployeeNumber en = 0, DepartmentNumber pn = 0);
};
```

FIGURE 9.5 *A class with a concatenated key*

A concatenated key consists of two key values that combine to form a primary key and that operate individually as secondary keys. Figure 9.6 shows the construction of a class with a concatenated key.

```
Assignment::Assignment(EmployeeNumber en, ProjectNumber pn) :
                    assignment(en, pn)
{
    // ...
}
```

FIGURE 9.6 *Constructing concatenated keys*

Concatenated keys have functions named *Key1* and *Key2* that return references to the two *Key<T>* objects of the concatenated key. You can use their *KeyValue* and *SetKeyValue* functions, or you can use the

KeyValue1, *SetKeyValue1*, *KeyValue2*, and *SetKeyValue2* functions of the concatenated key itself.

Retrieving Persistent Objects

You retrieve a persistent object by declaring one that exists in the database. Figure 9.7 shows this procedure.

```
Employee empl(123);
if (empl.ObjectExists())  {
    // --- the object exists
    // ...
}
```

FIGURE 9.7 *Retrieving a persistent object*

The *empl* object in Figure 9.7 is constructed from the 123 primary key value, which is the employee number in this example. The *ObjectExists* function returns a true value if PARODY found a matching object on the database. In either case, the object is instantiated.

If the object does not exist on the database, the object's memory copy contains the key value that you specified. The other data members are initialized to whatever values are assigned by the derived *Persistent* object constructor—in this case the constructor for the *Employee* object. The *Persistent* base class has initialized its data members to indicate that the object is not on the database.

If the object exists on the database, PARODY will have read its data members into its memory copy by calling the derived *Read* function that you provide in the class design.

After an object is instantiated, existing or not, the program may or may not change the object's data values and then call *AddObject*, *ChangeObject*, or *DeleteObject* as described later in this chapter. The program can also decline to call any of those functions allowing the object to go out of scope without modifying the database.

Creating Persistent Objects

You create a persistent object by declaring one that does not already exist on the database and then telling PARODY to add it to the database. Figure 9.8 shows this procedure.

```
Employee empl(123);
if (!empl.ObjectExists())   {
    // --- the object does not exist
    // ...
    empl.AddObject();
}
```

FIGURE 9.8 *Adding a persistent object*

The *empl* object in Figure 9.8 is constructed from the 123 primary key value, which is the *empl*oyee number in this example. This time, PARODY does not find a matching object, so the program calls the *AddObject* function to tell PARODY to add the object to the database. Calling *AddObject* does not immediately write the object to the database. It tells PARODY that the program intends to add the object to the database when the object goes out of scope. You can continue to make changes to the object; they are written to the database when the object goes out of scope.

Changing Persistent Objects

To change a persistent object, declare one that exists, change its data values, and call the *ChangeObject* function. Figure 9.9 is an example of that process.

```
Employee empl(123);
if (empl.ObjectExists())   {
    // --- the object exists
    // ... (change the data members) ...
    empl.ChangeObject();
}
```

FIGURE 9.9 *Changing a persistent object*

Calling *ChangeObject* does not immediately write the changed object to the database. It tells PARODY that the program has made modifications and intends to write the changed object to the database when the object goes out of scope. You can continue to make changes to the object after calling *ChangeObject*. Those changes are written to the database along with any others when the object goes out of scope.

Deleting Persistent Objects

To delete a persistent object, declare one that exists and call the *DeleteObject* function. Figure 9.10 is an example of that process.

```
Employee empl(123);
if (empl.ObjectExists())   {
    // --- the object exists
    // ...
    empl.DeleteObject();
}
```

FIGURE 9.10 *Deleting a persistent object*

Calling *DeleteObject* does not immediately delete the object from the database. It tells PARODY that the program intends to delete the object when the object goes out of scope. You can continue to work with the object in memory; the delete does not take effect until the object goes out of scope.

Integrity

The *AddObject*, *ChangeObject*, and *DeleteObject* functions return a true value if they permit the action and a false value if they do not. The functions do not permit the action if it would violate class integrity. *AddObject* and *ChangeObject* reject an object that attempts to relate itself to another object when the other object does not exist on the database. *DeleteObject* rejects the deletion of an object if other objects in the database are still related to it. Figure 9.11 shows how those functions work.

```
if (!empl.AddObject())
    // --- add was rejected
if (!empl.ChangeObject())
    // --- change was rejected
if (!empl.DeleteObject())
    // --- delete was rejected
```

FIGURE 9.11 *Maintaining object integrity*

These return values reflect the condition of the database when the functions execute. Nothing prevents the program from making further changes to the objects or to the rest of the database after the integrity tests are passed. Therefore, if you depend on return values from these functions to convey the condition of the database's integrity, make these function calls the last thing you do to the object before it goes out of scope.

Navigating the Database

You can navigate a database two ways: by associative access, which uses key index values to address objects, or by navigational access, which uses the addresses of the objects. The first method is relational, and the second reflects a more object-oriented approach.

Navigating by Key: Content-Addressable Objects

The relational data model uses key index values to locate objects. Although it is not a relational database management system, PARODY supports this technique. You have already seen that a program can retrieve a persistent object by instantiating it with a primary key value. You can find objects by using the values of the secondary keys as well. This facility permits the kind of content-addressable access normally associated with relational databases.

FindObject

The *FindObject* function locates an object by using the value assigned by the program to a secondary key. Figure 9.12 shows how that works.

```
Employee empl;
empl.SetDeptNo(1); // initialize the dept#
empl.FindObject(empl.DeptKey());
if (empl.ObjectExists())  {
    // --- at least one object exists
    // ...
}
```

FIGURE 9.12 *Finding an object with a secondary key*

In this example, the program instantiates an *Employee* object with no speci-fied primary key value. The default constructor for the class builds the object with a null key value, and PARODY does not try to find a matching object in the database—thus the importance of the *isNullValue* function described in Chapter 8. The *empl* object has no meaningful data member values yet. The program assigns one data value—the department number—which, in this example, is a secondary key. The program now tells the object to find the per-sistent object by using the initialized value in the secondary key.

The *FindObject* function, which accepts a pointer to a *PdyKey* class, does the retrieval. The *PdyKey* class is the base class for all *Key<T>* and *CatKey<T1,T2>* parameterized types. In this example, the *DeptKey* func-tion returns the address of the class's *Key<DepartmentNumber> deptno* data member.

If the database has at least one *Employee* object with a matching entry in its secondary department number key, PARODY initializes the *empl* object with the first such *Employee* object. The sequence of objects of the same type with identical values for a particular secondary key is coincidental. The call to *FindObject* retrieves the first coincidental one.

FirstObject AND *LastObject*

You can retrieve the first or last object in a primary or secondary key sequence by using the *FirstObject* and *LastObject* functions. These func-tions do not require that you initialize the key data value. They retrieve the objects from the beginning or end of the key sequence. Figure 9.13 is an example of using these functions.

```
Employee empl;
empl.FirstObject(empl.DeptKey());
if (empl.ObjectExists())   {
    // --- the object exists
    // ...
}
// ....
empl.LastObject(empl.DeptKey());
if (empl.ObjectExists())   {
    // --- the object exists
    // ...
}
```

FIGURE 9.13 *Finding the first and last object of a class*

These functions return false only if there are no objects of the derived *Persistent* class in the database that have non-null values in the secondary key. If you have specified a primary key, the functions return false only if the database has no objects of the derived *Persistent* class whatsoever.

If you call the *FirstObject* and *LastObject* functions without passing a pointer to a key, PARODY finds the first or last object in the sequence of the primary key. Figure 9.14 illustrates this usage.

```
Employee empl;
empl.FirstObject();
if (empl.ObjectExists())   {
    // --- the object exists
    // ...
}
// ....
empl.LastObject();
if (empl.ObjectExists())   {
    // --- the object exists
    // ...
}
```

FIGURE 9.14 *First and last object by primary key*

The same convention applies to *NextObject* and *PreviousObject* described next.

NextObject AND *PreviousObject*

The *NextObject* and *PreviousObject* functions return the next and previous sequential objects in the sequence of the key through which they are called, or through the primary key if they are called through the persistent object itself. These functions assume that either they, *FirstObject*, *LastObject*, or *FindObject* has positioned the key at an object. If not, *NextObject* works just like *FirstObject*, and *PreviousObject* works just like *LastObject*. Figure 9.15 illustrates their use.

This navigation uses the same object in memory to hold each of the successive retrieved objects. As long as there is a next or previous object in the key sequence, the object's *ObjectExists* function returns a true value. After *NextObject* has retrieved the last object and you call it again, it does not retrieve another object and the *ObjectExists* function returns a false value. Likewise, *ObjectExists* returns false after *PreviousObject* has gone past the first object in the key sequence.

```
// ----- navigate forward
Employee empl;
empl.FirstObject(empl.DeptKey());
while (empl.ObjectExists())   {
    // --- process the object
    empl.NextObject(empl.DeptKey());
    // ...
}
// ----- navigate backward
empl.LastObject(empl.DeptKey());
while (empl.ObjectExists())   {
    // --- process the object
    empl.PreviousObject(empl.DeptKey());
    // ...
}
```

FIGURE 9.15 *Navigating forward and backward*

Each key in a persistent class object keeps track of its own logical position in the thread of objects in its sequence. You could conceivably have several threads running at one time by doing retrievals on the same memory object with several of its keys or by declaring more than one instance of the class and running retrievals on all of them. Keep in mind, however, that if you try to instantiate the same object more than once, PARODY throws the *Persistent** exception.

NAVIGATING AMONG CLASSES

Sometimes a program must declare a persistent object and then retrieve, one by one, its related objects of another class. For example, Figure 9.16 retrieves the employees assigned to a particular department.

The program in Figure 9.16 instantiates a *Department* object with 321 as its primary key value. Next, it instantiates an empty *Employee* object, sets the same department number into that object's secondary key, and calls *FindObject* using the secondary key for the retrieval. The program processes that employee object and subsequent employee objects retrieved by the *NextObject* function until either the department number in the next employee object changes or the *ObjectExists* function returns a false value, indicating the end of the *Employee* class's department number key sequence.

```
Department dept(321);
if (dept.ObjectExists())  {
    Employee empl;
    empl.SetDeptNo(321);
    empl.FindObject(empl.DeptKey());
    while (empl.ObjectExists() &&
            empl.DeptNo() == dept.DeptNo())   {
        // ...
        empl.NextObject(empl.DeptKey());
    }
}
```

FIGURE 9.16 *Navigating among classes*

Navigating by Address: Position-Addressable Objects

We have stressed until now the strength of the relational approach to database navigation. There are times, however, when keyed indexes are not the best solution for database access and navigation. Sometimes you just want to retrieve a persistent object by using some kind of handle that the database manager provides when you create the object.

Perhaps you are using the object database to retain some number of single objects between invocations of a program or for passing the object from program to program. For example, a CAD/CAM database might contain one object each of several classes, among them the design model, some number of canned features, and perhaps some embedded text strings. The application does not need to retrieve objects from a collection on the basis of data values. It needs to retrieve the one and only object of a class or one of a very few objects of a class. This is a design decision, and you should know whether this data model applies to your application. As a general rule, if the database stores a large number of objects of the same class, the objects should be indexed by a key value. If the database stores a small number of objects of each class—small enough that the application does need to address them by unique data values—then the objects may be keyless.

PARODY supports the design of a database without keys and the retrieval of objects without indexing.

DESIGNING A CLASS WITHOUT KEYS

To design a class without keys, simply leave out the keys. If no data member is built with the *Key<T>* or *CatKey<T1,T2>* class, then the objects are *keyless*, and you must retrieve them by specifying their logical PARODY addresses. The class still has its *Read* and *Write* functions, the constructor still calls *LoadObject*, and the destructor still calls *SaveObject*.

The keyless class must recognize two constructors: one that allows it to be declared with no data values, and one that allows it to be declared with an *ObjAddr* parameter. Both constructions may be provided by one constructor that uses a default parameter value to set the *ObjAddr* parameter to zero. The constructor's call to *LoadObject* includes the *ObjAddr* parameter's value as a parameter. Figure 9.17 is a simple keyless class that stores a text string for an application.

```
class Text : public Persistent
{
    string text;
    void Read()
        { ReadObject(text); }
    void Write()
        { WriteObject(text); }
public:
    Text(const string& str) : text(str)
        { LoadObject(); }
    Text(ObjAddr objaddr = 0)
        { LoadObject(objaddr); }
    ~Text()
        { SaveObject(); }
    const string& GetText()
        { return text; }
    // ...
};
```

FIGURE 9.17 *A keyless class*

CREATING A KEYLESS OBJECT

You create a keyless object by instantiating it, assigning values to its data members, and calling *AddObject* just as you do with keyed objects. There are no integrity checks with keyless objects because there are no keys to relate classes.

After the call to *AddObject* you must get the logical PARODY address of the new persistent object. The *ObjectAddress* function returns the address of an object once it has been added to the database. It is the responsibility of the application to remember the address for subsequent retrievals of the object. Figure 9.18 creates an object of the *Text* class.

```
Text tx("Birth of the Cool");
tx.AddObject();
ObjAddr oa = tx.ObjectAddress();
```

FIGURE 9.18 *Creating a keyless object*

RETRIEVING BY OBJECT ADDRESS

To retrieve a keyless object, you instantiate it with its object address as a parameter. Figure 9.19 retrieves the *Text* object from the database by passing the object's address to its constructor.

```
void f(ObjAddr objadr)
{
    Text tx(objadr);
    cout << tx.GetText();
    // ...
}
```

FIGURE 9.19 *Retrieving a keyless object*

The example in Figure 9.19 assumes that the caller passes the correct object address to the function, which declares an object from the address. If PARODY determines that the address does not point to an object of that class, it does not call the class's *Read* function, and *ObjectExists*, if you call it, returns false. This condition would probably be a program bug rather than a user error, because the technique assumes that the program can always know the correct addresses for the objects it retrieves.

NAVIGATING BY OBJECT ADDRESS

You can use the *FirstObject*, *LastObject*, *NextObject*, and *PreviousObject* functions for a keyless class. These functions navigate the class in the coincidental physical sequence of the objects of the class in the database. This sequence is not necessarily the sequence in which the objects were created. The algorithm that allocates space in the database for new objects reuses deleted object space, so an object that you created yesterday might properly be found after one that you create today.

This form of navigation can be inefficient in a large database. PARODY maintains no pointers to or chains of keyless objects. When you call *FirstObject*, for example, PARODY scans the database from the beginning looking at every node to find the first node of the first object of the class. The other scans work similarly, scanning from the last node of the file or from the address of the object through which you call the function.

UPDATING AND DELETING KEYLESS OBJECTS

Updating and deleting keyless objects involve retrieving the object to be changed or deleted, changing the data members for a change, and calling *ChangeObject* or *DeleteObject* just as you do with keyed objects. There are no integrity checks other than to make sure that the object address points to an object of the class being changed or deleted.

Navigating Shorthand

Each of the navigating functions—*FindObject*, *FirstObject*, *LastObject*, *NextObject*, and *PreviousObject*—returns a reference to the object for which it was called. This convention allows you to use shorthand notation such as that shown in Figure 9.20.

```
Department dept;
if (dept.FirstObject().ObjectExists())
    // ...
```

FIGURE 9.20 *Navigating shorthand*

Converting PARODY Databases

A database that has been designed, implemented, and placed in use is not necessarily a fixed entity. Requirements for the application change, and from time to time you need to modify the format of an existing database. Such modifications imply a conversion of the existing database to the new format. There are several things to consider.

Adding Classes

If you are adding one or more classes to the database, your conversion is simple. Make no physical conversion of the database files at all. Design the classes, instantiate objects, and add them to the database. The database accepts the new classes without modification.

Removing Classes

To remove a class, delete all the objects. You do not need to make a physical conversion of the database file, and you can later reuse the class name for a new class.

Adding Data Items to an Existing Class

You can add data items to an existing class without converting the database if the following conditions are true. First, you must add the data items at the end of the series of calls to *ReadObject* and *WriteObject* from your *Read* and *Write* functions. Second, your constructor should initialize the new data items to zero values before it calls *ReadObject*. Third, the new data items should behave appropriately when they have zero values.

The *ReadObject* function does not read past the last node of an object. The last node of an object is padded with zeros. Therefore, if you initialize the additional data items with zeros and if *ReadObject* either reads padding bytes into the data item or reads nothing because there are no more nodes in the object's node string, then the data item contains zeros after the persistent object is instantiated.

The *WriteObject* function allows new or changed objects to grow to their proper lengths.

Removing Data Items from an Existing Class

If you remove a data item from an existing class, you should convert the database as described later in this section. You can avoid that conversion if the *Read* and *Write* functions continue to allow for the data item's space by reading and writing to and from unused variable space. In practice, however, you will find that such workarounds are inefficient and cloud the design. Residual data values remain in the database in old objects, and new or changed objects have useless holes. It's better to do a proper job and convert the database.

Adding Keys to an Existing Class

If you are changing an existing data item into a key, you might not need to convert the database as long as the data item's physical size and proximity to other data items in the class do not change. Replace the data item in the class definition with one parameterized by the *Key<T>* class. Then rebuild the indexes for the database as described in a later section.

   If you are adding a completely new key data item, use the procedures for adding any data item, add the *Key<T>* object to the class, and rebuild the indexes for the database as described later in this chapter.

Converting the Database

The changes you make will most likely affect only a small part of the database, perhaps only one class. You need to convert that class only, and you can do it within the database itself. Leave the original class intact and use a dummy name for the replacement class. For example, if you are changing the *Department* class, add the new class with the name *DepartmentNEW*. The conversion consists of the following six steps.

STEP 1

Design the *DepartmentNEW* class to reflect the changes you are making. Add the class design to the database schema. Leave the original *Department* class design in the schema.

Step 2

Write a conversion constructor to convert the *Department* class to the *DepartmentNEW* class.

Step 3

Write and run a conversion program that reads all the *Department* objects, converts them to *DepartmentNEW* objects, and deletes the *Department* objects. Figure 9.21 is an example of such a conversion program.

```
void main()
{
    Parody *personnel = new Parody("PERSONEL");
    // --- scan all the Department objects
    for (;;)   {
        Department dept;
        if (dept.FirstObject().ObjectExists() == false)
            break;
        // --- convert the Department object
        //     to the DepartmentNEW object
        DepartmentNEW deptnew(dept);
        deptnew.AddObject();
        // --- delete the Department object
        dept.DeleteObject();
    }
    delete personel;
}
```

FIGURE 9.21 *A class conversion program*

Step 4

Rename the *DepartmentNEW* class to *Department* and replace the old *Department* class definition in your source code header files.

Step 5

Make all appropriate modifications to the application that the changed database requires. Compile and link the entire application with the new class definition.

Step 6

Rebuild the database indexes as described below. This step removes the *DepartmentNEW* class identification from the index file and associates the *Department* class identification with the new modified class.

Rebuilding the Index File

The weakest link in a relational database is the integrity between the indexes and the data files. If a system error causes an index to point somewhere other than to the object it indexes, the database is in a state of disintegrity and is unstable and probably unusable. In other errors, the integrity of the index file itself can be disturbed.

Database Integrity Errors

These errors usually occur when the system fails while the indexes and objects are being changed. Until the changes are completed, the system is unstable. The failure causes the instability to remain when you restart the system. The symptom of such instability is the inability of the application to retrieve valid and logical objects. Therefore, the first thing that a database user should try when those symptoms occur is rebuilding the indexes. You should provide such a program for each database that you build. As you learned in the previous section, database conversion tasks need utility programs to rebuild indexes.

The Index Rebuilding Program

Each database needs its own program that rebuilds indexes. The program is not complex, and Figure 9.22 is an example of such a program.

The example conversion program in Figure 9.22 rebuilds the indexes for a database that contains objects of two classes. The program gets PARODY's internal class identification codes for the classes in the database by calling the *GetClassID* function and passing the names of the classes.

The program scans all the nodes from number 1 to the highest node used. It reads each node's object header to see whether the node is the first node of an object. If so, the program calls the *RebuildIndexes* function to tell the database to rebuild the indexes to point to the current node for the next persistent object instantiated. Then the program instantiates an object of whatever type the object header indicates. PARODY and the object read the data values from the database through the *Read* and *ReadObject* functions invoked by the object's constructor. PARODY does not try to find the object from its index value because the program told it that it was rebuilding indexes. Instead, PARODY uses the node number that the program passed to the *RebuildIndexes* function to position the database to read the data values. When the object goes out of scope—which it does right away—PARODY rebuilds the object's indexes from the data values in the keys.

```c
#include <stdio.h>
#include "personel.h"   // application-specific header
#define dbname "PERSONEL"
void BuildIndex()
{
    remove(dbname ".ndx");  // delete old index file
    Parody *personnel = new Parody(dbname);
    ObjectHeader objhdr;
    ClassID EMPLOYEE =
        personnel->GetClassID(typeid(Employee).name());
    ClassID DEPARTMENT =
        personnel->GetClassID(typeid(Department).name());
    NodeNbr nd = 1;
    NodeNbr end = personnel->datafile.HighestNode();
    // ------- scan Parody nodes
    while (nd <= end) {
        // --- read the object header for this node
        personnel->GetObjectHeader(nd, objhdr);
        // --- object relative node# 0 is 1st node of object
        if (objhdr.ndnbr == 0) {
            // --- tell Parody to rebuild indexes this object
            personnel->RebuildIndexes(nd);
            // ----- rebuild depending on class type
            if (objhdr.classid == EMPLOYEE) {
                Employee empl;
            }
```

FIGURE 9.22 *An index rebuilding program*

```
                else if (objhdr.classid == DEPARTMENT)
                    Department dept;
            }
        }
        nd++;
    }
    delete personnel;
}
int main()
{
    BuildIndex();
    return 0;
}
```

FIGURE 9.22 *Continued*

The program's *main* function does not do the work. It calls the *BuildIndex* function, which is the name that you must use. That function name is a C++ *friend* of the *Parody* class, which gives it access to the *GetClassID*, *RebuildIndexes*, and *GetObjectHeader* functions and to the datafile object to determine when the scan of the database has reached the end.

Summary

This chapter taught you how to use PARODY's persistent objects, how to perform database conversion, and how to rebuild database indexes. Chapter 10 presents case studies that are examples of PARODY applications. It also introduces some utility classes that you can use as data types to build data members in your persistent objects.

Chapter 10

PARODY in Applications

Few things are harder to put up with than the annoyance of a good example.

—*Mark Twain*

This chapter presents four small working applications that use PARODY. You can use these examples to learn more about how PARODY works and to guide you when you develop your own applications.

The first example uses keyless objects to store and retrieve simple payroll records. It demonstrates how the *PersistentObject<T>* template class encapsulates the persistence of simple, flat structure objects.

The second example implements a classic computer simulation, the Game of Life, using a string key to store and retrieve Life patterns.

The third example, a personnel management system, uses the almost-relational properties of PARODY to implement a personnel management system that maintains indexed objects for departments, projects, employees, and assignments. You will recognize much of the personnel application from the examples in earlier chapters. This example illustrates persistent object inheritance.

The fourth example maintains a family tree database. It illustrates the use of persistent reference objects in a PARODY application.

Before discussing the example applications, this chapter addresses some supporting software. PARODY uses several general-purpose data structure classes that you might find useful in your own applications. This discussion also describes *GUI*, the generic user interface class that the example applications use.

> **Note:** Please realize that the programs in this chapter are not intended to be models of user interface excellence. Their purpose is to show how to build applications that store, retrieve, and maintain persistent objects in a PARODY database. They are kept simple in the interest of brevity and to avoid the distractions that come from cluttered code examples. Your use of these techniques will, I hope, occur within a more comprehensive application framework than the one used here.

The source code for these classes and the example applications is in Appendix C. This chapter refers to them by their source code file names, and the discussion of each example application begins with a list of the pertinent files. A table of contents at the beginning of the appendix tells you where to find each of the listings. You should read the discussions while looking at the files that they address.

Utility Classes

The following source files are discussed:

- ♦ bool.h
- ♦ linklist.h
- ♦ money.cpp
- ♦ money.h
- ♦ date.cpp
- ♦ date.h

PARODY defines several utility classes for use in building persistent objects. The first class, *bool*, emulates the Boolean type that the ANSI committee is considering for inclusion in standard C++. The second class, *LinkedList<T>*, is a template class that implements a doubly linked list data structure to manage lists of objects. PARODY uses the *LinkedList* class internally to maintain lists of keys and objects. The other two classes—*Money* and *Date*—are used by the example applications as user-defined data types.

The string Class

The previous version of PARODY included a *String* class. The ANSI committee has proposed a standard *string* class, which Borland compilers implement. PARODY now uses the ANSI *string* class instead of its own. Current developments in the committee indicate that the *string* class definition might soon use templates to support strings with international character widths. PARODY's use of strings might necessarily have to change at some time in the future whenever the standardization activity settles down.

The bool Class

The ANSI committee has proposed a *bool* data type to implement Boolean—two-state—objects with *true* and *false* values, and automatic type conversions with integer objects that have nonzero and zero values. The definition is not approved as of this writing, but its details are generally understood. The *bool* class implemented in **bool.h** emulates the ANSI *bool* data type. An application program uses the *bool* type as shown in Figure 10.1.

```
#include "bool.h"
bool PgmSwitch = true; // or false
if (PgmSwitch)
    // ...
if (!PgmSwitch)
    // ...
```

FIGURE 10.1 *Using the bool data type*

You can compare a *bool* object to an integer. The comparison reflects the relative truth of the two objects rather than the numerical relationship. When you assign an integer to a *bool* object, the assigned value is converted to *true* or *false* depending on the nonzero/zero value of the integer being assigned.

> **Note:** After the ANSI *bool* type is implemented, *bool* becomes a C++ keyword. When and if that happens, the declarations in

bool.h will not compile with contemporary compilers. Simply eliminate the preprocessing directives that include **bool.h**, and, if my assumptions about the implementation of *bool* are correct, the programs will compile and execute properly.

LinkedList<T>

PARODY uses linked lists in several places. A *linked list* is a data structure that links objects in a list that the program can navigate. A linked list consists of a list head that points to the first and last objects in the list and list entries that are themselves the listed objects. Each list entry includes its own data values, a pointer to the list head, and pointers to the next and previous entries in the list. A program can append entries to the list, insert an entry at a specified position relative to another entry, delete entries, and navigate the list forward and backward starting at either end or at a chosen entry in the middle of the list. Figure 10.2 illustrates the architecture of a linked list.

LinkedListHead   **LinkedListEntries**

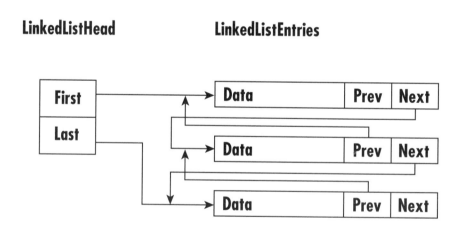

FIGURE 10.2 *Linked list architecture*

No doubt the ANSI committee will approve a standard linked list class. Until then, PARODY uses the one defined as a template in **linklist.h**. You can use the template yourself in your programs by declaring objects of type *LinkedList<T>* as shown in Figure 10.3.

```
LinkedList<int> IntList;    // a list of integers
int i = 123;
IntList.AppendEntry(&i);    // append an entry to the list
// ...
// navigate the list
int *ls = IntList.FirstEntry();
while (ls != 0)    {
    // ... (use the int pointed to by ls)
    ls = IntList.NextEntry();
}
```

FIGURE 10.3 *Using the LinkedList<T> class*

There are member functions to insert and remove entries from the list based on entry position or relative to a specified other entry. You can retrieve an entry based on its position in the list. Appendix A includes a full reference guide to the *LinkedList<T>* template class and its member functions.

The Date Class

The *Date* class defined in **date.h** and **date.cpp** implements a simple month/day/year structure with overloaded relational and stream insertion operators.

The Money Class

The *Money* class defined in **money.h** and **money.cpp** implements a currency data type from a *float* type with overloaded relational and insertion operators. Its constructor rounds the fractional part of the numerical value to even hundredths to emulate the behavior of dollars and cents.

The GUI Class, a Generic User Interface

The following source files are discussed:

♦ gui.cpp
♦ gui.h

Every software development activity targets a user environment and must, therefore, code to a particular user interface model. The example programs in this chapter are no exception. They are launched from the ubiquitous command-line interface, and they use a simple text-mode screen model to display information. To encapsulate the console functions, this book includes the *GUI* class, which manages menus, data and error message displays, and keyboard input through a combination of ANSI protocols and PC-specific BIOS calls.

Do not expect to use the *GUI* class outside the example applications in this chapter. Most programmers write programs for far more sophisticated user interface environments. The *GUI* class provides support for the example programs at the lowest common console denominator. If you use something other than an ANSI terminal or a PC with MS-DOS or OS/2, you must modify the *GUI* class.

The use of this class in these examples does not in any way tie PARODY to text-mode, *iostream* applications. The *GUI* class is not a part of PARODY, which is independent of any particular user interface. PARODY is a class library that implements persistent objects without regard to the user interface of the application that uses the persistent object classes.

The Display

To run the example progams without modification to the screen display software, you need an ANSI-compatible terminal or a software driver that emulates the ANSI protocols for cursor positioning and clearing the screen.

If you are using MS-DOS to run these programs, make sure that the **CONFIG.SYS** file in the root directory of the boot disk contains this statement:

```
DEVICE=ANSI.SYS
```

It may be necessary to add a DOS path to the file name.

If you are using OS/2 to run these programs and the displays appear to be jibberish, enter this command at the OS/2 command line:

```
ANSI ON
```

The Keyboard

The *GUI* class uses functions from MS-DOS and OS/2 C++ compilers to test for keyboard input and read the keyboard. The standard *cin* object does not satisfactorily provide for single key input, which menu selections use. The object has no way to test for the presence of a keystroke without actually reading it, and the sample applications require such a feature. Furthermore, there is no consensus among C++ compiler vendors for the implementation standards of *iostreams*. All the compilers behave differently in small ways. The *GUI* class uses *iostreams*, but not for everything. Instead, it uses platform-specific, compiler-supplied function calls into the BIOS of the PC.

The gui Object

The **gui.h** and **gui.cpp** source files define and implement the *GUI* class. The example applications declare a global pointer to an object of that class named *gui* and use the *new* operator to build a *GUI* object. The *GUI* class consists mostly of methods that manage keyboard input and screen output. The **gui.h** header file defines constant values to establish screen dimensions and the values returned for certain function keys. If you use function key values other than those defined in **gui.h**, you should add constants to that list. The discussion on the *GetKBChar* member function explains that process.

The *GUI* class manages menus, data input, output to the screen, and keyboard operations.

DATA INPUT

The *GUI* class includes several overloaded *UserInput* functions that prompt the user to enter a data value and then read the value into a specified object. Figure 10.4 shows the use of these functions.

The *UserInput* call to load a *string* object specifies the length of the string to be read. The object's length is adjusted to reflect the specified length.

```
// ----- character input
char c;
UserInput(&c, "Enter a letter");
// ----- integer input
int i;    // could be long
UserInput(&i, "Enter a number");
// ----- string input
string name;
UserInput(&name, "Enter your name", 25);
// ----- Date input
Date dt;
UserInput(&dt, "Enter your birthday");
// ----- Money input
Money wage;
UserInput(&wage, "Enter your hourly wage");
```

FIGURE 10.4 *Calling the UserInput function*

SCREEN OUTPUT

The *GUI* class includes these four member functions to perform screen output:

- ♦ *SetCursor* positions the screen and keyboard cursor at a specified x/y coordinate.
- ♦ *ClearScreen* clears the screen.
- ♦ *WriteChar* writes a single character at a specified x/y coordinate.
- ♦ *StatusLine* writes a line of text at the bottom of the screen, padding the line with spaces.

Figure 10.5 shows the use of these functions.

```
gui->ClearScreen();          // clear the screen
gui->SetCursor(5,10);        // position cursor:x=5,y=10
cout << "Hello, Dolly";      // written at 5/10
gui->WriteChar('!',17,10);   // punctuate the message
gui->StatusLine("All done"); // write a status line
```

FIGURE 10.5 *Screen output*

KEYBOARD INPUT

The *GUI* class includes three member functions for keyboard input of a single keystroke:

♦ *KBCharWaiting* returns *true* if there is a keystroke waiting to be read.

♦ *GetKBChar* waits for a keystroke, reads it, and returns its value.

♦ *PutBack* stuffs a keystroke into the input buffer so that it is returned by the next *GetKBChar* call.

Figure 10.6, which assumes the presence of the *gui* pointer declared by the example applications, shows the operation of the keyboard functions.

```
if (gui->KBCharWaiting())
    c = gui->GetKBChar();
gui->PutBack(ESC);
```

FIGURE 10.6 *Keyboard input*

When the user presses a function key, the *GetKBChar* function returns the key's ASCII scan value logically OR'd with the value 0x80. The constant integers in **gui.h** define those values for the PC's cursor arrow keys and the **Escape** key. If your application needs other function key values, you can add to that list. To determine the values, write a program such as the one in Figure 10.7.

```
#include <iostream.h>
#include "gui.h"
void main()
{
    char c;
    cout << "Type keys. Esc when done" << endl;
    while ((c = gui.GetKBChar()) != ESC)
        cout << "That key's value is: "
             << ((int) c & 255) << endl;
}
```

FIGURE 10.7 *Finding the key values*

DIALOGS

The *GUI* class includes three simple dialogs that the applications use. The *YesNo* function displays a question, reads the user's answer, and returns *true* if the user answered yes, and *false* if the user answered no. The *Error* function displays a specified error message along with an audible alarm and prompts the user to enter any key to continue. The *AnyKey* function prompts the user to enter any key. Figure 10.8 shows the use of these three dialogs.

```
if (!gui->YesNo("Is that OK?"))
    gui->Error("Sorry");
else
    gui->AnyKey();
```

FIGURE 10.8 *User dialogs*

Menus

Two menu formats are supported by the *GUI* framework: a full-screen menu and a one-liner menu. They are implemented by the *ScreenMenu* and *OneLineMenu* classes, which are defined in **gui.h** and **gui.cpp**. An application declares an object of the particular menu class, provides the menu details as arguments to the constructor, and calls the class's *Execute* member function.

FULL-SCREEN MENUS

Figure 10.9 illustrates how an application invokes a full-screen menu by declaring and initializing a *ScreenMenu* object.

```
void AddEmployee(); // declare menu selection functions
// etc...
ScreenMenu("Employees",  // menu title
           // --- menu selections
           "Add",       AddEmployee,
           "Change",    ChangeEmployee,
           "Delete",    DeleteEmployee,
           "List",      ListEmployees,
           "Projects", ListEmployeeProjects,
           // --- terminate selection list & execute
           NULL).Execute();
```

FIGURE 10.9 *Executing a full-screen menu*

The first argument in the *ScreenMenu* constructor is the menu title. Subsequent arguments are pairs of menu selection labels and command functions to execute when the user chooses the selection. Because the constructor uses a C-style variable argument list, the last argument must be a null pointer. You must use the NULL global identifier here instead of a constant zero. The constructor is declared with one parameter and an ellipse to form a variable argument list. The compiler would not know to convert a zero argument to a null character pointer. In an environment where integers and pointers are different lengths—such as typical MS-DOS 16-bit programs—the conversion would be wrong, so use NULL to be sure.

> **Note:** Many C++ purists deprecate the use of variable argument lists because of the absence of type checking. There are other C++ techniques that I could have used to implement the *ScreenMenu* class. One such approach is to define a menu selection class, declare arrays of menu selection objects, and pass the address of the arrays to the constructor. That convention would remain within the spirit of strong type checking and would keep the purists happy. I find, however, that the variable argument list notation is convenient and expressive for these types of operations. If it offends you, then by all means change it. The NULL global identifier is out of favor as well, for very good reasons. C++ programmers prefer to use the constant 0 instead, using the compiler's automatic type conversion of integer zero to address zero where a pointer type is expected. In this case, the type conversion does not work for the reasons stated above.

By using the dot operator after the constructor to call the *Execute* function, you do not have to name the menu object. This practice is for notational convenience to obviate unnecessary identifier declarations. All you can do to a *ScreenMenu* object is declare it and call its *Execute* function. An application might declare and name all menus globally and then execute them in appropriate places in the program. Either way works.

The *ScreenMenu* declaration in Figure 10.9 clears the screen and displays the menu shown in Figure 10.10.

The user selects a menu command by typing its number. The program executes the function associated with the command.

When the command function returns, ScreenMenu clears the screen and displays the menu again. If the command function displays information that the user must see before returning to the menu, the command

mand function should call the *GUI* object's *AnyKey* function to prompt the user to press a key before proceeding. When the user presses the **Esc** key at the menu's *Select>* prompt, the *ScreenMenu* constructor is completed, and the statement following the constructor executes.

```
              Employees
                 1: Add
                 2: Change
                 3: Delete
                 4: List
                 5: Projects
               Esc: Return
               Select>
```

FIGURE 10.10 *A GUI full-screen menu*

ONE-LINER MENUS

One-liner menus are different from full-screen menus in these respects: First, one-liner menus do not clear the screen. Second, rather than displaying in the center of the screen, the menu text is displayed wherever the cursor happens to be when you declare the *OneLineMenu* object. Third, the one-liner menu does not loop while waiting for the user to press **Esc** or any other exit key. Instead, the menu takes one selection from the user and then returns. Fourth, there is no menu title; the menu text consists of one line that describes the menu selections. Finally, instead of using digits for menu selection keystrokes, the one-liner menu figures out which keystroke matches each selection based on the first character of each selection's text. Figure 10.11 is an example of the code that invokes a one-liner menu.

```
void ChangeName(), ChangeDept();
OneLineMenu("N-ame, D-epartment",
    ChangeName, ChangeDept).Execute();
```

FIGURE 10.11 *Invoking a one-line menu*

The code in Figure 10.11 constructs a *OneLineMenu* object, which displays the first text argument on the screen and waits for the user to press

N or D. Depending on which key the user presses, the object executes one of the two functions named as the second and third arguments. There is no need to have a NULL final argument because the constructor uses the number of discrete words in the text to determine not only the command keys but also the number of selections on the menu. This means that each discrete selection must be represented by a label that includes no white space.

Navigational Access: The Payroll Application

The following source files are discussed:

- **payroll.cpp**
- **payroll.h**

Needless to say, the code in **payroll.h** and **payroll.cpp** does not implement a complete payroll system. These files demonstrate the use of the *PersistentObject<T>* template class to add persistence to simple flat structures without key data members.

The **payroll.h** header file declares the *PayrollRcd* structure, which contains only fixed-length data members. It contains no virtual functions and no pointer or reference data members. You can store and retrieve objects of this structure in and from a PARODY persistent object database by using the type as the argument when declaring objects of the *PersistentObject<T>* template class. The program's *main* function declares *GUI* and *Parody* objects and uses a *ScreenMenu* object to run the program. The menu has selections to add records to the database and to list the records in the database. The essence of adding a record is shown in Figure 10.12.

```
PayrollRcd pr;
// ... put some data into pr
PersistentObject<PayrollRcd> ppr(pr);
ppr.AddObject();
```

FIGURE 10.12 *Adding a PersistentObject<T> object*

The example in Figure 10.12 represents the simplest use of PARODY. It contains all the code necessary to store a flat, simple object into the database. The object itself is an instance of the structure. The persistent object is an instance of the *PersistentObject* template class with the structure as the parameterized type.

The *PersistentObject* template assumes that the size of the structure is the size of the object's record. The template further assumes that everything within the structure is persistent and independent of its original memory address, which means that the record may be read into a different instance of the structure in a different program at a different time with no attendant problems. Had it needed to, the program could have obtained the object's database address by calling the *Persistent::ObjectAddress* function while the object was still in scope. Figure 10.13 shows how that would have worked.

```
ObjAddr oa = ppr.ObjectAddress();
```

FIGURE 10.13 *The address of a persistent object*

The *ListRecords* function in **payroll.cpp** navigates all the *PayrollRcd* objects in the database in the coincidental order in which they were added. Figure 10.14 illustrates this process.

```
PersistentObject<PayrollRcd> ppr;
ppr.FirstObject();
while (ppr.ObjectExists())  {
    // ...
    ppr.NextObject();
}
```

FIGURE 10.14 *Navigating PersistentObject<T> Objects*

This simple payroll application represents the requirements for keyless objects. Without keys, the application itself keeps track of where the individual objects are in the database. Many applications would use this strategy. Many others use a unique data member value to identify persistent objects. Those applications are best served by key data members, and the next example demonstrates that usage.

Associative Access: The Game of Life Application

The following source file is discussed:

♦ **life.cpp**

The Game of Life, used here to demonstrate keyed persistent objects, dates to the early days of computer simulation. The game was invented by British mathematician John Conroy and was published in *Scientific American* in 1970.

The simulation is small enough to lend itself well to an illustration of persistent objects. The game involves relatively few lines of code, and the condition of its simulation at any time is an object that can be stored and retrieved in an object database.

The Concept of Life

Life simulates a world of neighboring cells. Each cell, identified by its x/y address in the screen coordinate system, may have one of two possible states. The cell is either populated or unpopulated and is surrounded by eight neighboring cells, as shown in Figure 10.15.

FIGURE 10.15 *A Life world*

The neighborhood wraps around. Cells in the margins are neighbors with adjacent cells in the opposite margins.

The game consists of a sequence of generations. Each generation examines each cell to see whether the cell is populated and how many neighbors it has. A neighbor is one of the eight adjacent cells in the 3x3 array of nine in which the target cell is the center cell.

A cell is born and survives or expires depending on the population of its neighborhood. Its survival depends on having enough neighbors for company and support and not too many with whom to share resources. With each generation, a cell is born—becomes populated—if there are enough adjacent neighbors to spawn it. The cell dies—becomes depopulated—if there are either too few neighbors to support it or too many neighbors with which it must share resources. More specifically, if an unpopulated cell has three—no more, no less—populated neighbors, the cell becomes populated in the next generation. Conversely, if a populated cell has fewer than two or more than three neighbors, its population expires in the next generation.

The implementation of Life in this book uses screen character positions to represent cells, and the world of cells is limited to the number of screen character positions.

An Evolution of Generations

The Game of Life simulates the evolution of generations. To play the game, you create the world by specifying which cells are initially populated. Then you run the evolution and observe how each generation modifies the pattern of populated cells. You can run the evolution continuously or by stepping through it one generation at a time. The world often takes on interesting symmetrical patterns as the generations pass. Some patterns result in a totally depopulated world after a few generations. Some patterns result in a stable, populated world. Some patterns endlessly repeat cycles of births and deaths. A culture of Life players blossomed at MIT and elsewhere in the 1970s, and they often published and shared interesting starting patterns.

The Life Program

Life.cpp is the source file that implements the game. It uses persistent objects of type *Life* to save and retrieve patterns. You can design a pattern and save it as a persistent object, or you can stop an evolution mid-way and save the current pattern. To save an object, you must provide a name. The program adjusts the size of the name to a fixed-length *string* object and uses the name as the object's key. Later, you can retrieve patterns by their names and play the game by beginning with the retrieved pattern.

The persistent *Life* object is built from the state of the in-memory *Life* object when the program adds it to the database. The object in the database consists of the object's name, a count of populated cells, and a list of the x/y coordinates of the populated cells. The persistent object is, therefore, a variable-length data structure that does not resemble the in-memory object at all. The *Life::Write* and *Life::Read* functions define the database object format.

This is an important example. Unlike the records of traditional databases, a persistent object's representation does not necessarily resemble the object's in-memory representation. Instead, the persistent representation contains sufficient data to reconstruct the in-memory representation. The details of that representation and reconstruction are provided by the class's *Read* and *Write* member functions.

Rules for Survival

The in-memory object includes a table of rules for cell survival. As published, the rules reflect those of the traditional Game of Life as Conroy designed it. You can modify this table to achieve different results during the evolution of a Life session. The *Life::Rules* array consists of true/false state indicators. The outer dimension contains two inner arrays: the first applies to a cell that is unpopulated; the second applies to a cell that is populated. The inner array has one entry for each possible count of neighbors. For example, if the cell has four neighbors, then the fifth entry specifies whether that cell is to be populated in the next generation.

Running the Program

When you run the program, it displays the menu shown in Figure 10.16.

```
                    The Game of Life
                       1: New
                       2: Change
                       3: Delete
                       4: List
                       5: Display
                       6: Run
                       7: Step
                       8: Load
                       9: Save
                     Esc: Return
                    Select>
```

FIGURE 10.16 *Running the Game of Life*

Select **1** to build a new world. The program displays a mostly blank screen with a status line at the bottom. Use the cursor arrow keys to move the cursor around, and press the space bar or the **Enter** key to toggle the population of a cell. A populated cell displays as a happy face character on a PC. You can change the display character by changing the value of the *Pop* constant in **life.cpp**. Figure 10.17 shows the screen with a typical pattern.

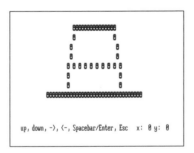

FIGURE 10.17 *A Game of Life pattern*

When the screen has the population configuration you want, press **Esc** to return to the menu. Table 10.1 lists the Game of Life menu actions.

TABLE 10.1 *Game of Life menu selections*

SELECTION	ACTION
1	Builds a new world pattern of populated and depopulated cells.
2	Returns to the pattern screen and allows you to make further modifications to the pattern.
3	Deletes from the database the Life object that you loaded with selection 8.
4	Displays the names of all the Life objects in the database.
5	Displays the current pattern.
6	Runs the evolution of generations nonstop, displaying the patterns while you watch. Interrupt the process by pressing Esc.
7	Displays the current generation and allows you to step through subsequent generations a step at a time by pressing the S key.
8	Retrieves a Life object from the PARODY database. The program prompts you to enter the pattern's name.
9	Saves the current pattern in its current generation as a persistent object in the PARODY database named LIFE.DAT. The program prompts you to provide a name for the pattern in the database.

Almost Relational: The Personnel Application

The following source files are discussed:

- ♦ assign.cpp
- ♦ assign.h
- ♦ dept.cpp
- ♦ dept.h
- ♦ employee.cpp
- ♦ employee.h
- ♦ index.cpp
- ♦ manager.cpp
- ♦ manager.h
- ♦ personel.cpp

- ♦ personel.h
- ♦ project.cpp
- ♦ project.h
- ♦ projview.cpp

This section describes the Personnel system, a PARODY application that maintains a database of departments, employees, projects, and employee-to-project assignments. This system uses PARODY's almost-relational properties to maintain indexed objects and interclass relationships. Figure 10.18 illustrates the relational and hierarchical architectures of the Personnel application database.

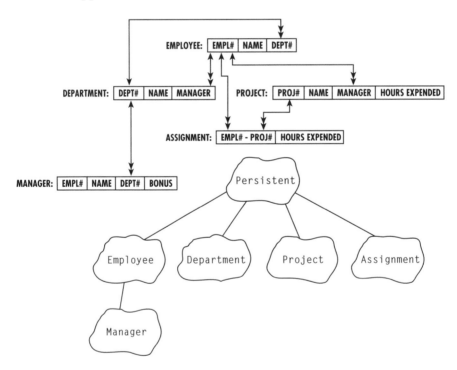

FIGURE 10.18 *Personnel application object architectures*

The Personnel application stores records of departments, employees, projects, and employee-to-project assignments. An employee may work for only one department. Departments and projects may have one manager each. The managers are employees. Employees are assigned to projects and log labor hours against those projects. An employee may work on several projects. A project may have several employees assigned to it.

We will first discuss the Personnel application's persistent classes and then we will address how the application uses them.

The Department Class

Dept.h and **dept.cpp** define and implement the *Department* class, which is typical of a simple persistent object class. In addition to its *deptno* primary key, it includes data members that define the department name and, as a secondary key, the *manager* object, which is the employee number of the department manager. The *EmployeeNumber* type is defined in **employee.h**, which you will see later, so the **dept.h** file includes it prior to the *Department* class definition.

There are the usual *Read* and *Write* member functions to support persistence and some member functions to read and change the data values.

The *Department* class encapsulates certain aspects of the user interface required to retrieve, display, and modify the object. This approach is consistent in the design of the other classes in the system, and it consists of member functions to display the object, read its data member values from the keyboard, and prompt for and retrieve or build instances of the object. The related member functions are *Input*, *InputName*, *InputManager*, *TryChange*, *SelectChange*, *Get*, *GetExisting*, *Header*, and an overloaded *ostream* insertion operator.

The Employee Class

Employee.h and **employee.cpp** define and implement the *Employee* class, with its *emplno* primary key. The *Employee* class has a secondary key as well, the *deptno* object, which specifies the department to which the employee is assigned. The only other data member is the employee's name. The remaining class definitions consist of member functions that access and modify data values and that encapsulate the user interface in the same way that the *Department* class does.

The Project Class

Project.h and **project.cpp** define and implement the *Project* class, which is similar in construction to the *Department* class. It includes a *projno* primary key and a *manager* secondary key to identify the employee number of the project manager. The other two data members are the project name and an integer that represents the hours expended against the project. The member functions include the usual data member access and modification functions as well as one that allows a using program to add to the hours expended. The user interface is encapsulated just as in the *Department* and *Employee* classes.

The Assignment Class

Assign.h and **assign.cpp** implement the *Assignment* class, an example of a relational connector class that forms the many-to-many relationship between objects of the *Employee* class and objects of the *Project* class. The *assignment* object is the concatenated key that makes the connection. It is built from the *CatKey<T1,T2>* class template and it contains two member objects built from *EmployeeNumber* and *DepartmentNumber* objects. In addition to forming the concatenated primary key, the two objects are secondary keys. The rest of the class definition is similar to the other classes with member functions that access and change data values and with an encapsulated user interface.

The Manager Class

Manager.h and **manager.cpp** implement the *Manager* class, which demonstrates deriving a class from a persistent class. In this case, the *Manager* class is derived from the *Employee* class. All that it adds to the class is a *bonus* data member of type *Money*.

To use persistent classes in a class hierarchy, the base class must cooperate with the inheritance. Its *Read* and *Write* member functions must be *virtual*, and it must be prevented from calling *LoadObject* from its constructor and *SaveObject* from its destructor. Except for those differences, a base persistent class is identical to any other persistent class.

The *Employee* class is not an abstract base class. You can have *Employee* objects that are of type *Employee* rather than a derived type. Therefore, the class needs to know, during construction and destruction, whether it is operating as a base class. Normally, C++ classes have no way of knowing that. Therefore, we must contrive something.

Observe the *Employee* constructor and destructor in **employee.cpp.** They call *LoadObject* and *SaveObject* only if the employee number is not –1. We have set that convention for classes that will derive from

Employee. You can use other methods of a similar nature in your designs. The idea is to have the derived constructor and destructor notify the base constructor and destructor that the derivation exists. Inasmuch as –1 is not a valid employee number (according to a rule that we just made up to fit the occasion), we can use that value as a signal to the base class.

The *Manager* constructor in **manager.cpp** initializes the *Employee* constructor with the value –1 in the parameter initialization list. That value tells the *Employee* constructor not to call *LoadObject.* Then, the *Manager* constructor calls *Employee::SetEmplNo* to set the employee number to a valid value. After that, the constructor calls *LoadObject.*

This sequence is important because while the *Employee* constructor is running, the *Manager* object does not yet exist. The *Manager* object's *Read* function would not be called, and PARODY would associate the indexes with the *Employee* class rather than the *Manager* class.

The *Manager* destructor calls *SaveObject* and then sets the employee number to –1 so that the *Employee* destructor does not call *SaveObject.*

Observe that the relationships established between *Employee* and other classes are not automatically inherited by the *Manager* class. It is a class unto itself—albeit a derived one—and if relationships are to be maintained, you must establish them separately from those of the base class.

The Personnel Program

Personel.h and **personel.cpp** implement the Personnel application. The header file declares the *typedefs* for the application's key data elements, includes the header files that define the persisent classes, and declares the external pointer to the GUI object.

Personel.cpp implements the application with a series of *GUI* menus that allow you to enter data into the database and display the database contents. The first menu has selections for employees, departments, projects, and assignments. Each of these selections allows you to add, change, list, or delete objects of the chosen class as well as some unique processes for each class. The add, change, list, and delete processes are similar in all the classes, so this discussion covers those functions in general and then discusses the unique processes for the classes that illustrate different ways that an application uses PARODY where objects are related.

ADDING AN OBJECT:

This discussion relates to the *AddEmployee*, *AddDepartment*, *AddProject*, and *AddAssignment* functions in **personel.cpp**.

The add functions for the classes first call the static *Get* function for the class, which prompts the user to enter a value for the primary key— employee number, for example—and then instantiates an object from the key value. The *Get* functions use the *new* operator to instantiate the objects on the heap and return their pointers, which the caller must destroy with the *delete* operator or *Persistent::Destroy* member function. If the object's *ObjectExists* function returns *true*, the add function displays the object along with an error message that the user is trying to add an object that already exists.

CHANGING AN OBJECT

This discussion relates to the *ChangeEmployee*, *ChangeDepartment*, *ChangeProject*, and *ChangeAssignment* functions in **personel.cpp**.

The change function calls the object's *GetExisting* function, which prompts the user for a primary key and instantiates an object from the key value. If the object does not exist in the database, *GetExisting* displays an error message, destroys the empty object, and returns a null pointer. Otherwise, it displays the object and returns the address of the object, which the caller must later destroy by using the *delete* operator or *Persistent::Destroy* member function. The change function calls the object's *SelectChange* function, which prompts for one of the various data fields in the object and accepts the user's input to change the data. If PARODY rejects the change due to an integrity violation, *SelectChange* displays an error message.

LISTING AN OBJECT

This discussion relates to the *ListEmployee*, *ListDepartment*, *ListProject*, and *ListAssignment* functions in **personel.cpp**.

The list function calls *FirstObject* to retrieve the first object for the class. Then, as long as the object's *ObjectExists* function returns *true*, the list function displays the object on *cout* and retrieves the next object in its primary key sequence by calling its *NextObject* function.

DELETING AN OBJECT

This discussion relates to the *DeleteEmployee*, *DeleteDepartment*, *DeleteProject*, and *DeleteAssignment* functions in **personel.cpp**.

The delete function uses *GetExisting* the same way that the change function does. If *GetExisting* returns a valid object pointer, the delete function asks the user to verify the deletion in a *GUI::YesNo* dialog. Then the delete function calls *DeleteObject* to delete the object from the database, displaying an error message if PARODY rejects the deletion due to an integrity violation.

LISTING AN EMPLOYEE'S PROJECTS AND A PROJECT'S EMPLOYEES

The *ListEmployeeProjects* and *ListProjectEmployees* functions illustrate how a program navigates a connector class by using a secondary key component of its concatenated primary key. The program calls *GetExisting* to get an instance of the project or employee, depending on which secondary key you are searching. Then it instantiates an empty *Assignments* object, adding the partial concatenated key value to the object. Next, it calls *FindObject*, specifying the secondary part of the concatenated key to find the first instance on the database of an *Assignment* object with the specified project or employee number. Then, as long as the object's *ObjectExists* function returns *true* and its partial key value is equal to the original value entered by the user, the program instantiates an object of the other type in the concatenated key, displays that object, and calls *NextObject* for the connector class.

ADDING A MANAGER AND LISTING MANAGERS

These processes resemble those of the same operations for employees. The program does not attempt to validate that managers are employees or that department and project managers are manager objects. The *Manager* class is added to illustrate persistent class inheritance only.

The Project View Program

Recall from Chapter 8 that PARODY throws an exception when you try to instantiate more than one copy of the same persistent object. The **projview.cpp** program demonstrates how you can use that feature to advantage, and Figure 10.19 illustrates that logic.

```
Project *proj1, *proj2;
try
{
    // --- get two project numbers (could be the same)
    proj1 = Project::Get();
    proj2 = Project::Get();
}
catch(Persistent *obj)
{
    // --- both Gets got the same project number
    proj2 = static_cast<Project*>(obj);
}
// --- use proj1 and proj2 (same or different)
// ...
Persistent::Destroy(proj1);   // delete proj1
Persistent::Destroy(proj2);   // delete proj2
```

FIGURE 10.19 *Multiple-copy objects*

The program displays two *Project* objects from the database so that the user can compare them. It calls the *Project::Get* function twice to prompt the user for the project numbers and to instantiate the selected *Project* objects. If the user enters two valid and different unique project numbers, the program displays those two projects and terminates. If, however, the user enters the same project number twice, the *Project::Get* function tries to instantiate the object a second time, and PARODY throws the *Persistent** exception. If a program ignores this exception, the program aborts. *Projview.cpp* does not ignore the exception; it catches the exception, displays a message to that effect, and copies the thrown pointer into the second pointer. The second pointer is null prior to the copy because the construction failed as a result of the exception. Now, when the program uses the two pointers, they point to the same object. PARODY maintains a count of the number of times a persistent object has been instantiated. The *Persistent::Destroy* function decrements this count and does not actually delete the object until the count goes to zero.

Rebuilding the Index

Index.cpp is a utility program that rebuilds the indexes for the Personnel application database. It follows the logic described in Chapter 9 for rebuilding indexes and is aware of all five classes that the Personnel system uses.

Persistent References: The Family Tree Application

The following source files are discussed:

- ◆ **family.cpp**
- ◆ **family.h**
- ◆ **famtree.cpp**

This application maintains a family tree database, that contains objects of family members. Each object records the family member's name, sex, dates of birth and death, and parents. The example demonstrates the use of the *Reference<T>* template class in recording persistent references to related objects in a class. In this case, the parents of a family member are represented by persistent references to their persistent family member objects in the database.

Although this example application is not a comprehensive family tree maintenance system, its data members comprise the minimum necessary data elements needed for a family tree. Most such systems add a memo field to record biographical notes about the family member. They also usually include a marriage object that records the spouses and dates of marriage and divorce for each such union. A database with these few data members can support virtually all functional requirements for a family tree system.

The FamilyMember Class

The **family.h** header file and the **family.cpp** source file define the *FamilyMember* class, the one persistent object class in the family tree database. The *name* field is a *string* object and is the key data member that identifies the object. The *sex* field is an *enum* that can contain the values *unknown*, *male*, and *female*. The dates of birth and death are objects of the *Date* class used earlier in this chapter. The *mother* and *father* data members are objects of the template class *Reference<FamilyMember>*. The database stores references to other objects of the same class within these members.

Because the *FamilyMember* class can be referenced by a *Reference<T>* object, it has a conversion constructor that constructs the object from its *ObjAddr* identity. The application does not usually use this constructor, but it is required for the *Reference<T>* template class to use to construct a referenced object when a referencing object is constructed. In this example, the referencing object and the referenced object are of the same class. This circumstance is not always the case.

The *FamilyMember* class includes member functions that set and retrieve its data members. Observe that the member functions to set the parent objects simply assign *FamilyMember* objects to the *Reference<FamilyMember>* data members. This action is all that is needed to establish a persistent reference to another persistent object.

Maintaining a Family Tree

The **famtree.cpp** source code file implements the family tree application. Remember that this application maintains the database only. It does not perform relationship retrievals, build ancestor and descendant diagrams, or support any of the other complex operations that a full family tree system supports. The data values are there, but to go beyond the simple operations of this example you must add functionality to the algorithms that they support.

The program displays a menu with three selections: add a record, list the records, and view a record. The primary key to this database file is the family member's name. To complete the design, you would have to augment this key with a suffix that permitted several family members to have the same name, which is a common occurrence in most families.

Adding a record consists of providing a name, the sex, and the dates of birth and death. Enter three space-separated zeros for the date of death when the family member is still alive.

Viewing a member prompts you for the member's name. The *GetListedMember* function lets you supply a portion of a name and lists those that are close to the specification. If a name matches what you enter, that name is used; otherwise, the program displays the list and lets you select from the list.

After displaying the specified family member's record, the program uses a one-liner menu that allows you to change or delete the record. If you choose to change it, another one-liner menu lets you choose to change the name, sex, dates, or parents. Of interest here is how the program changes the parents.

When you have specified a name for a parent and when the program has determined that the selected parent is of the correct sex, the program establishes a persistent reference from the offspring to the parent's *FamilyMember* object by assigning that object to the offspring object's *Reference<FamilyMember>* data member.

Summary

This chapter provides example applications and utility programs for the PARODY developer. Appendix A shows you how to build the software by using one of the MS-DOS or OS/2 C++ compilers. Appendix B is a programmer's reference guide to PARODY. The complete source code for PARODY and the example applications is in Appendix C.

Appendix *A*

Building the Software

This appendix describes how to build the programs in this book by using one of the supported compilers. PARODY compiles with Borland C++ 4.0 for DOS and Borland C++ 1.5 for OS/2. Those are the only PC compilers that support all the new ANSI features that PARODY uses. Eventually, more compilers will support the new features, and I will add support for those compilers. The features themselves will probably change as the committee proceeds with its work. There are new features under consideration—such as namespaces—that are not yet implemented. As they become available, PARODY will change to incorporate the ones that benefit the software.

The procedures in this appendix use the command-line environments of the compiler products. Both compilers have integrated development environments, and you might want to install PARODY and the example applications into one of them. However, as published here, PARODY uses the command-line MAKE, compiler, librarian, and linker programs that come with the compiler products.

There are two files, other than the source code itself, that are needed to build the software. They are **makefile**, which is the command file read by the MAKE utility program, and **parody.bld**, the command file that the librarian uses to build the PARODY object library. The listings for these files are at the end of this appendix.

General Instructions

These instructions apply to both compiler environments. Follow them first and then proceed to the instructions related to your compiler. If there are additional compilers supported after the publication of this book or if newer versions of the compilers necessitate changes to these procedures, the companion diskette will describe the changes in a file named **README.DOC**.

Install Your Compiler

To use either of the compilers, first install it according to the vendor's instructions. Make sure that you have set the DOS or OS/2 path to include the subdirectory where you installed the compiler's executable files. Most compiler installations offer to do this for you. The symptoms that occur when your compiler is not properly installed usually point to missing configuration file items. The compilers use these controls to tell them where to find the system's header and library files.

Many of the letters I have received from readers about their problems building the code from the first edition of *C++ Database Development* were, in fact, problems with their installation of the compiler. Before you assume that a problem originates in the PARODY code or these instructions, verify that your compiler will compile something else. Build the ubiquitous **HELLO.C** program that most C language texts begin with and make sure that you can compile, link, and run that program. Use the command-line compiler to build the test program. Often a compiler is configured correctly for the integrated development environment but is not configured to work from the command line.

Install the PARODY Source Code

Make a subdirectory to contain the source code and copy the associated **makefile** and **parody.bld** files into that subdirectory. Copy the source code from Appendix C into the same subdirectory.

Log into the subdirectory where you copied the PARODY source code.

Modifying Makefile

If you wish to build programs for a memory model other than the large model, change the MODEL macro in **makefile** from 'l' to 's' for the small model, 'c' for the compact model, or 'm' for the medium model. Note that an OS/2 installation is not concerned with memory models, and you must comment out the definition of the MODEL macro in **makefile**.

Building the Executable Programs

Enter the following command at the DOS or OS/2 command line to run the Borland C++ MAKE program and build the software.

```
make
```

The MAKE program builds these files:

- **parody.lib**—The PARODY object library with which all applications link.
- **index.exe**—An example of a program to rebuild a database's indexes.
- **personel.exe**—The Personnel application.
- **projview.exe**—A program that illustrates instantiating multiple copies of objects.
- **payroll.exe**—The Payroll application.
- **life.exe**—Conway's Game of Life.
- **famtree.exe**—The Family Tree application.

Testing the Software

Observe the screen while the compiler's MAKE utility builds the software. There should be no error messages. There will probably be no warning messages either, but compiler warnings are not consistent, and future versions of compilers might issue warnings where current ones do not.

If everything went smoothly, the files listed above will be in the subdirectory where you installed the source code.

ANSI.SYS

Before you run the applications, make sure that the DOS **ansi.sys** device driver is installed in **config.sys**. For OS/2, make sure that the ANSI ON command is in effect. If it is not, you will see a display similar to the one shown in Figure A.1 when you run **life.exe**.

```
D:\PARODY2>life
←[2J←[7;21HThe Game of Life←[9;23H1: New←[10;23H2: Change←[11;23H3: Delete←[12;2
3H4: List←[13;23H5: Display←[14;23H6: Run←[15;23H7: Step←[16;23H8: Load←[17;23H9
: Save←[18;21HEsc: Return←[20;21HSelect>
```

FIGURE A.1 *The Game of Life without ANSI protocols*

The display just shown contains the ANSI command protocols that clear the screen and position the cursor embedded in the menu text. If the DOS **ansi.sys** device driver is not installed or if the OS/2 ANSI ON command has not been issued, the operating system displays those commands on the screen as if they were common text.

Run the Example Application Programs

Run the **life.exe** program. Exit it immediately. There should now be two additional files: **life.dat** and **life.ndx**. They are the PARODY database for the example Life application. Each will be only four bytes long, because you have not added any objects.

Run the **personel.exe** program. Exit it immediately. There should now be two additional files: **personel.dat** and **personel.ndx**. They are the PARODY database for the example Personnel application. Each will be only four bytes long, because you have not added any objects.

Run the **personel.exe** program and add, change, list, and delete employee, department, project, and assignment objects by using the menu commands. Exit and rerun the application to see that the objects are, in fact, persistent.

Run the **life.exe** program. Build and save worlds of populated cells by using the menu commands. Exit and rerun the application to load those objects.

Test the **payroll.exe, projview.exe,** and **famtree.exe** programs by running them, adding objects where appropriate, and viewing those objects to see that the database is updated correctly.

Rebuild the Indexes

Run the **index.exe** program. It displays each of the objects in the Personnel database as it finds them and rebuilds the indexes. You can verify that **index.exe** works by deleting or renaming the **personel.ndx** file before you run **index.exe.** After the program is done, the **personel.ndx** file will be reestablished, which you can verify by running **personel.exe** again and retrieving objects.

Listings

Following are listings of the files that build the PARODY library and the example applications.

Makefile

```
# ========================================================
# makefile - Borland C++ 4.0 for DOS and 1.5 for OS/2
# ========================================================
# ========================================================
# Comment out this macro to remove debugging
# ========================================================
DEBUG= -v -vi
# ========================================================
# Comment out this macro for OS/2
# ========================================================
MODEL= -ml
# ========================================================
```

continued

continued

```
CMPL= $(DEBUG) $(MODEL)
.cpp.obj:
    bcc $(CMPL) -c {$* }
all : index.exe    \
     personel.exe \
     projview.exe \
     payroll.exe  \
     life.exe     \
     famtree.exe  \
    echo all done
# ================================================
# define the Personnel system class library
# ================================================
APOBJ=employee.obj dept.obj project.obj assign.obj manager.obj
PLINK=$&.obj $(APOBJ)
index.exe : index.obj $(APOBJ) parody.lib
    bcc $(CMPL) $(PLINK) parody.lib
personel.exe : personel.obj $(APOBJ) parody.lib
    bcc -M $(CMPL) $(PLINK) parody.lib
projview.exe : projview.obj $(APOBJ) parody.lib
    bcc $(CMPL) $(PLINK) parody.lib
life.exe : life.obj parody.lib
    bcc -M $(CMPL) life.obj parody.lib
payroll.exe : payroll.obj parody.lib
    bcc $(CMPL) payroll.obj parody.lib
famtree.exe : famtree.obj family.obj parody.lib
    bcc $(CMPL) famtree.obj family.obj parody.lib
# ================================================
# Build the PARODY.LIB class library
# ================================================
parody.lib : parody.obj \
             btree.obj  \
             key.obj    \
             tnode.obj  \
             node.obj   \
             gui.obj    \
             money.obj  \
             date.obj
    tlib parody @parody.bld
```

Parody.bld

```
-+parody.obj    &
-+btree.obj     &
-+key.obj       &
-+tnode.obj     &
-+node.obj      &
-+gui           &
-+money.obj     &
-+date.obj
```

Appendix *B*

PARODY Reference Guide

This appendix is the programmer's reference guide to PARODY. It describes:

- ♦ Constants and *typedefs* that alter PARODY's behavior.
- ♦ Class interface member functions.
- ♦ Exceptions.
- ♦ PARODY data structures.

Modifying PARODY

You can change the way PARODY works by altering the values assigned to some constants and by changing some *typedef* declarations.

Constants

Table B.1 shows the global constants that you can change to make compile-time modifications to the way PARODY operates.

TABLE B.1 *Global constants*

CONSTANT	DESCRIPTION	DEFAULT	HEADER FILE
SCREENHEIGHT	Screen height	25	gui.h
SCREENWIDTH	Screen width	80	gui.h
MAXCOMMANDS	Maximum menu commands	9	gui.h
nodelength	Length of a PARODY disk node	128	parody.h

The first three constants affect the *GUI* class behavior. As such they do not affect PARODY. You can change them if you plan to use the *GUI* class in your applications. One possible change is to increase the *SCREENHEIGHT* constant to 43 or 50 and use the DOS or OS/2 command-line MODE command to set the video mode to 43 or 50 lines. Try that with the Game of Life example application to have larger world patterns with which to experiment.

typedefs

Node.h declares *NodeNbr,* a *typedef* that you can change to affect the range and size of files. The type is a scalar representing a serial node number. The internal object identity of a persistent object is a *NodeNbr* value relative to the value one. Zero represents a null value. The type width determines the maximum number of *Nodes* that you can have in a database. As published, *NodeNbr* is a *short* integer. In a typical PC implementation, this means that a database may have 65,536 physical nodes. If no object exceeds one node in length (as defined by the *nodelength* constant described above), there can be as many as 65,536 objects in the database. To increase this limit, change the *typedef* to *int* (on 32-bit compilers) or *long* and recompile the software before you build the database. Because the index and datafiles contain *NodeNbr* objects, changing *NodeNbr*'s width changes not only the ranges of the files but also their sizes. As a result, you cannot change *NodeNbr* and subsequently use the software with a database built before the change. You must rebuild the database from scratch.

Date.h declares *DtEl,* an integer *typedef* that stores the month, day, and year components of a calendar date. As used in the examples, the type is an *unsigned char.* If you need to record years with values greater than 255, you must change this *typedef* or modify the *Date* class.

Class Library Reference

This section describes the application program interface (API) to PARODY. It identifies each of the API classes, the header file where the class is defined, and the member functions that using programs call.

bool *(bool.h)*

```
class bool;
```

A Boolean data type that may have one of two enumerated values: *true* or *false*. You can assign an integer value to a *bool* object, which stores the value as *true* or *false* rather than as the integer's numerical value.

CatKey *(key.h)*

```
template <class T1,class T2> class CatKey;
```

A template that implements concatenated keys for a *Persistent* derived class. The key consists of two data types that, if not intrinsic C++ types, must overload *operator==*, *operator=*, and *operator>*. The types must include conversion constructors that accept a constant zero argument to build null values.

Constructor

```
CatKey(const T1& key1, const T2& key2)
```

Constructs the concatenated key with two data types.

Key1

```
Key<T1>& Key1()
```

Returns a reference to the first (leftmost) half of the concatenated key as an object of type *Key<T1>*.

KeyValue1   `T1& KeyValue1()`

Returns a reference to the object parameterized as the first (leftmost) half of the concatenated key.

`const T1& KeyValue1() const`

Returns a *const* reference to the object parameterized as the first (leftmost) half of the concatenated key.

SetKeyValue1   `void SetKeyValue1(const T1& key1)`

Sets the value of the argument into the first (leftmost) half of the concatenated key.

Key2   `Key<T2>& Key2()`

Returns a reference to the second (rightmost) half of the concatenated key as an object of type *Key<T2>*.

KeyValue2   `T2& KeyValue2()`

Returns a reference to the object parameterized as the second (rightmost) half of the concatenated key.

`const T2& KeyValue2() const`

Returns a *const* reference to the object parameterized as the second (rightmost) half of the concatenated key.

SetKeyValue2   `void SetKeyValue2(const T2& key2)`

Sets the value of the argument into the second (rightmost) half of the concatenated key.

operator=   `PdyKey& operator=(const PdyKey& key)`

operator==   `int operator==(const PdyKey& key) const`

operator>   `int operator>(const PdyKey& key) const`

Overloaded operators for assignment and comparison between *CatKey* objects.

Date (date.h)

```
class Date;
```

Implements a calendar date with month, day, and year values.

Constructor

```
Date(DtEl m=0,DtEl d=0,DtEl y=0)
```

Month

```
DtEl Month() const
```

Returns the month as a *DtEl* object.

Day

```
DtEl Day() const
```

Returns the day as a *DtEl* object.

Year

```
DtEl Year() const
```

Returns the year as a *DtEl* object.

SetMonth

```
void SetMonth(DtEl m)
```

Sets the month value.

SetDay

```
void SetDay(DtEl d)
```

Sets the day value.

SetYear

```
void SetYear(DtEl y)
```

Sets the year value.

operator==

```
int operator==(const Date& dt) const
```

operator<

```
int operator<(const Date& dt) const
```

operator!=

```
int operator!=(const Date& dt) const
```

operator>

```
int operator>(const Date& dt) const
```

operator<=

```
int operator<=(const Date& dt) const
```

operator>=	`int operator>=(const Date& dt) const`
	Overloaded operators for comparison between *Date* objects.

GUI *(gui.h)*

class GUI;

The *GUI* class implements the generic user interface with the standard *cin* and *cout* objects.

Constructor	`GUI()`
AnyKey	`void AnyKey() const`
	Displays an "Any key..." message and waits for the user to type a key.
ClearScreen	`void ClearScreen() const`
	Clears the screen.
Error	`void Error(const char *message) const`
	Displays the *message* string, sounds the console's audible alarm, and calls the *AnyKey* function.
GetKBChar	`unsigned char GetKBChar() const`
	Reads the next key from the keyboard. If no key is waiting, waits for the next keystroke.
KBCharWaiting	`bool KBCharWaiting() const`
	Tests for keyboard input. Returns *true* if the user has pressed a key; otherwise, returns *false*.
PutBack	`void PutBack(char c)`
	Sets the character argument *c* as the next value returned from *GetKBChar*.
SetCursor	`void SetCursor(short int x, short int y) const`
	Positions the cursor at the screen character coordinates specified by x and y.

StatusLine

```
void StatusLine(const string& s) const
```

Displays a status line at the bottom of the screen.

UserInput

```
void UserInput(string *s, const char *prompt, short len)
void UserInput(char *c, const char *prompt)
void UserInput(short int *i, const char *prompt)
void UserInput(long int *i, const char *prompt)
void UserInput(Date *dt, const char *prompt)
void UserInput(Money *m, const char *prompt)
```

These functions display the prompt string and read the user's input into the variable pointed to by the first argument. The *string* version of the function uses the third argument to specify the length of the input string data.

YesNo

```
bool YesNo(const char *question)
```

Displays the *question* string and prompts the user to enter "Y" or "N" (case-insensitive). The function returns *true* if the user enters "Y" and *false* if the user enters "N".

WriteChar

```
void WriteChar(char c, short x, short y) const
```

Writes a single character on the screen at the x/y coordinate.

Key *(key.h)*

```
template <class T> class Key;
```

A template that implements keys into a *Persistent* derived class. The key consists of one data type that, if not an intrinsic C++ type, must overload *operator==*, *operator=*, and *operator>*. The type must include a conversion constructor that accepts a constant zero argument to build a null value.

Constructor

```
CatKey(const T& key)
```

Constructs the concatenated key with one data type.

KeyValue

`T& KeyValue()`

Returns a reference to the object parameterized as the key.

`const T& KeyValue() const`

Returns a *const* reference to the object parameterized as the key.

SetKeyValue

`void SetKeyValue(const T& key)`

Sets the value of the argument into the key.

operator=

`PdyKey& operator=(const PdyKey& key)`

operator==

`int operator==(const PdyKey& key) const`

operator>

`int operator>(const PdyKey& key) const`

Overloaded operators for assignment and comparison between *Key* objects.

LinkedList *(linklist.h)*

`template <class T> class LinkedList;`

A template that implements a doubly linked list data structure. A program constructs the list and adds entries that consist of pointers to objects that the program declares. The list does not make copies of the entries, so the user's copies must remain in scope as long as the entries are in the list.

Constructor

`LinkedList()`

Constructs a linked list of pointers to objects of a specified (parameterized) type.

AppendEntry

`void AppendEntry(T *entry)`

Appends an entry to the linked list.

InsertEntry

```
void InsertEntry(T *entry, T *curr)
```

Inserts an entry in the list ahead of a specified existing entry. If *curr* is null, *InsertEntry* works just like *AppendEntry*.

RemoveEntry

```
void RemoveEntry(T *entry)
```

Removes a specified entry from the linked list.

FindEntry

```
T *FindEntry(int pos)
```

Returns the address of the entry in the position specified by the *pos* argument. Zero is the first entry.

```
short int FindEntry(T *entry)
```

Returns the position of the entry pointed to by the argument. Zero is the first entry.

FirstEntry

```
T *FirstEntry()
```

Returns the address of the first entry in the list.

LastEntry

```
T *LastEntry()
```

Returns the address of the last entry in the list.

NextEntry

```
T *NextEntry()
```

Returns the address of the next entry in the list following the most recent access of the list. If no access has occurred or if the last access retrieved the last entry, returns the address of the first entry in the list.

```
T *NextEntry(T *entry)
```

Returns the address of the entry following the entry specified by the argument.

PrevEntry

```
T *PrevEntry()
```

Returns the address of the entry in the list ahead of the most recent access of the list. If no access has occurred or if the last access retrieved the first entry, returns the address of the last entry in the list.

```
T *PrevEntry(T *entry)
```

Returns the address of the entry ahead of the entry specified by the argument.

ClearList

```
void ClearList()
```

Clears all entries from the list. The objects themselves are not deleted. They are the property of the using program. Only the list entries that point to the objects are deleted.

Money *(money.h)*

```
class Money;
```

The Money class implements a numeric class consisting of dollars and cents.

Constructor

```
Money(float v=0, unsigned char w = 6)
```

Constructs a *Money* object with the *v* argument value rounded to the nearest cent. The *w* argument specifies the width that the object assumes when displayed.

Value

```
float& Value()
```

Returns the value of the *Money* object.

operator<

```
int operator<(const Money& m) const
```

operator==

```
int operator==(const Money& m) const
```

operator!=

```
int operator!=(const Money& m) const
```

operator>

```
int operator>(const Money& m) const
```

operator<=

```
int operator<=(const Money& m) const
```

operator>=

```
int operator>=(const Money& m) const
```

Overloaded operators for comparison between *Money* objects.

ObjAddr *(parody.h)*

```
struct ObjAddr;
```

An integer type that specifies a persistent object's address.

Constructor

```
ObjAddr(NodeNbr nd = 0)
```

Constructs an object address from a *NodeNbr* object.

Conversion

```
operator NodeNbr() const
```

Converts an *ObjAddr* object to a *NodeNbr* object.

OneLineMenu *(gui.h)*

```
class OneLineMenu;
```

Implements a one-line screen menu with selections determined from the first letter of each word in the one-line text string.

Constructor

```
OneLineMenu(const char *menu, ...)
```

Constructs a *OneLineMenu* object consisting of the menu text and a variable list of function pointer arguments. The function pointers point to the functions to be called when the user chooses the corresponding selection from the menu.

Execute

```
void Execute()
```

Displays the menu text and waits for the user to press a key. If the user presses a character corresponding to the first letter or number of a word in the menu text, *Execute* calls the function from the constructor's variable argument list that corresponds to the selection. When the called function returns, the *Execute* function returns. If the user presses **Esc**, the *Execute* function returns immediately. If the user presses any other key, the function sounds the audible alarm and waits for another keypress.

Parody *(parody.h)*

```
class Parody;
```

The persistent object database. A program declares an object of this type to establish a database in which to store and from which to retrieve persistent objects.

Constructor
```
Parody(const string& name)
```

Constructs the database object. The argument is the file name of the database. The file name conforms to the operating system's file name conventions. PARODY builds two physical files. The first has the file name extension **.DAT** and contains the persistent objects. The second has the file name extension **.NDX** and contains indexes into the persistent objects. This constructor opens the files if they exist and creates them if they do not.

Destructor
```
~Parody()
```

The *Parody* class destructor closes the database files.

OpenDataBase
```
static Parody *OpenDatabase()
```

Returns the address of the most recently declared *Parody* object.

Persistent   *(parody.h)*

```
class Persistent;
```

An abstract base class from which persistent object classes are derived.

Constructors

```
Persistent()
```

Constructs a persistent object to be retrieved from and stored in the most recently declared (and still in scope) *Parody* database.

```
Persistent(Parody& db)
```

Constructs a persistent object to be retrieved from and stored in the specified *Parody* database.

Read

```
virtual void Read() = 0
```

Write

```
virtual void Write() = 0
```

Functions provided by the derived class to read and write the data values of the persistent object. These functions call *ReadObject* and *WriteObject* function templates for each of the data members.

LoadObject

```
void LoadObject(ObjAddr nd = 0)
```

Called from the derived persistent object's constructor to load the object into memory from the database. If the *nd* parameter is nonzero, the object is assumed to be keyless.

SaveObject

```
void SaveObject()
```

Called from the persistent object's destructor to save the object from memory into the PARODY database.

AddObject

```
bool AddObject()
```

Tells PARODY to add a newly created object to the database when the destructor calls *SaveObject*.

Returns *false* if the addition cannot be made due to integrity violations.

ChangeObject
```
bool ChangeObject()
```
Tells PARODY to write a changed object back to the database when the destructor calls *SaveObject*. Returns *false* if the change cannot be made due to integrity violations.

DeleteObject
```
bool DeleteObject()
```
Tells PARODY to delete the object from the database when the destructor calls *SaveObject*. Returns *false* if the delete cannot be made due to integrity violations.

ObjectExists
```
bool ObjectExists()
```
Returns *true* if PARODY found the specified object in the database. Valid after the object is instantiated and after calls to the next six functions discussed.

FindObject
```
Persistent& FindObject(PdyKey *key)
```
Finds the object associated with the value in the key parameter.

CurrentObject
```
Persistent& CurrentObject(PdyKey *key = 0)
```

FirstObject
```
Persistent& FirstObject(PdyKey *key = 0)
```

LastObject
```
Persistent& LastObject(PdyKey *key = 0)
```

NextObject
```
Persistent& NextObject(PdyKey *key = 0)
```

PreviousObject
```
Persistent& PreviousObject(PdyKey *key = 0)
```
Finds the object by position relative to the specified key. If the *key* parameter is 0, uses the prima-

ry key. If the class has no key (a keyless object), the retrieval uses the incidental position of the object in the physical database.

ObjectAddress

```
ObjAddr ObjectAddress()
```

Returns the object's address in the PARODY database.

Destroy

```
static void Destroy(Persistent *pp)
```

Deletes the persistent object, which is assumed to have been constructed from the free store. If there are multiple instances of the object intercepted by a *catch* of the *Persistent** exception, the delete does not take effect until the last of the instances is being destroyed.

PersistentObject *(parody.h)*

```
template <class T> PersistentObject:
```

A template class derived from the *Persistent* class that encapsulates most of the persistence cooperation normally provided by derived persistent classes. This template works with keyless objects that are flat structures with no references or pointers. The using program instantiates objects of the template class. The class provides its own persistent constructors, destructor, and *Read* and *Write* functions. The using program dereferences the object value through the public *Obj* data member. The program calls the following *Persistent* class member functions to manage the persistent object.

- ◆ *AddObject*
- ◆ *ChangeObject*
- ◆ *DeleteObject*
- ◆ *ObjectExists*
- ◆ *FindObject*

- ♦ *CurrentObject*
- ♦ *FirstObject*
- ♦ *LastObject*
- ♦ *NextObject*
- ♦ *PreviousObject*
- ♦ *ObjectAddress*
- ♦ *Destroy*

Constructors

```
PersistentObject(const T& obj)
```

Construct a *PersistentObject<T>* object from a reference to a *T* object.

```
PersistentObject(ObjAddr oa = 0)
```

Construct a *PersistentObject<T>* object from an *Objaddr* value. If the value is nonzero, PARODY retrieves from the database the object located at the specified object address.

Reference   (parody.h)

```
template <class T> class Reference;
```

A template that encapsulates a persistent reference in one persistent object to another persistent object in the database. The *T* type must be derived from the *Persistent* class, and the declaration of the *Reference<T>* object must be a data member of a class derived from the *Persistent* class. The using class dereferences the object through the *Reference* template's public *obj* data member.

Constructor

```
Reference()
```

Constructs a persistent reference data member in a persistent class. When an object of the class is instantiated and read from the database, the referenced object—if one has been established—is instantiated at the same time.

ReadObject   `void ReadObject()`

Used in the *Read* function of the *Persistent* derived class that contains the *Reference<T>* object to instantiate and read the referenced object into memory.

WriteObject   `void WriteObject()`

Used in the *Write* function of the *Persistent* derived class that contains the *Reference<T>* object to write the referenced object to the data base.

operator=   `void operator=(T& to)`

The overloaded assignment operator establishes the persistent reference. The using program assigns a persistent object of a matching type to the *Reference<T>* object in the referencing object.

RemoveReference   `void RemoveReference()`

Removes the persistent reference from the referencing object.

ScreenMenu *(gui.h)*

`class ScreenMenu;`

Implements a full screen menu.

Constructor   `ScreenMenu(const char *title, ...)`

Constructs a *ScreenMenu* object consisting of the menu title text and a variable list of argument pairs. Each pair consists of a test for the menu selection and a function pointer. The function pointers point to the functions to be called when the user chooses the corresponding selection from the menu.

Execute　　　　`void Execute()`

Clears the screen, displays the menu, and waits for the user to press a key. Each menu selection is numbered starting with 1. A final selection is displayed specifying the **Esc** key for the selection to exit from the menu. If the user presses a digit corresponding to one of the selections, *Execute* calls the corresponding function from the constructor's variable argument list. When the called function returns, the *Execute* function repeats its process beginning with the screen clear operation. If the user presses **Esc**, the *Execute* function returns immediately. If the user presses any other key, the function sounds the audible alarm and waits for another keypress.

Exceptions Thrown

Parody throws several exceptions. Most of them represent errors in the using program. One is used to manage multiple copies of the same persistent object.

Program Error Exceptions

Table B.2 shows the PARODY program error exceptions.

TABLE B.2 *PARODY program error exceptions*

EXCEPTION	CONDITION CAUSING EXCEPTION TO BE THROWN
PdyExceptions	Not thrown. Base class for program error exceptions.
NotInConstructor	*ReadObject* called from outside a persistent object constructor.
NotInDestructor	*WriteObject* called outside a persistent object destructor.
NoDatabase	Database operations attempted with no open database.
NotLoaded	*LoadObject* not called for a persistent object.
NotSaved	*SaveObject* not called for a persistent object.
MustDestroy	*delete* operator used on an object with multiple copies.
ZeroLengthKey	*string* object used for key with no length specified.
BadKeyLength	*string* object used for key with length different from that established for the index.
BadReference	Declared *Reference<T>* object when *T* not derived from *Persistent*.
BadObjAddr	Bad object address provided to retrieve persistent object.

PdyExceptions is not thrown. It is a base class from which the other exception classes in Table B.2 are derived. You can *catch* the derived exceptions individually or *catch* the *PdyExceptions* exception to catch them all in the same place.

Persistent* Exception

PARODY throws the *Persistent** exception when the using program instantiates a persistent object that is already in scope. The constructor throws the exception, which means that the construction is not completed. The thrown variable contains the address of the existing persistent object.

GUI Exceptions

The menu classes throw exceptions as listed in Table B.3

TABLE B.3 *Menu program error exceptions*

EXCEPTION	CONDITION CAUSING EXCEPTION TO BE THROWN
NoGUI	Declared a *ScreenMenu* or *OneLineMenu* object with no *GUI* object in scope.
BadMenu	Invalid argument list in *ScreenMenu* or *OneLineMenu* constructor call.

Disk Data Structures

This section contains a technical description of the PARODY file structures. You do not need to understand these structures in order to use PARODY, but knowledge of them is helpful when you get into detailed database troubleshooting. Data structures on disk are not always obvious in view of the class definitions from which they are written. This discussion describes how PARODY organizes data on disk and the format of each physical record.

Disk Files

A PARODY database consists of two files: the data file, which contains the objects; and the index file, which contains key indexes to the objects.

The *Parody* object opens or creates these two files when the program declares the object. The data file has the file extension **.DAT**, and the index file has the file extension **.NDX**. The file architecture must support:

- Variable-length persistent objects.
- Indexes into and objects of multiple classes.
- Persistent objects that can grow or shrink in length or be deleted between the time a program declares one and when the program destroys it.
- Reuse of deleted file space.

To support these objectives, PARODY uses a system of file nodes, described next.

Nodes

Both files in a PARODY database are managed by an input/output system of fixed-length file nodes in a thread. Nodes are logically addressed by node numbers starting with 1. PARODY uses the node system two ways. The index files are organized into fixed-length nodes, which inherit the behavior of the *Node* class, declared in **node.h**. The objects are unformatted variable-length data streams that could extend beyond the boundaries of a node, so they declare *Node* objects and copy their data values into and out of the nodes.

Both files are represented by a File Header Block at the beginning of the file and a variable number of fixed-length Data Nodes, as shown in Figure B.1.

FILE HEADER BLOCK

The header record contains two node numbers. The first node number points to the first node in a chain of deleted nodes. The second node number points to the highest node that has been allocated. Header records are implemented as objects of the *FileHeader* type, declared in **node.h**.

DATA NODES

Each file consists of a variable number of fixed-length nodes. The first node is node number 1, and so on. Each node begins with a *NodeNbr* variable that points to the next node in a logical list of nodes that form a set. The last node in the set has a value of zero in the *NodeNbr* variable. If the node has been deleted by its user, the set is a list of nodes the first of which is pointed to by the deleted node pointer in the File Header block. Nodes are implemented as objects of the *Node* type, declared in **node.h**.

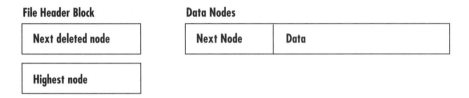

File Header Block

Next deleted node

Highest node

Data Nodes

Next Node	Data

FIGURE B.1 *File header block and data nodes*

NODE THREADS

A node thread consists of a number of nodes. PARODY maintains a pointer to the first node in the thread. The node pointer at the front of the first node points to the second node, which points to the third, and so on, until a node is reached that has zero in its node pointer, which marks the end of the thread. The nodes in a thread are in no particular sequence in the file.

DELETING NODES

When PARODY is finished with a node, it tells the *Node* class to delete the node. This action clears the node's data area to zeros and adds it to the deleted node thread, which is pointed to by the deleted node pointer in the header record. The pointer actually points to the most recently deleted node. At first, before any nodes have been deleted, the deleted node pointer is zero. When a node is deleted, its constructor moves the deleted node pointer from the header into its next node pointer and moves the deleted node's address into the deleted node pointer in the header.

ALLOCATING NODES

When PARODY needs a new node, it looks first at the deleted node pointer in the header. If the pointer is nonzero, PARODY appropriates that node for the new usage and writes the next node pointer from the node into the deleted node pointer.

If the deleted node thread has no nodes, PARODY appropriates a node from the end of the file by using the node number of the highest node allocated as recorded in the file header.

Persistent Objects

The persistent object data file consists of a File Header Block and Data Nodes. Each persistent object is stored in a set of nodes. Each node in the set has the *NodeNbr* variable mentioned above to form the set followed by the Object Header and Object Data, as shown in Figure B.2.

Object Header		Object Data	
Next Node	**Class ID**	**Relative Node #**	**Data Byte Stream**

FIGURE B.2 *Object header and data*

OBJECT HEADER

The Object Header is an object of type *ObjectHeader*, declared in **parody.h**. It contains an integer class identification code for the object followed by a relative *NodeNbr* variable for the object. The first relative node number is zero, signifying that the node is the first node of the object. Subsequent relative node numbers are numbered sequentially. This pattern allows PARODY to identify the first node of an object without an index reference to it and is used in rebuilding the index file, described in Chapter 9.

OBJECT DATA

PARODY stores objects in node threads. Each object starts on a node boundary. The node number is the object's address. The data bytes of the object follow the Object Header.

If the object's length is greater than that of a node, the object spills over into the next node in the thread, continuing that way until the entire object is recorded. The balance of the last node in an object's thread is padded with zeros. Figure B.3 shows the relationship between the index file and the object file.

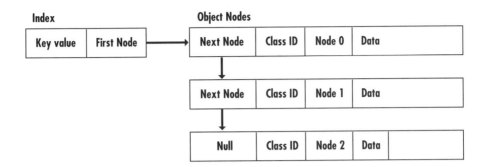

Index **Object Nodes**

Key value	First Node

Next Node	Class ID	Node 0	Data

Next Node	Class ID	Node 1	Data

Null	Class ID	Node 2	Data

FIGURE B.3 *Index and object file*

The same physical file of nodes holds all the objects of all the classes in a database. Every class can support objects of different sizes and formats, and objects of a class can have variable lengths as well. A class that has a string data type might have objects with many different string lengths, for example. A class with an array can have objects with different numbers of elements in the array.

Without the class definitions and the member functions that support the objects, the object file is meaningless. Nothing that stands alone in the file itself tells the database the types of the objects or anything about their formats. For PARODY to correctly locate an object, it needs the address of the object's first node. That address is maintained by the indexes, described next.

Indexes

The database index file contains indexes that associate key values with object node addresses in the object file. An index file holds one logical index table for every primary and secondary key in the persistent classes. The indexes are implementations of the B-tree algorithm.

The index file consists of a File Header Block and Data Nodes. There is a set of data nodes that contains the Index Header Records, and there are individual one-node sets that contain the B-Tree Node Header and an array of fixed-length key values.

CLASS HEADER TABLES

Node 1 in the index file is the first node in a set of nodes that contain Index Header Blocks for the persistent classes. Each Index Header Node represents one persistent class. The node contains a fixed-length class name *string* object and an array of Index Header Blocks. The first node in the set contains the array for class identification zero; the second set contains the array for class identification one; and so on. The first entry in the array is for the primary key of the class; the second entry is for the first secondary key; and so on. Figure B.4 shows the Index Header Node set.

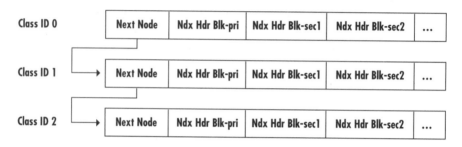

FIGURE B.4 *Index Header Nodes*

INDEX HEADER BLOCKS

Each Index Header Block for a class contains two data items: the node number of the root node for the index, and the length in bytes of the index key value. The software assigns the root node number when the index is first built. The key lengths are determined from the *Key<T>* objects.

B-TREES

PARODY uses the B-tree data structure to implement the indexes. The B-tree is an index structure that R. Bayer and E. McCreight developed in 1970. It is a balanced tree of key values used to locate the object node that matches a specified key argument. The tree is a hierarchy of nodes in which each node contains from one to a fixed number of keys.

A B-tree consists of a root node and usually two or more lower nodes. If the total number of keys in the tree is equal to or less than the number that a node can contain, then only the root node exists. When that number exceeds the capacity of a node, the root node splits into two lower nodes, retaining the key that is logically between the key values of the two new nodes. Higher nodes are parents of the lower nodes in the hierarchy.

Nodes store keys in key value sequence. Each key consists of the key index value provided by the object and the object's node address in the database provided by PARODY. When the tree has multiple levels, each key in a parent node points to the lower node that contains keys greater than the parent key and less than the next adjacent key in the parent. The nodes at the lowest level are called *leaves* and do not contain pointers to lower nodes.

Figure B.5 is an example of a B-tree that uses the letters of the alphabet as keys to locate matching words from the phonetic alphabet. The letters are analogous to the data values for key data elements in a class; the phonetic alphabet words, incomplete in the example, are equivalent to the objects that the B-tree indexes.

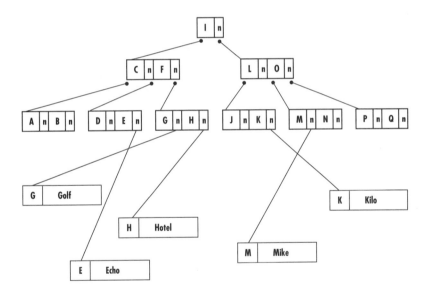

FIGURE B.5 *The B-tree*

When a node becomes overpopulated by key value insertions, the insertion algorithm splits it into two nodes and inserts the middle key value into the parent node of the original, unsplit node. If the root node splits, a new root node is grown as the parent of the split nodes.

When a node becomes underpopulated as the result of key value deletions, it combines with an adjacent node. The key value that is between the two nodes and that is in the common parent node of the two is moved into the combined node and deleted from the parent node. If the deleted key is the last key in the root node, the old root node is deleted, and the newly combined node becomes the root node.

In the example in Figure B.5, the root node has one key value, and each of the other nodes has two keys. This example makes for a simple illustration of the structure, but, in practice, a typical B-tree has as many keys as will fit in a node.

The B-tree algorithms provide that the tree always remains in balance—that is, the number of levels from the root node to the bottom of the tree is always the same no matter which branch is taken by the search. This property gives the B-tree its name. The "B" stands for "balanced."

B-TREE NODE HEADER AND KEYS

The Data Nodes in a B-tree contain the B-tree Node Header block followed by a fixed-length array of keys.

The B-tree Node Header Block is in the format shown in its structure in Figure B.6.

```
struct TNodeHeader  {
    bool isleaf;            // true if node is a leaf
    NodeNbr parent;         // parent to this node
    NodeNbr leftsibling;    // left sibling node
    NodeNbr rightsibling;   // right sibling node
    int keycount;           // number of keys in this node
    NodeNbr lowernode;      // lower node associated with
                            // keys < keys in this node
};
```

FIGURE B.6 *The B-tree Node Header*

A key in the array consists of its key data value followed by the *NodeNbr* address of the object in the data file to which the key points. If the node is not a leaf node, each key array entry also includes a *NodeNbr* variable that points to the B-tree node at the next lower level in the tree that contains keys with collating sequence values greater than the current key value and less than the next adjacent key value in the array.

References

Fundamentals of Data Structures, Horowitz and Sahni, 1976, Computer Science Press, Inc.

The Art of Computer Programming, *Volume 3*, Donald E. Knuth, 1973, Addison-Wesley

Appendix *C*

Table of Contents

Listings by Category

PARODY

PAYROLL APPLICATION

THE GAME OF LIFE

PERSONNEL APPLICATION

EXAMPLE INDEX BUILDER

Family Tree Application

Listings Alphabetically by File Name

Listings

LISTING C.1 GUI.H

```
 1| // ----------- gui.h
 2|
 3| #ifndef GUI_H
 4| #define GUI_H
 5|
 6| // ===========================
 7| // Generic User Interface (GUI)
 8| // ===========================
 9|
10| #include <iostream.h>
11| #include <stdarg.h>
12| #include <cstring.h>
13| #include "bool.h"
14| #include "date.h"
15| #include "money.h"
16|
17| // ------ exceptions
18| class BadMenu{};
19| class NoGUI{};
20|
21| // -------- screen dimensions
22| const short int SCREENHEIGHT = 25;
23| const short int SCREENWIDTH  = 80;
```

```
24|
25| // ------- function key values
26| const short int UPARROW    = 200;
27| const short int DOWNARROW  = 208;
28| const short int RIGHTARROW = 205;
29| const short int LEFTARROW  = 203;
30| const short int ESC        = 27;
31|
32| // --------- the Generic User Interface class
33| class GUI   {
34|     char putback;
35| public:
36|     GUI()
37|         { putback = 0; gui = this; }
38|     ~GUI()
39|         { gui = 0; }
40|     // ---- data field entry
41|     void UserInput(string *s, const char *prompt, short len);
42|     void UserInput(char *c, const char *prompt);
43|     void UserInput(short int *i, const char *prompt);
44|     void UserInput(long int *i, const char *prompt);
45|     void UserInput(Date *dt, const char *prompt);
46|     void UserInput(Money *m, const char *prompt);
47|     // ---- standard dialogs
48|     bool YesNo(const char *question);
49|     void Error(const char *message) const;
50|     void AnyKey() const;
51|     // ----- screen operations
52|     void SetCursor(short int x, short int y) const;
53|     void ClearScreen() const;
54|     void WriteChar(char c, short x, short y) const;
55|     void StatusLine(const string& s) const;
56|     // ----- keyboard operations
57|     bool KBCharWaiting() const;
58|     unsigned char GetKBChar() const;
59|     void PutBack(char c);
60|     static GUI *gui;
61| };
```

```
62|
63| typedef void (*Mfunc)();
64| // ------ maximum commands in a menu
65| const short int MAXCOMMANDS = 9;
66| // ------- where to display menus
67| const short int menux = (SCREENWIDTH/2-SCREENWIDTH/4);
68| const short int menuy = (SCREENHEIGHT/2-SCREENHEIGHT/4);
69|
70| // ============================
71| // Generic Menu Class
72| // ============================
73| class Menu  {
74| protected:
75|     Mfunc sels[MAXCOMMANDS];
76|     char selcodes[MAXCOMMANDS];
77|     short int selection;
78|     short int cmdno;
79|     void Select(bool clearscreen = false);
80| public:
81|     Menu() throw (NoGUI);
82|     virtual void Execute() = 0;
83| };
84|
85| class ScreenMenu : public Menu  {
86|     string title;
87|     string labels[MAXCOMMANDS];
88| public:
89|     ScreenMenu(const char *title, ...) throw (BadMenu);
90|     void Execute();
91| };
92|
93| class OneLineMenu : public Menu {
94|     short int cmdct;
95|     string menuline;
96| public:
97|     OneLineMenu(const char *menu, ...) throw (BadMenu);
98|     void Execute();
99| };
```

```
100|
101| #endif
```

LISTING C.2 GUI.CPP

```
 1| // ---------- gui.cpp
 2|
 3| // ============================
 4| // Generic User Interface (GUI)
 5| // ============================
 6|
 7| #include <iostream.h>
 8| #include <iomanip.h>
 9| #include <stdarg.h>
10| #include <ctype.h>
11| #include <conio.h>
12| #include "gui.h"
13|
14| GUI *GUI::gui;
15|
16| // --------------------------------
17| // Menu user interface
18| // --------------------------------
19| Menu::Menu() throw (NoGUI)
20| {
21|     selection = 0;
22|     cmdno = 0;
23|     if (GUI::gui == 0)
24|         throw NoGUI();
25| }
26|
27| void Menu::Select(bool clearscreen)
28| {
29|     for (;;)    {
30|         unsigned char sl = GUI::gui->GetKBChar();
31|         if (isprint(sl))
32|             cout << sl << '\b';
33|
```

```
34|          if (sl == ESC)  {
35|              selection = ESC;
36|              break;
37|          }
38|          // --- search for a match among the selections
39|          for (selection = 0; selection < cmdno; selection++) {
40|              if (selcodes[selection] == tolower(sl)) {
41|                  // --- execute the command
42|                  if (clearscreen)
43|                      GUI::gui->ClearScreen();
44|                  (*sels[selection])();
45|                  break;
46|              }
47|          }
48|          if (selection < cmdno)
49|              break;
50|          cout << '\a';
51|      }
52| }
53|
54| // -------------------------------
55| // full screen menu user interface
56| // -------------------------------
57| ScreenMenu::ScreenMenu(const char *ttl, ...)
58|              throw (BadMenu)
59| {
60|     title = ttl;
61|     va_list ap;
62|     va_start(ap, ttl);
63|     char cc = '1';
64|     // ----- gather the menu from the caller's parameters
65|     while (cmdno < MAXCOMMANDS) {
66|         char *sp = va_arg(ap, char*);
67|         if (sp == 0)
68|             break;
69|         labels[cmdno] = sp;
70|         selcodes[cmdno] = cc++;
71|         sels[cmdno] = va_arg(ap, Mfunc);
```

```
72|              if (sels[cmdno++] == 0)
73|                  throw BadMenu();
74|          }
75| }
76|
77| void ScreenMenu::Execute()
78| {
79|      selection = 0;
80|      while (selection != ESC)    {
81|          GUI::gui->ClearScreen();
82|          GUI::gui->SetCursor(menux, menuy);
83|          // ------ display the menu
84|          cout << title;
85|          for (short int i = 0; i < cmdno; i++)   {
86|              GUI::gui->SetCursor(menux+2, menuy+2+i);
87|              cout << (i+1) << ": " << labels[i];
88|          }
89|          GUI::gui->SetCursor(menux, menuy+2+i);
90|          cout << "Esc: Return";
91|
92|          // ----- get the user's selection
93|          GUI::gui->SetCursor(menux, menuy+4+i);
94|          cout << "Select> ";
95|          Select(true);
96|      }
97| }
98|
99| // -------------------------------
100| // one line menu user interface
101| // -------------------------------
102| OneLineMenu::OneLineMenu(const char *menu, ...)
103|              throw (BadMenu)
104| {
105|      menuline = menu;
106|      // ---- collect and count the menu commands
107|      const char *cp = menu;
108|      cmdct = 0;
109|      for (short sel = 0; sel < MAXCOMMANDS && *cp; sel++)    {
```

```
110|            while (*cp && isspace(*cp))
111|                cp++;
112|            selcodes[cmdct++] = tolower(*cp);
113|            while (*cp && !isspace(*cp))
114|                cp++;
115|        }
116|    // ----- gather the menu functions
117|    va_list ap;
118|    va_start(ap, menu);
119|
120|    while (cmdno < cmdct)    {
121|        sels[cmdno] = va_arg(ap, Mfunc);
122|        if (sels[cmdno++] == 0)
123|            throw BadMenu();
124|    }
125| }
126|
127|
128| void OneLineMenu::Execute()
129| {
130|    // --- display the menu
131|    cout << endl << menuline << ": ";
132|
133|    selection = 0;
134|    // --- get the user's selection
135|    Select();
136| }
137|
138| // --------------------------------
139| // character input
140| // --------------------------------
141| void GUI::UserInput(char *c, const char *prompt)
142| {
143|    cout << endl << prompt << ": ";
144|    cout.flush();
145|    *c = GetKBChar();
146| }
147|
```

```
148|  // ----------------------------------
149|  // short integer input
150|  // ----------------------------------
151|  void GUI::UserInput(short int *i, const char *prompt)
152|  {
153|      cout << endl << prompt << ": ";
154|      cout.flush();
155|      cin >> ws >> *i;
156|  }
157|
158|  // ----------------------------------
159|  // long integer input
160|  // ----------------------------------
161|  void GUI::UserInput(long int *l, const char *prompt)
162|  {
163|      cout << endl << prompt << ": ";
164|      cout.flush();
165|      cin >> ws >> *l;
166|  }
167|
168|  // ----------------------------------
169|  // Date input
170|  // ----------------------------------
171|  void GUI::UserInput(Date *dt, const char *prompt)
172|  {
173|      cout << endl << prompt << " (mm dd yy): ";
174|      cout.flush();
175|      unsigned short mo, da, yr;
176|      cin >> ws >> mo >> da >> yr;
177|      *dt = Date(mo,da,yr);
178|  }
179|
180|  // ----------------------------------
181|  // Money input
182|  // ----------------------------------
183|  void GUI::UserInput(Money *m, const char *prompt)
184|  {
185|      cout << endl << prompt << ": ";
```

```
186|      cout.flush();
187|      cin >> ws >> m->Value();
188| }
189|
190| // -------------------------------
191| // string input
192| // -------------------------------
193| void GUI::UserInput(string *s, const char *prompt, short len)
194| {
195|      cout << endl << prompt << ": ";
196|      cout.flush();
197|      char *bf = new char[len+1];
198|      cin >> ws;
199|      cin.getline(bf, len+1);
200|      *s = bf;
201|      s->resize(len);
202| }
203|
204| // -------------------------------
205| // yes/no user interface
206| // -------------------------------
207| bool GUI::YesNo(const char *question)
208| {
209|      char c = ' ';
210|      while (c != 'y' && c != 'n')     {
211|          cout << endl << question << "? (y/n) ";
212|          cout.flush();
213|          c = GetKBChar();
214|          c = tolower(c);
215|          if (c != 'y' && c != 'n')
216|              cout << '\a';
217|      }
218|      cout.flush();
219|      return c == 'y';
220| }
221|
222| // -------------------------------
223| // error message
```

```
224|  // --------------------------------
225|  void GUI::Error(const char *message) const
226|  {
227|      cout << endl << '\a' << message << endl;
228|      AnyKey();
229|  }
230|
231|  // --------------------------------
232|  // get a keyboard char
233|  // --------------------------------
234|  unsigned char GUI::GetKBChar() const
235|  {
236|      short int c;
237|      if (putback)    {
238|          c = putback;
239|          (const_cast<GUI*>(this))->putback = 0;
240|      }
241|      else    {
242|          c = getch();
243|          if (c == 0)
244|              // --- convert function key
245|              c = getch() | 0x80;
246|          else
247|              // --- strip scan code
248|              c &= 0xff;
249|      }
250|      return static_cast<unsigned char>(c);
251|  }
252|
253|  // --------------------------------
254|  // put back a keyboard char
255|  // --------------------------------
256|  void GUI::PutBack(char c)
257|  {
258|      putback = c;
259|  }
260|
261|  // --------------------------------
```

```
262|  // Display a status line
263|  // --------------------------------
264|  void GUI::StatusLine(const string& s) const
265|  {
266|      SetCursor(0, SCREENHEIGHT-1);
267|      cout << s;
268|      cout.flush();
269|      short int len = strlen(s.c_str());
270|      while (len++ < SCREENWIDTH-1)
271|          cout << ' ';
272|      cout.flush();
273|  }
274|
275|
276|  // --------------------------------
277|  // Prompt for and read any key
278|  // --------------------------------
279|  void GUI::AnyKey() const
280|  {
281|      cout << endl << "Any key..." << endl;
282|      GetKBChar();
283|  }
284|
285|  // --------------------------------
286|  // Position the cursor
287|  // --------------------------------
288|  void GUI::SetCursor(short int x, short int y) const
289|  {
290|      cout << "\033[" << (y+1) << ';' << (x+1) << 'H';
291|      cout.flush();
292|  }
293|
294|  // --------------------------------
295|  // Clear the screen
296|  // --------------------------------
297|  void GUI::ClearScreen() const
298|  {
299|      cout << "\033[2J";
```

```
300|     cout.flush();
301| }
302|
303| // --------------------------------
304| // Write a single character to the screen
305| // --------------------------------
306| void GUI::WriteChar(char c, short int x, short int y) const
307| {
308|     SetCursor(x, y);
309|     cout << c;
310|     cout.flush();
311| }
312|
313| // --------------------------------
314| // Test for a keyboard character waiting
315| // --------------------------------
316| bool GUI::KBCharWaiting() const
317| {
318|     return kbhit();
319| }
```

LISTING C.3 LINKLIST.H

```
 1| // ------------ linklist.h
 2| // a template for a linked list
 3|
 4| #ifndef LINKLIST_H
 5| #define LINKLIST_H
 6|
 7| // --- the linked list entry
 8| template <class T>
 9| class ListEntry    {
10|     friend class LinkedList<T>;
11|     T *thisentry;
12|     ListEntry<T> *nextentry;
13|     ListEntry<T> *preventry;
14|     ListEntry(T *entry);
15| };
```

```
16|
17| template <class T>
18| // ---- the linked list
19| class LinkedList    {
20|     // --- the listhead
21|     ListEntry<T> *firstentry;
22|     ListEntry<T> *lastentry;
23|     ListEntry<T> *iterator;
24|     T *CurrentEntry();
25|     void RemoveEntry(ListEntry<T> *entry);
26|     void InsertEntry(T *entry);
27|     void InsertEntry(T *entry, short int pos);
28|     void RemoveEntry(short int pos);
29| public:
30|     LinkedList();
31|     virtual ~LinkedList()
32|         { ClearList(); }
33|     void AppendEntry(T *entry);
34|     void InsertEntry(T *entry, T *curr);
35|     void RemoveEntry(T *entry);
36|     T *FindEntry(short int pos);
37|     short int FindEntry(T *entry);
38|     T *FirstEntry();
39|     T *LastEntry();
40|     T *NextEntry();
41|     T *PrevEntry();
42|     T *NextEntry(T *entry);
43|     T *PrevEntry(T *entry);
44|     void ClearList();
45| };
46|
47| template <class T>
48| // ---- construct a linked list
49| LinkedList<T>::LinkedList()
50| {
51|     iterator = 0;
52|     firstentry = 0;
53|     lastentry = 0;
```

```
54|  }
55|
56|  template <class T>
57|  // ---- remove all entries from a linked list
58|  void LinkedList<T>::ClearList()
59|  {
60|      ListEntry<T> *lentry = firstentry;
61|      while (lentry != 0) {
62|          ListEntry<T> *nxt = lentry->nextentry;
63|          delete lentry;
64|          lentry = nxt;
65|      }
66|      iterator = 0;
67|      firstentry = 0;
68|      lastentry = 0;
69|  }
70|
71|  // ---- construct a linked list entry
72|  template <class T>
73|  ListEntry<T>::ListEntry(T *entry)
74|  {
75|      thisentry = entry;
76|      nextentry = 0;
77|      preventry = 0;
78|  }
79|
80|  template <class T>
81|  // ---- append an entry to the linked list
82|  void LinkedList<T>::AppendEntry(T *entry)
83|  {
84|      ListEntry<T> *newentry = new ListEntry<T>(entry);
85|      newentry->preventry = lastentry;
86|      if (lastentry)
87|          lastentry->nextentry = newentry;
88|      if (firstentry == 0)
89|          firstentry = newentry;
90|      lastentry = newentry;
91|  }
```

```
 92|
 93| template <class T>
 94| // ---- return the current linked list entry
 95| T *LinkedList<T>::CurrentEntry()
 96| {
 97|     return iterator ? iterator->thisentry : 0;
 98| }
 99|
100| template <class T>
101| // ---- return the first entry in the linked list
102| T *LinkedList<T>::FirstEntry()
103| {
104|     iterator = firstentry;
105|     return CurrentEntry();
106| }
107|
108| template <class T>
109| // ---- return the last entry in the linked list
110| T *LinkedList<T>::LastEntry()
111| {
112|     iterator = lastentry;
113|     return CurrentEntry();
114| }
115|
116| template <class T>
117| // ---- return the next entry following the specified one
118| T *LinkedList<T>::NextEntry(T *entry)
119| {
120|     FindEntry(entry);
121|     return NextEntry();
122| }
123|
124| template <class T>
125| // ---- return the next entry in the linked list
126| T *LinkedList<T>::NextEntry()
127| {
128|     if (iterator == 0)
129|         iterator = firstentry;
```

```
130|     else
131|         iterator = iterator->nextentry;
132|     return CurrentEntry();
133| }
134|
135| template <class T>
136| // ---- return the previous entry ahead of the specified one
137| T *LinkedList<T>::PrevEntry(T *entry)
138| {
139|     FindEntry(entry);
140|     return PrevEntry();
141| }
142|
143| template <class T>
144| // ---- return the previous entry in the linked list
145| T *LinkedList<T>::PrevEntry()
146| {
147|     if (iterator == 0)
148|         iterator = lastentry;
149|     else
150|         iterator = iterator->preventry;
151|     return CurrentEntry();
152| }
153|
154| template <class T>
155| // ---- remove an entry from the linked list by position
156| void LinkedList<T>::RemoveEntry(short int pos)
157| {
158|     FindEntry(pos);
159|     if (iterator != 0)
160|         RemoveEntry(iterator);
161| }
162|
163| template <class T>
164| // ---- remove an entry from the linked list by entry address
165| void LinkedList<T>::RemoveEntry(ListEntry<T> *lentry)
166| {
167|     if (lentry == 0)
```

```
168|        return;
169|    if (lentry == iterator)
170|        iterator = lentry->preventry;
171|    // ---- repair any break made by this removal
172|    if (lentry->nextentry)
173|        lentry->nextentry->preventry = lentry->preventry;
174|    if (lentry->preventry)
175|        lentry->preventry->nextentry = lentry->nextentry;
176|    // --- maintain listhead if this is last and/or first
177|    if (lentry == lastentry)
178|        lastentry = lentry->preventry;
179|    if (lentry == firstentry)
180|        firstentry = lentry->nextentry;
181|    delete lentry;
182| }
183|
184| template <class T>
185| // ---- remove an entry from the linked list by entry
186| void LinkedList<T>::RemoveEntry(T *entry)
187| {
188|    FindEntry(entry);
189|    RemoveEntry(iterator);
190| }
191|
192| template <class T>
193| // ---- insert an entry into the linked list ahead of another
194| void LinkedList<T>::InsertEntry(T *entry, T *curr)
195| {
196|    FindEntry(curr);
197|    InsertEntry(entry);
198| }
199|
200| template <class T>
201| // ---- insert an entry into the linked list by position
202| void LinkedList<T>::InsertEntry(T *entry, short int pos)
203| {
204|    FindEntry(pos);
205|    InsertEntry(entry);
```

```
206| }
207|
208| template <class T>
209| // ---- insert an entry into the linked list ahead of iterator
210| void LinkedList<T>::InsertEntry(T *entry)
211| {
212|     if (iterator == 0)
213|         AppendEntry(entry);
214|     else    {
215|         ListEntry<T> *newentry = new ListEntry<T>(entry);
216|         newentry->nextentry = iterator;
217|         if (iterator)    {
218|             newentry->preventry = iterator->preventry;
219|             iterator->preventry = newentry;
220|         }
221|         if (newentry->preventry)
222|             newentry->preventry->nextentry = newentry;
223|         if (iterator == firstentry)
224|             firstentry = newentry;
225|         iterator = newentry;
226|     }
227| }
228|
229| template <class T>
230| // ---- return a specific linked list entry
231| T *LinkedList<T>::FindEntry(short int pos)
232| {
233|     iterator = firstentry;
234|     while (iterator && pos--)
235|         iterator = iterator->nextentry;
236|     return CurrentEntry();
237| }
238|
239| template <class T>
240| // ---- return a specific linked list entry number
241| short int LinkedList<T>::FindEntry(T *entry)
242| {
243|     short int pos = 0;
```

```
244|     if (entry != 0) {
245|         iterator = firstentry;
246|         while (iterator)    {
247|             if (entry == iterator->thisentry)
248|                 break;
249|             iterator = iterator->nextentry;
250|             pos++;
251|         }
252|     }
253|     return pos;
254| }
255|
256| #endif
```

LISTING C.4 BOOL.H

```
 1| // --------- bool.h
 2|
 3| #ifndef BOOL_H
 4| #define BOOL_H
 5|
 6| // ----- Boolean type
 7| class bool {
 8|     unsigned char state;
 9| public:
10|     bool(int st = 0) { state = !!st; }
11|     operator int() const { return state; }
12| };
13|
14| const bool true = 1;
15| const bool false = 0;
16|
17| #endif
```

LISTING C.5 MONEY.H

```
 1| // ------ money.h
 2|
```

```
 3| #ifndef MONEY_H
 4| #define MONEY_H
 5|
 6| #include <iostream.h>
 7|
 8| class Money {
 9|     float value;
10|     unsigned char wd; // display width
11| public:
12|     Money(float v=0, unsigned char w = 6);
13|     float& Value()
14|         { return value; }
15|     int operator<(const Money& m) const
16|         { return value < m.value; }
17|     int operator==(const Money& m) const
18|         { return value == m.value; }
19|     int operator!=(const Money& m) const
20|         { return value != m.value; }
21|     int operator>(const Money& m) const
22|         { return value > m.value; }
23|     int operator<=(const Money& m) const
24|         { return value <= m.value; }
25|     int operator>=(const Money& m) const
26|         { return value >= m.value; }
27|     friend ostream& operator<<(ostream&os,const Money& m);
28| };
29|
30| #endif
```

LISTING C.6 MONEY.CPP

```
 1| // ------ money.cpp
 2|
 3| #include "money.h"
 4| #include <math.h>
 5|
 6| // --- construct Money from float
 7| //     adjust to even cents
```

```
 8| Money::Money(float v, unsigned char w)
 9| {
10|     float vl = fabs(v);
11|     long dol = vl;
12|     unsigned short ct = (vl - dol) * 100;
13|     value = ct;
14|     value /= 100;
15|     value += dol;
16|     if (v < 0)
17|         value *= -1;
18|     wd = w;
19| }
20|
21| // ---- ostream Money insertion operator
22| ostream& operator<<(ostream&os,const Money& m)
23| {
24|     os << '$';
25|     os.width(m.wd);
26|     os.precision(2);
27|     os.setf(ios::fixed | ios::right);
28|     os << m.value;
29|     return os;
30| }
```

LISTING C.7 DATE.H

```
 1| // ----- date.h
 2|
 3| #ifndef DATE_H
 4| #define DATE_H
 5|
 6| #include <iostream.h>
 7|
 8| typedef unsigned char DtEl;
 9|
10| class Date {
11|     DtEl mo, da, yr;
12| public:
```

```
13|     Date(DtEl m=0,DtEl d=0,DtEl y=0) : mo(m),da(d),yr(y)
14|         { /* ... */ }
15|     DtEl Month() const
16|         { return mo; }
17|     DtEl Day() const
18|         { return da; }
19|     DtEl Year() const
20|         { return yr; }
21|     void SetMonth(DtEl m)
22|         { mo = m; }
23|     void SetDay(DtEl d)
24|         { da = d; }
25|     void SetYear(DtEl y)
26|         { yr = y; }
27|     int operator<(const Date& dt) const;
28|     int operator==(const Date& dt) const
29|         { return mo == dt.mo && da == dt.da && yr == dt.yr; }
30|     int operator!=(const Date& dt) const
31|         { return !(*this == dt); }
32|     int operator>(const Date& dt) const
33|         { return !(*this == dt || *this < dt); }
34|     int operator<=(const Date& dt) const
35|         { return (*this == dt || *this < dt); }
36|     int operator>=(const Date& dt) const
37|         { return (*this == dt || *this > dt); }
38|     friend ostream& operator<<(ostream&os, const Date& dt);
39| };
40|
41|
42| #endif
```

Listing C.8 DATE.CPP

```
1| // --------- date.cpp
2| #include "date.h"
3|
4| // ---- overloaded relational less-than
5| int Date::operator<(const Date&dt) const
```

```
 6|  {
 7|      if (yr < dt.yr)
 8|          return 1;
 9|      if (yr == dt.yr)    {
10|          if (mo < dt.mo)
11|              return 1;
12|          if (mo == dt.mo)
13|              return da < dt.da;
14|      }
15|      return 0;
16|  }
17|
18|  // ---- ostream insertion operator
19|  ostream& operator<<(ostream&os, const Date& dt)
20|  {
21|      os.setf(ios::right);
22|      os.fill(' ');
23|      os.width(2);
24|      os << static_cast<unsigned short>(dt.mo) << '/';
25|      os.fill('0');
26|      os.width(2);
27|      os << static_cast<unsigned short>(dt.da) << '/';
28|      os.width(2);
29|      os << static_cast<unsigned short>(dt.yr);
30|      os.fill(' ');
31|      return os;
32|  }
```

LISTING C.9 PARODY.H

```
 1|  // ------- parody.h
 2|
 3|  #ifndef DATABASE_H
 4|  #define DATABASE_H
 5|
 6|  #include <fstream.h>
 7|  #include <typeinfo.h>
 8|  #include <cstring.h>
```

```
 9|
10| // =================================================
11| // Parody exceptions representing program errors
12| // =================================================
13| class PdyExceptions {};
14| // --- ReadObject from non-ctor
15| class NotInConstructor : public PdyExceptions {};
16| // --- WriteObject from non-dtor
17| class NotInDestructor : public PdyExceptions {};
18| // --- No database open
19| class NoDatabase : public PdyExceptions {};
20| // --- LoadObject was not called
21| class NotLoaded : public PdyExceptions {};
22| // --- SaveObject was not called
23| class NotSaved : public PdyExceptions {};
24| // --- Multireference object deleted
25| class MustDestroy : public PdyExceptions {};
26| // --- string key w/out size
27| class ZeroLengthKey : public PdyExceptions {};
28| // --- Key length != btree key length
29| class BadKeylength : public PdyExceptions {};
30| // --- Bad reference object
31| class BadReference : public PdyExceptions {};
32| // --- Bad ObjAddr specified
33| class BadObjAddr : public PdyExceptions {};
34|
35| // ===========================
36| // Class Identification
37| // ===========================
38| typedef short int ClassID;
39|
40| // ===================================
41| // Class Identification structure
42| // ===================================
43| struct Class {
44|     char *classname;
45|     ClassID classid;
46|     streampos headeraddr;
```

```
47|      Class(char *cn = 0) :
48|              classname(cn), classid(0), headeraddr(0)
49|          { /* ... */ }
50| };
51|
52| // ============================
53| // Key Controls
54| // ============================
55| typedef short int IndexNo;
56| typedef short int KeyLength;
57|
58| #include "bool.h"
59| #include "linklist.h"
60| #include "btree.h"
61|
62| // ============================
63| // Object Address
64| // ============================
65| struct ObjAddr  {
66|     NodeNbr oa;
67|     ObjAddr(NodeNbr nd = 0) : oa(nd)
68|         { /* ... */ }
69|     operator NodeNbr() const
70|         { return oa; }
71| };
72|
73| // ============================
74| // Persistent Object Header Rcd
75| // ============================
76| struct ObjectHeader {
77|     ClassID classid;    // class identification
78|     NodeNbr ndnbr;       // relative node number within object
79|     ObjectHeader() : classid(0), ndnbr(0)
80|         { /* ... */ }
81| };
82|
83| // ==================================
84| // Persistent object abstract base class
```

```
 85|  // ======================================
 86|  class Persistent    {
 87|      friend class Parody;
 88|      friend class PdyKey;
 89|      friend class PdyReference;
 90|      ObjectHeader objhdr;
 91|      ObjAddr objectaddress;  // Node address for this object
 92|      Parody& parody;         // database for this object
 93|      short int indexcount;   // number of keys in the object
 94|      short int instances;    // number of instances of object
 95|      Node *node;             // current node for reading/writing
 96|      short int offset;       // current char position
 97|      bool changed;           // true if user changed the object
 98|      bool deleted;           // true if user deleted the object
 99|      bool newobject;         // true if user is adding the object
100|      bool loaded;            // true if LoadObject called
101|      bool saved;             // true if SaveObject called
102|      static bool usingnew;   // true if object built with new
103|      streampos filepos;      // for saving file position
104|
105|      // --- pointers to associate keys with objects
106|      Persistent *prevconstructed;
107|      static Persistent *objconstructed;
108|      static Persistent *objdestroyed;
109|
110|      LinkedList<PdyKey> keys;
111|      LinkedList<PdyKey> orgkeys; // original keys in the object
112|
113|      // --- private copy constructor & assignment prevent copies
114|      Persistent(Persistent&) : parody(Parody())
115|          { /* ... */ }
116|      Persistent& operator=(Persistent&)
117|          { return *this; }
118|
119|      // ---- methods used from within Persistent class
120|      void RegisterKey(PdyKey *key)
121|          { keys.AppendEntry(key); }
122|      void ObjectOut();
```

```
123|     void RecordObject();
124|     void RemoveObject();
125|     void RemoveOrgKeys();
126|     void AddIndexes();
127|     void DeleteIndexes();
128|     void UpdateIndexes();
129|     void PositionNode() throw (BadObjAddr);
130|     void ReadObjectHeader();
131|     void WriteObjectHeader();
132|     void SearchIndex(PdyKey *key);
133|     void ReadDataMembers();
134|     PdyBtree *FindIndex(PdyKey *key);
135|     bool TestRelationships();
136|     void ScanForward(NodeNbr nd);
137|     void ScanBackward(NodeNbr nd);
138|     void BuildObject() throw (NoDatabase);
139|     void TestDuplicateObject() throw (Persistent*);
140| public:
141|     // --- These are public members because template functions
142|     //     cannot be friends or member functions, and some
143|     //     template functions need to call them.
144|     //     Users should not call these member functions.
145|     static Persistent *ObjectBeingConstructed()
146|         throw (NotInConstructor);
147|     static Persistent *ObjectBeingDestroyed()
148|         throw (NotInDestructor);
149|     void PdyReadObject(void *buf, short int length);
150|     void PdyWriteObject(const void *buf, short int length);
151|     void ReadStrObject(string& str);
152|     void WriteStrObject(const string& str);
153|     // --- s/b called only from Reference template
154|     void AddReference()
155|         { instances++; }
156| protected:
157|     Persistent();
158|     Persistent(Parody& db);
159|     virtual ~Persistent()
160|         throw (NotLoaded, NotSaved, MustDestroy);
```

```
161|     // --- provided by derived class
162|     virtual void Write() = 0;
163|     virtual void Read() = 0;
164|     // ---- called from derived class's constructor
165|     void LoadObject(ObjAddr nd = 0);
166| public:
167|     // ---- called from derived class's destructor
168|     //      or by user to force output to database
169|     void SaveObject() throw (NoDatabase);
170|
171|     // --- class interface methods for modifying database
172|     bool AddObject();
173|     bool ChangeObject();
174|     bool DeleteObject();
175|     bool ObjectExists() const
176|         { return objectaddress != 0; }
177|
178|     // ---- class interface methods for searching database
179|     Persistent& FindObject(PdyKey *key);
180|     Persistent& CurrentObject(PdyKey *key = 0);
181|     Persistent& FirstObject(PdyKey *key = 0);
182|     Persistent& LastObject(PdyKey *key = 0);
183|     Persistent& NextObject(PdyKey *key = 0);
184|     Persistent& PreviousObject(PdyKey *key = 0);
185|     // ---- return the object identification
186|     ObjAddr ObjectAddress() const
187|         { return objectaddress; }
188|     // ----- pseudo delete operator for multiple instances
189|     static void Destroy(Persistent *pp);
190| };
191|
192| // =========================
193| // DataFile class
194| // =========================
195| class DataFile : public NodeFile    {
196| public:
197|     DataFile(const string& name) : NodeFile(name+".dat")
198|         { /* ... */ }
```

```
199|  };
200|
201|  // =========================
202|  // the Parody database
203|  // =========================
204|  class Parody    {
205|      friend Persistent;
206|      DataFile datafile;                  // the object datafile
207|      IndexFile indexfile;                // the b-tree file
208|      LinkedList<Persistent> objects;  // instantiated objects
209|      LinkedList<Class> classes;       // registered classes
210|      LinkedList<PdyBtree> btrees;     // btrees in the database
211|      // --- for Index program to rebuild indexes
212|      ObjAddr rebuildnode;                // object being rebuilt
213|      Parody *previousdatabase;          // previous open database
214|      static Parody *opendatabase;       // latest open database
215|      void GetObjectHeader(ObjAddr nd, ObjectHeader& objhdr);
216|      void RebuildIndexes(ObjAddr nd)
217|          { rebuildnode = nd; }
218|      bool FindClass(Class *cls, NodeNbr *nd = 0);
219|      ClassID GetClassID(const char *classname);
220|      friend void BuildIndex();
221|      // --- private copy constructor & assignment prevent copies
222|      Parody(Parody&) : datafile(string()), indexfile(string())
223|          { /* ... */ }
224|      Parody& operator=(Parody&)
225|          { return *this; }
226|      void RegisterIndexes(Class *cls, const Persistent& pcls)
227|              throw (ZeroLengthKey);
228|      ClassID RegisterClass(const Persistent& cls);
229|      Class *Registration(const Persistent& pcls);
230|      void AddClassToIndex(Class *cls);
231|  public:
232|      Parody(const string& name);
233|      ~Parody();
234|      static Parody *OpenDatabase()
235|          { return opendatabase; }
236|  };
```

```
237|
238| // ---- Persistent constructor using last declared database
239| inline Persistent::Persistent() :
240|                    parody(*Parody::OpenDatabase())
241| {
242|     BuildObject();
243| }
244|
245| // ---- Persistent constructor using specified database
246| inline Persistent::Persistent(Parody& db) : parody(db)
247| {
248|     BuildObject();
249| }
250|
251| template <class T>
252| void ReadObject(T& t)
253| {
254|     Persistent *oc = Persistent::ObjectBeingConstructed();
255|     oc->PdyReadObject(&t, sizeof(T));
256| }
257|
258| template <class T>
259| void WriteObject(const T& t)
260| {
261|     Persistent *od = Persistent::ObjectBeingDestroyed();
262|     od->PdyWriteObject(&t, sizeof(T));
263| }
264|
265| inline void ReadObject(string& s)
266| {
267|     Persistent *oc = Persistent::ObjectBeingConstructed();
268|     oc->ReadStrObject(s);
269| }
270|
271| inline void WriteObject(const string& s)
272| {
273|     Persistent *od = Persistent::ObjectBeingDestroyed();
274|     od->WriteStrObject(reinterpret_cast<const string&>(s));
```

```
275| }
276|
277| // =====================================
278| // PersistentObject template
279| // =====================================
280| template <class T>
281| class PersistentObject : public Persistent  {
282|     void Read()
283|     {PdyReadObject(reinterpret_cast<void*>(&Obj), sizeof(T));}
284|     void Write()
285|     {PdyWriteObject(reinterpret_cast<void*>(&Obj), sizeof(T));}
286| public:
287|     T Obj;
288|     PersistentObject(const T& obj) : Obj(obj)
289|         { LoadObject(); }
290|     PersistentObject(ObjAddr oa = 0)
291|         { LoadObject(oa); }
292|     virtual ~PersistentObject()
293|         { SaveObject(); }
294| };
295|
296| // =====================================
297| // Reference template
298| // =====================================
299| template <class T>
300| class Reference {
301| public:
302|     T *obj;
303|     Reference();
304|     ~Reference();
305|     void ReadObject();
306|     void WriteObject();
307|     void operator=(T& to) throw (BadReference);
308|     void RemoveReference();
309| };
310|
311| template <class T>
312| Reference<T>::Reference()
```

```
313|  {
314|      obj = 0;
315|  }
316|
317|  template <class T>
318|  Reference<T>::~Reference()
319|  {
320|      Persistent::Destroy(obj);
321|  }
322|
323|  template <class T>
324|  void Reference<T>::ReadObject()
325|  {
326|      Persistent::Destroy(obj);
327|      obj = 0;
328|
329|      ObjAddr oa;
330|      ::ReadObject(oa);
331|      if (oa != 0)
332|          obj = new T(oa);
333|  }
334|
335|  template <class T>
336|  void Reference<T>::WriteObject()
337|  {
338|      ObjAddr oa = 0;
339|      if (obj != 0)
340|          oa = obj->ObjectAddress();
341|      ::WriteObject(oa);
342|  }
343|
344|  template <class T>
345|  void Reference<T>::operator=(T& to)
346|          throw (BadReference)
347|  {
348|      Persistent *po = dynamic_cast<Persistent*>(&to);
349|      if (po == 0)
350|          throw BadReference();
```

```
351|      Persistent::Destroy(obj);
352|      obj = static_cast<T*>(po);
353|      obj->AddReference();
354| }
355|
356| template <class T>
357| void Reference<T>::RemoveReference()
358| {
359|      Persistent::Destroy(obj);
360|      obj = 0;
361| }
362|
363| #include "key.h"
364|
365| #endif
```

Listing C.10 PARODY.CPP

```
 1| // ---------- parody.cpp
 2|
 3| // ==========================================
 4| // Parody persistent object member functions
 5| // ==========================================
 6|
 7| #include <new.h>
 8| #include <stdlib.h>
 9| #include <string.h>
10| #include "parody.h"
11|
12| Parody *Parody::opendatabase;   // latest open database
13|
14| // ======================================
15| // Parody member functions
16| // ======================================
17|
18| // ---------- construct a Parody database
19| Parody::Parody(const string& name) :
20|               datafile(name), indexfile(name)
```

```
21| {
22|     rebuildnode = 0;
23|     previousdatabase = opendatabase;
24|     opendatabase = this;
25| }
26|
27| // ---------- close the Parody database
28| Parody::~Parody()
29| {
30|     PdyBtree *bt = btrees.FirstEntry();
31|     while (bt != 0) {
32|         delete bt;
33|         bt = btrees.NextEntry();
34|     }
35|     Class *cls = classes.FirstEntry();
36|     while (cls != 0)    {
37|         delete [] cls->classname;
38|         delete cls;
39|         cls = classes.NextEntry();
40|     }
41|     opendatabase = previousdatabase;
42| }
43|
44| // ------- read an object header record
45| void Parody::GetObjectHeader(ObjAddr nd,ObjectHeader &objhdr)
46| {
47|     // --- constructing this node seeks to the first data byte
48|     Node(&datafile, nd);
49|     datafile.ReadData(&objhdr, sizeof(ObjectHeader));
50| }
51|
52| Class *Parody::Registration(const Persistent& pcls)
53| {
54|     Class *cls = classes.FirstEntry();
55|     while (cls != 0)    {
56|         const char *ty = typeid(pcls).name();
57|         if (strcmp(cls->classname, ty) == 0)
58|             break;
```

```
59|            cls = classes.NextEntry();
60|        }
61|     return cls;
62| }
63|
64| bool Parody::FindClass(Class *cls, NodeNbr *nd)
65| {
66|     char classname[classnamesize];
67|     ClassID cid = 0;
68|     if (!indexfile.NewFile())   {
69|         Node tmpnode;
70|         NodeNbr nx = 1;
71|         // ------- locate the class header
72|         while (nx != 0) {
73|             tmpnode = Node(&indexfile, nx);
74|             indexfile.ReadData(classname, classnamesize);
75|             if (strcmp(classname, cls->classname) == 0) {
76|                 cls->headeraddr = indexfile.FilePosition();
77|                 cls->classid = cid;
78|                 return true;
79|             }
80|             // --- this node is not the class header
81|             cid++;
82|             nx = tmpnode.NextNode();
83|         }
84|         if (nd != 0)    {
85|             *nd = indexfile.NewNode();
86|             tmpnode.SetNextNode(*nd);
87|         }
88|     }
89|     cls->classid = cid;
90|     return false;
91| }
92|
93| ClassID Parody::GetClassID(const char *classname)
94| {
95|     Class cls(const_cast<char*>(classname));
96|     FindClass(&cls);
```

```
 97|     return cls.classid;
 98| }
 99|
100|
101| void Parody::AddClassToIndex(Class *cls)
102| {
103|     NodeNbr nd = 0;
104|
105|     if (FindClass(cls, &nd) == false)   {
106|         indexfile.ResetNewFile();
107|         nd = nd ? nd : indexfile.NewNode();
108|         // ------- build the class header for new class
109|         Node tmpnode(&indexfile, nd);
110|
111|         // -----  write class name into class record
112|         indexfile.WriteData(cls->classname, classnamesize);
113|
114|         // ---- save disk address of tree headers
115|         cls->headeraddr = indexfile.FilePosition();
116|
117|         // ----- pad the residual node space
118|         int residual = nodedatalength-classnamesize;
119|         char *residue = new char[residual];
120|         memset(residue, 0, residual);
121|         indexfile.WriteData(residue, residual);
122|         delete residue;
123|
124|         tmpnode.MarkNodeChanged();
125|     }
126| }
127|
128| // ----- register a class's indexes with the database manager
129| void Parody::RegisterIndexes(Class *cls, const Persistent& pcls)
130|             throw (ZeroLengthKey)
131| {
132|     Persistent& cl = const_cast<Persistent&>(pcls);
133|     PdyKey *key = cl.keys.FirstEntry();
134|     while (key != 0)    {
```

```
135|            if (key->GetKeyLength() == 0)
136|                throw ZeroLengthKey();
137|            PdyBtree *bt = new PdyBtree(indexfile, cls, key);
138|            bt->SetClassIndexed(cls);
139|            btrees.AppendEntry(bt);
140|            key = cl.keys.NextEntry();
141|        }
142| }
143|
144| // ---- register a persistent class with the database manager
145| ClassID Parody::RegisterClass(const Persistent& pcls)
146| {
147|     Class *cls = Registration(pcls);
148|     if (cls == 0)   {
149|         cls = new Class;
150|         const char *cn = typeid(pcls).name();
151|         cls->classname = new char[strlen(cn)+1];
152|         strcpy(cls->classname, cn);
153|
154|         // ---- search the index file for the class
155|         AddClassToIndex(cls);
156|
157|         // ---- register the indexes
158|         RegisterIndexes(cls, pcls);
159|
160|         classes.AppendEntry(cls);
161|     }
162|     return cls->classid;
163| }
164|
165| // ==========================================
166| // Persistent base class member functions
167| // ==========================================
168|
169| Persistent *Persistent::objconstructed = 0;
170| Persistent *Persistent::objdestroyed = 0;
171| bool Persistent::usingnew = false;
172|
```

```
173|  // ------ common constructor code
174|  void Persistent::BuildObject() throw (NoDatabase)
175|  {
176|      if (Parody::OpenDatabase() == 0)
177|          throw NoDatabase();
178|      prevconstructed = objconstructed;
179|      objconstructed = this;
180|      changed = false;
181|      deleted = false;
182|      newobject = false;
183|      loaded = false;
184|      saved = false;
185|      offset = 0;
186|      indexcount = 0;
187|      node = 0;
188|      objectaddress = 0;
189|      instances = 0;
190|  }
191|
192|  // ------ destructor
193|  Persistent::~Persistent()
194|      throw (NotLoaded, NotSaved, MustDestroy)
195|  {
196|      if (Parody::OpenDatabase() == 0)
197|          throw NoDatabase();
198|      RemoveObject();
199|      keys.ClearList();
200|      delete node;
201|      if (!loaded)
202|          throw NotLoaded();
203|      if (!saved)
204|          throw NotSaved();
205|      if (instances != 0)
206|          throw MustDestroy();
207|  }
208|
209|  void Persistent::Destroy(Persistent *pp)
210|  {
```

```
211|    if (pp != 0)    {
212|        if (pp->instances == 0)
213|            delete(pp);
214|        else
215|            --(pp->instances);
216|    }
217| }
218|
219| Persistent *Persistent::ObjectBeingConstructed()
220|        throw (NotInConstructor)
221| {
222|    Persistent *oc = objconstructed;
223|    if (oc == 0)
224|        throw NotInConstructor();
225|    return oc;
226| }
227|
228| Persistent *Persistent::ObjectBeingDestroyed()
229|        throw (NotInDestructor)
230| {
231|    Persistent *dc = objdestroyed;
232|    if (dc == 0)
233|        throw NotInDestructor();
234|    return dc;
235| }
236|
237| // ------ search the collected Btrees for this key's index
238| PdyBtree *Persistent::FindIndex(PdyKey *key)
239| {
240|    PdyBtree *bt = 0;
241|    if (key == 0)
242|        key = keys.FirstEntry();
243|    if (key != 0)    {
244|        bt = parody.btrees.FirstEntry();
245|        while (bt != 0) {
246|            const char *ty = typeid(*this).name();
247|            if (strcmp(ty, bt->ClassIndexed()->classname) == 0)
248|                if (bt->Indexno() == key->indexno)
```

```
249|                    break;
250|              bt = parody.btrees.NextEntry();
251|          }
252|      }
253|      return bt;
254| }
255|
256| // ----- remove copies of the original keys
257| void Persistent::RemoveOrgKeys()
258| {
259|     PdyKey *ky = orgkeys.FirstEntry();
260|     while (ky != 0) {
261|         delete ky;
262|         ky = orgkeys.NextEntry();
263|     }
264|     orgkeys.ClearList();
265| }
266|
267| // --------------- record the object's state
268| void Persistent::RecordObject()
269| {
270|     // --- remove object from the list of instantiated objects
271|     RemoveOrgKeys();
272|     // --- remove copies of the original keys
273|     parody.objects.RemoveEntry(this);
274|     // ---- put the object's address in a parody list of
275|     //       instantiated objects
276|     parody.objects.AppendEntry(this);
277|     // ---- make copies of the original keys for later update
278|     PdyKey *key = keys.FirstEntry();
279|     while (key != 0)    {
280|         PdyKey *ky = key->MakeKey();
281|         *ky = *key;
282|         orgkeys.AppendEntry(ky);
283|         // --- instantiate the index b-tree (if not already)
284|         FindIndex(ky);
285|         key = keys.NextEntry();
286|     }
```

```
287| }
288|
289| //  ---- remove the record of the object's state
290| void Persistent::RemoveObject()
291| {
292|     // --- remove object from the list of instantiated objects
293|     parody.objects.RemoveEntry(this);
294|     // --- remove copies of the original keys
295|     RemoveOrgKeys();
296| }
297|
298| void Persistent::TestDuplicateObject()
299|         throw (Persistent*)
300| {
301|     if (objectaddress != 0) {
302|         // --- search for a previous instance of this object
303|         Persistent *obj = parody.objects.FirstEntry();
304|         while (obj != 0)    {
305|             if (objectaddress == obj->objectaddress)    {
306|                 // ---- object already instantiated
307|                 obj->instances++;
308|                 saved = true;
309|                 throw obj;
310|             }
311|             obj = parody.objects.NextEntry();
312|         }
313|     }
314| }
315|
316| // -- called from derived constructor after all construction
317| void Persistent::LoadObject(ObjAddr nd)
318| {
319|     loaded = true;
320|     objconstructed = 0;
321|     objhdr.classid = parody.RegisterClass(*this);
322|     objectaddress = nd;
323|     if (parody.rebuildnode)
324|         objectaddress = parody.rebuildnode;
```

```
325|     if (objectaddress == 0)
326|         // --- position at object's node
327|         SearchIndex(keys.FirstEntry());
328|     ReadDataMembers();
329|     objconstructed = prevconstructed;
330| }
331|
332| // ------ write the object to the database
333| void Persistent::ObjectOut()
334| {
335|     Persistent *hold = objdestroyed;
336|     objdestroyed = this;
337|     // --- tell object to write its data members
338|     Write();
339|     objdestroyed = hold;
340|     // --- pad the last node
341|     short int padding = nodedatalength - offset;
342|     if (padding)    {
343|         char *pads = new char[padding];
344|         memset(pads, 0, padding);
345|         parody.datafile.WriteData(pads, padding);
346|         delete pads;
347|     }
348|     NodeNbr nx = node->NextNode();
349|     node->SetNextNode(0);
350|     delete node;
351|     node = 0;
352|     // --- if node was linked, object got shorter
353|     while (nx != 0) {
354|         Node nd(&parody.datafile, nx);
355|         nx = nd.NextNode();
356|         nd.MarkNodeDeleted();
357|     }
358|     parody.datafile.Seek(filepos);
359| }
360|
361| // ----- write the object's node header
362| void Persistent::WriteObjectHeader()
```

```
363|  {
364|      // --- write the relative node number and class id
365|      parody.datafile.WriteData(&objhdr, sizeof(ObjectHeader));
366|      offset = sizeof(ObjectHeader);
367|  }
368|
369|  // ----- read the object's node header
370|  void Persistent::ReadObjectHeader()
371|  {
372|      // --- read the relative node number and class id
373|      parody.datafile.ReadData(&objhdr, sizeof(ObjectHeader));
374|      offset = sizeof(ObjectHeader);
375|  }
376|
377|  // --- called from derived destructor before all destruction
378|  //          a new or existing object is being saved
379|  void Persistent::SaveObject()
380|          throw (NoDatabase)
381|  {
382|      if (Parody::OpenDatabase() == 0)
383|          throw NoDatabase();
384|      saved = true;
385|      if (parody.rebuildnode) {
386|          AddIndexes();
387|          return;
388|      }
389|      if (newobject)  {
390|          if (!deleted && ObjectExists()) {
391|              AddIndexes();
392|              PositionNode();
393|              ObjectOut();
394|              RecordObject();
395|          }
396|      }
397|      else if (deleted || changed && ObjectExists())  {
398|          // --- position the parody file at the object's node
399|          PositionNode();
400|          if (deleted)     {
```

```
401|                  // --- delete the object's nodes from the database
402|                  while (node != 0)   {
403|                      node->MarkNodeDeleted();
404|                      NodeNbr nx = node->NextNode();
405|                      delete node;
406|                      if (nx)
407|                          node = new Node(&parody.datafile, nx);
408|                      else
409|                          node = 0;
410|                  }
411|                  DeleteIndexes();
412|                  objectaddress = 0;
413|              }
414|          else    {
415|                  // --- tell object to write its data members
416|                  ObjectOut();
417|                  // ---- update the object's indexes
418|                  UpdateIndexes();
419|                  RecordObject();
420|              }
421|          parody.datafile.Seek(filepos);
422|      }
423|      newobject = false;
424|      deleted = false;
425|      changed = false;
426| }
427|
428| // --- read one data member of the object from the database
429| void Persistent::PdyReadObject(void *buf, short int length)
430| {
431|      while (node != 0 && length > 0) {
432|          if (offset == nodedatalength)   {
433|              NodeNbr nx = node->NextNode();
434|              delete node;
435|              node = nx ? new Node(&parody.datafile, nx) : 0;
436|              ReadObjectHeader();
437|          }
438|          if (node != 0)   {
```

```
439|              short int len = min(length,
440|                  static_cast<short>(nodedatalength-offset));
441|              parody.datafile.ReadData(buf, len);
442|              buf = reinterpret_cast<char*>(buf) + len;
443|              offset += len;
444|              length -= len;
445|          }
446|      }
447| }
448|
449| // --- write one data member of the object to the database
450| void Persistent::PdyWriteObject(const void *buf, short length)
451| {
452|     while (node != 0 && length > 0) {
453|         if (offset == nodedatalength)   {
454|             NodeNbr nx = node->NextNode();
455|             if (nx == 0)
456|                 nx = parody.datafile.NewNode();
457|             node->SetNextNode(nx);
458|             delete node;
459|             node = new Node(&parody.datafile, nx);
460|             WriteObjectHeader();
461|             objhdr.ndnbr++;
462|         }
463|         short int len = min(length,
464|             static_cast<short>(nodedatalength-offset));
465|         parody.datafile.WriteData(buf, len);
466|         buf = reinterpret_cast<const char*>(buf) + len;
467|         offset += len;
468|         length -= len;
469|     }
470| }
471|
472| void Persistent::ReadStrObject(string& str)
473| {
474|     short int len;
475|     PdyReadObject(&len, sizeof(short int));
476|     char *s = new char[len+1];
```

```
477|     PdyReadObject(s, len);
478|     s[len] = '\0';
479|     str = s;
480|     delete s;
481| }
482|
483| void Persistent::WriteStrObject(const string& str)
484| {
485|     short int len = strlen(str.c_str());
486|     PdyWriteObject(&len, sizeof(short int));
487|     PdyWriteObject(str.c_str(), len);
488| }
489|
490| // ---- add the index values to the object's index btrees
491| void Persistent::AddIndexes()
492| {
493|     PdyKey *key = keys.FirstEntry();
494|     while (key != 0)    {
495|         if (!key->isNullValue())    {
496|             PdyBtree *bt = FindIndex(key);
497|             key->fileaddr = objectaddress;
498|             bt->Insert(key);
499|         }
500|         key = keys.NextEntry();
501|     }
502| }
503|
504| // ---- update the index values in the object's index btrees
505| void Persistent::UpdateIndexes()
506| {
507|     PdyKey *oky = orgkeys.FirstEntry();
508|     PdyKey *key = keys.FirstEntry();
509|     while (key != 0)    {
510|         if (!(*oky == *key))    {
511|             // --- key value has changed, update the index
512|             PdyBtree *bt = FindIndex(oky);
513|             // --- delete the old
514|             if (!oky->isNullValue())    {
```

```
515|                        oky->fileaddr = objectaddress;
516|                        bt->Delete(oky);
517|                    }
518|                    // --- insert the new
519|                    if (!key->isNullValue())    {
520|                        key->fileaddr = objectaddress;
521|                        bt->Insert(key);
522|                    }
523|                }
524|            oky = orgkeys.NextEntry();
525|            key = keys.NextEntry();
526|        }
527| }
528|
529| // -- delete the index values from the object's index btrees
530| void Persistent::DeleteIndexes()
531| {
532|     PdyKey *key = orgkeys.FirstEntry();
533|     while (key != 0)    {
534|         if (!key->isNullValue())    {
535|             PdyBtree *bt = FindIndex(key);
536|             key->fileaddr = objectaddress;
537|             bt->Delete(key);
538|         }
539|         key = orgkeys.NextEntry();
540|     }
541| }
542|
543| // ----- position the file to the specifed node number
544| void Persistent::PositionNode()
545|         throw (BadObjAddr)
546| {
547|     filepos = parody.datafile.FilePosition();
548|     if (objectaddress)  {
549|         delete node;
550|         node = new Node(&parody.datafile, objectaddress);
551|         offset = sizeof(ObjectHeader);
552|         ObjectHeader oh;
```

```
553|            parody.datafile.ReadData(&oh, sizeof(ObjectHeader));
554|            if (oh.ndnbr != 0 || oh.classid != objhdr.classid)
555|                throw BadObjAddr();
556|        }
557| }
558|
559| // ------- search the index for a match on the key
560| void Persistent::SearchIndex(PdyKey *key)
561| {
562|     objectaddress = 0;
563|     if (key != 0 && !key->isNullValue())    {
564|         PdyBtree *bt = FindIndex(key);
565|         if (bt != 0 && bt->Find(key))   {
566|             if (key->indexno != 0)  {
567|                 PdyKey *bc;
568|                 do
569|                     bc = bt->Previous();
570|                 while (bc != 0 && *bc == *key);
571|                 key = bt->Next();
572|             }
573|             objectaddress = key->fileaddr;
574|         }
575|     }
576| }
577|
578| // --- scan nodes forward to the first one of next object
579| void Persistent::ScanForward(NodeNbr nd)
580| {
581|     ObjectHeader oh;
582|     while (nd++ < parody.datafile.HighestNode())    {
583|         parody.GetObjectHeader(nd, oh);
584|         if (oh.classid == objhdr.classid && oh.ndnbr == 0)  {
585|             objectaddress = nd;
586|             break;
587|         }
588|     }
589| }
590|
```

```
591|  // --- scan nodes back to first one of the previous object
592|  void Persistent::ScanBackward(NodeNbr nd)
593|  {
594|      ObjectHeader oh;
595|      while (--nd > 0)    {
596|          parody.GetObjectHeader(nd, oh);
597|          if (oh.classid == objhdr.classid && oh.ndnbr == 0)  {
598|              objectaddress = nd;
599|              break;
600|          }
601|      }
602|  }
603|
604|  // --------- find an object by a key value
605|  Persistent& Persistent::FindObject(PdyKey *key)
606|  {
607|      RemoveObject();
608|      SearchIndex(key);
609|      ReadDataMembers();
610|      return *this;
611|  }
612|
613|  // --- retrieve the current object in a key sequence
614|  Persistent& Persistent::CurrentObject(PdyKey *key)
615|  {
616|      RemoveObject();
617|      PdyBtree *bt = FindIndex(key);
618|      if (bt != 0)    {
619|          if ((key = bt->Current()) != 0)
620|              objectaddress = key->fileaddr;
621|          ReadDataMembers();
622|      }
623|      return *this;
624|  }
625|
626|  // --- retrieve the first object in a key sequence
627|  Persistent& Persistent::FirstObject(PdyKey *key)
628|  {
```

```
629|      RemoveObject();
630|      objectaddress = 0;
631|      PdyBtree *bt = FindIndex(key);
632|      if (bt == 0)
633|          // ----- keyless object
634|          ScanForward(0);
635|      else if ((key = bt->First()) != 0)
636|          objectaddress = key->fileaddr;
637|      ReadDataMembers();
638|      return *this;
639| }
640|
641| // --- retrieve the last object in a key sequence
642| Persistent& Persistent::LastObject(PdyKey *key)
643| {
644|      RemoveObject();
645|      objectaddress = 0;
646|      PdyBtree *bt = FindIndex(key);
647|      if (bt == 0)
648|          // ----- keyless object
649|          ScanBackward(parody.datafile.HighestNode());
650|      else if ((key = bt->Last()) != 0)
651|          objectaddress = key->fileaddr;
652|      ReadDataMembers();
653|      return *this;
654| }
655|
656| // --- retrieve the next object in a key sequence
657| Persistent& Persistent::NextObject(PdyKey *key)
658| {
659|      RemoveObject();
660|      ObjAddr oa = objectaddress;
661|      objectaddress = 0;
662|      PdyBtree *bt = FindIndex(key);
663|      if (bt == 0)
664|          // ----- keyless object
665|          ScanForward(oa);
666|      else if ((key = bt->Next()) != 0)
```

```
667|         objectaddress = key->fileaddr;
668|     ReadDataMembers();
669|     return *this;
670| }
671|
672| // --- retrieve the previous object in a key sequence
673| Persistent& Persistent::PreviousObject(PdyKey *key)
674| {
675|     RemoveObject();
676|     ObjAddr oa = objectaddress;
677|     objectaddress = 0;
678|     PdyBtree *bt = FindIndex(key);
679|     if (bt == 0)
680|         // ----- keyless object
681|         ScanBackward(oa);
682|     else if ((key = bt->Previous()) != 0)
683|         objectaddress = key->fileaddr;
684|     ReadDataMembers();
685|     return *this;
686| }
687|
688| // ------- read an object's data members
689| void Persistent::ReadDataMembers()
690| {
691|     if (objectaddress != 0) {
692|         PositionNode();
693|         // --- tell object to read its data members
694|         Persistent *hold = objconstructed;
695|         objconstructed = this;
696|         Read();
697|         objconstructed = hold;
698|         delete node;
699|         node = 0;
700|         TestDuplicateObject();
701|         // --- post object instantiated and
702|         //     put secondary keys in table
703|         RecordObject();
704|         parody.datafile.Seek(filepos);
```

```
705|        }
706| }
707|
708| // -------- add an object to the Parody database
709| bool Persistent::AddObject()
710| {
711|     newobject = (objectaddress == 0 && TestRelationships());
712|     if (newobject)  {
713|         delete node;  // (just in case)
714|         node = new Node(&parody.datafile,
715|                         parody.datafile.NewNode());
716|         objectaddress = node->GetNodeNbr();
717|         WriteObjectHeader();
718|         objhdr.ndnbr++;
719|     }
720|     return newobject;
721| }
722|
723| // ---------- mark a persistent object for change
724| bool Persistent::ChangeObject()
725| {
726|     changed = TestRelationships();
727|     return changed;
728| }
729|
730| // ---------- mark a persistent object for delete
731| bool Persistent::DeleteObject()
732| {
733|     PdyKey *key = keys.FirstEntry();
734|     bool related = false;
735|
736|     if (!key->isNullValue())    {
737|         // --- scan for other objects related to this one
738|         PdyBtree *bt = parody.btrees.FirstEntry();
739|         while (bt != 0 && !related) {
740|             // --- test only secondary keys
741|             if (bt->Indexno() != 0) {
742|                 const Type_info *relclass =
```

```
743|                        bt->NullKey()->relatedclass;
744|                if (relclass != 0)  {
745|                    if (typeid(*this) == *relclass) {
746|                        PdyKey *ky = bt->MakeKeyBuffer();
747|                        if (ky->isObjectAddress())  {
748|                            const ObjAddr *oa =
749|                                ky->ObjectAddress();
750|                            ObjectHeader oh;
751|                            parody.GetObjectHeader(*oa, oh);
752|                            if (oh.classid == objhdr.classid)
753|                                if (oh.ndnbr == 0)
754|                                    related = true;
755|                        }
756|                        else    {
757|                            ky->CopyKeyData(key);
758|                            related = bt->Find(ky);
759|                        }
760|                    }
761|                }
762|            }
763|            bt = parody.btrees.NextEntry();
764|        }
765|    }
766|    deleted = !related;
767|    return deleted;
768| }
769|
770| // ------ test an object's relationships
771| //       return false if it is related to a
772| //       nonexistent object
773| //       return false if its primary key is already in use
774| bool Persistent::TestRelationships()
775| {
776|     PdyKey *key = keys.FirstEntry();
777|     if (key == 0)
778|         return true;
779|     PdyBtree *bt;
780|     if (objectaddress == 0) {
```

```
781|          bt = FindIndex(key);
782|          if (bt != 0 && bt->Find(key))
783|              return false;
784|      }
785|      bool unrelated = true;
786|
787|      while ((key = keys.NextEntry()) != 0)    {
788|          const Type_info *relclass = key->relatedclass;
789|          if (key->isObjectAddress()) {
790|              const ObjAddr *oa = key->ObjectAddress();
791|              if (oa != 0)    {
792|                  ObjectHeader oh;
793|                  parody.GetObjectHeader(*oa, oh);
794|                  if (oh.ndnbr == 0)  {
795|                      // --- find classid of related class
796|                      Class *cls = parody.classes.FirstEntry();
797|                      const char *cn = relclass->name();
798|                      while (cls != 0)    {
799|                          if (strcmp(cn, cls->classname)==0)
800|                              break;
801|                          cls = parody.classes.NextEntry();
802|                      }
803|                      if (cls && cls->classid == oh.classid)
804|                          continue;
805|                  }
806|                  unrelated = false;
807|              }
808|          }
809|          else if (!key->isNullValue() && relclass != 0)  {
810|              const char *kc = relclass->name();
811|              bt = parody.btrees.FirstEntry();
812|              while (bt != 0 && unrelated)    {
813|                  // --- test only primary keys
814|                  if (bt->Indexno() == 0) {
815|                      // --- primary key of related class?
816|                      const char *bc =
817|                          bt->ClassIndexed()->classname;
818|                      if (strcmp(bc, kc) == 0)    {
```

```
819|                          PdyKey *ky = bt->MakeKeyBuffer();
820|                          ky->CopyKeyData(key);
821|                          unrelated = bt->Find(ky);
822|                      }
823|                  }
824|                  bt = parody.btrees.NextEntry();
825|              }
826|          }
827|      }
828|      return unrelated;
829| }
```

LISTING C.11 KEY.H

```
 1| // ------------- key.h
 2|
 3| #ifndef KEY_H
 4| #define KEY_H
 5|
 6| // ============================
 7| // PdyKey abstract base class
 8| // ============================
 9| class PdyKey    {
10|     friend class Parody;
11|     friend class PdyBtree;
12|     friend class TNode;
13|     friend class Persistent;
14|     NodeNbr fileaddr;    // object address -> by this key
15|     NodeNbr lowernode;   // lower node of keys > this key
16|     virtual void WriteKey(IndexFile& bfile) = 0;
17|     virtual void ReadKey(IndexFile& bfile) = 0;
18|     virtual bool isNullValue() const = 0;
19|     virtual void CopyKeyData(const PdyKey *key) = 0;
20|     virtual bool isObjectAddress() const = 0;
21|     virtual const ObjAddr *ObjectAddress() const = 0;
22|     virtual PdyKey *MakeKey() const = 0;
23| protected:
24|     const Type_info *relatedclass; // related class
```

```
25|      IndexNo indexno;     // 0=primary key, >0 =secondary key
26|      KeyLength keylength; // length of the key
27| public:
28|      PdyKey(NodeNbr fa = 0);
29|      virtual ~PdyKey()
30|          { /* ... */ }
31|      virtual int operator>(const PdyKey& key) const = 0;
32|      virtual int operator==(const PdyKey& key) const = 0;
33|      virtual PdyKey& operator=(const PdyKey& key);
34|      void Relate(const Type_info *ti)
35|          { relatedclass = ti; }
36|      KeyLength GetKeyLength() const
37|          { return keylength; }
38|      void SetKeyLength(KeyLength kylen)
39|          { keylength = kylen; }
40| };
41|
42| // ===========================
43| // Key class
44| // ===========================
45| template <class T>
46| class Key : public PdyKey   {
47|      T ky;
48|      bool isObjectAddress() const
49|          { return typeid(T) == typeid(ObjAddr); }
50|      const ObjAddr *ObjectAddress() const
51|          { return reinterpret_cast<const ObjAddr*>(&ky); }
52|      void CopyKeyData(const PdyKey *key);
53|      PdyKey *MakeKey() const;
54| public:
55|      Key(const T& key);
56|      virtual ~Key()
57|          { /* ... */ }
58|      PdyKey& operator=(const PdyKey& key);
59|      int operator>(const PdyKey& key) const;
60|      int operator==(const PdyKey& key) const;
61|      T& KeyValue()
62|          { return ky; }
```

```
63|      void SetKeyValue(const T& key)
64|          { ky = key; }
65|      const T& KeyValue() const
66|          { return ky; }
67|      virtual void WriteKey(IndexFile& ndx);
68|      virtual void ReadKey(IndexFile& ndx);
69|      bool isNullValue() const;
70| };
71|
72| template <class T>
73| Key<T>::Key(const T& key) : ky(key)
74| {
75|      keylength = sizeof(T);
76| }
77|
78| template <class T>
79| void Key<T>::CopyKeyData(const PdyKey *key)
80| {
81|      const Key<T> *kp =
82|          static_cast<const Key<T>*>(key);
83|      ky = kp->ky;
84| }
85|
86| template <class T>
87| PdyKey& Key<T>::operator=(const PdyKey& key)
88| {
89|      if (this != &key)   {
90|          PdyKey::operator=(key);
91|          CopyKeyData(&key);
92|      }
93|      return *this;
94| }
95|
96| template <class T>
97| int Key<T>::operator>(const PdyKey& key) const
98| {
99|      const Key<T> *kp =
100|          static_cast<const Key<T>*>(&key);
```

```
101|     return ky > kp->ky;
102| }
103|
104| template <class T>
105| int Key<T>::operator==(const PdyKey& key) const
106| {
107|     const Key<T> *kp =
108|         static_cast<const Key<T>*>(&key);
109|     return ky == kp->ky;
110| }
111|
112| template <class T>
113| PdyKey *Key<T>::MakeKey() const
114| {
115|     PdyKey *newkey = new Key<T>(T(0));
116|     newkey->SetKeyLength(keylength);
117|     return newkey;
118| }
119|
120| // --- ReadKey must be specialized if key != simple data type
121| template <class T>
122| void Key<T>::ReadKey(IndexFile& ndx)
123| {
124|     if (keylength > 0)
125|         ndx.ReadData(&ky, keylength);
126| }
127|
128| // --- WriteKey must be specialized if key != simple data type
129| template <class T>
130| void Key<T>::WriteKey(IndexFile& ndx)
131| {
132|     if (keylength > 0)
133|         ndx.WriteData(&ky, keylength);
134| }
135|
136| template <class T>
137| bool Key<T>::isNullValue() const
138| {
```

```
139|    return ky == T(0);
140| }
141|
142| // ================================================
143| // specialized Key<string> template member functions
144| // ================================================
145| inline Key<string>::Key(const string& key) : ky(key)
146| {
147|    keylength = key.length();
148| }
149|
150| inline void Key<string>::ReadKey(IndexFile& ndx)
151| {
152|    char *cp = new char[keylength+1];
153|    ndx.ReadData(cp, keylength);
154|    *(cp+keylength) = '\0';
155|    ky = string(cp);
156|    delete cp;
157| }
158|
159| inline void Key<string>::WriteKey(IndexFile& ndx)
160| {
161|    ky.resize(keylength);
162|    ndx.WriteData(ky.c_str(),keylength);
163| }
164|
165| inline PdyKey *Key<string>::MakeKey() const
166| {
167|    PdyKey *newkey =
168|        new Key<string>(string('\0',keylength));
169|    newkey->SetKeyLength(keylength);
170|    return newkey;
171| }
172|
173| inline bool Key<string>::isNullValue() const
174| {
175|    return ky.is_null();
176| }
```

```
177|
178| // ===========================
179| // Concatenated key class
180| // ===========================
181| template <class T1, class T2>
182| class CatKey : public PdyKey    {
183|     Key<T1> ky1;
184|     Key<T2> ky2;
185|     bool isObjectAddress() const
186|         { return false; }
187|     const ObjAddr *ObjectAddress() const
188|         { return 0; }
189|     void CopyKeyData(const PdyKey *key);
190|     // --- ReadKey/WriteKey must be specialized
191|     //     if key(s) != simple data types
192|     virtual void ReadKey(IndexFile& ndx)
193|         { ky1.ReadKey(ndx); ky2.ReadKey(ndx); }
194|     virtual void WriteKey(IndexFile& ndx)
195|         { ky1.WriteKey(ndx); ky2.WriteKey(ndx); }
196|     PdyKey *MakeKey() const;
197|     bool isNullValue() const
198|         { return ky1.isNullValue() && ky2.isNullValue(); }
199| public:
200|     CatKey(const T1& key1, const T2& key2);
201|     ~CatKey() {}
202|     PdyKey& operator=(const PdyKey& key);
203|     int operator>(const PdyKey& key) const;
204|     int operator==(const PdyKey& key) const;
205|     Key<T1>& Key1()
206|         { return ky1; }
207|     T1& KeyValue1()
208|         { return ky1.KeyValue(); }
209|     const T1& KeyValue1() const
210|         { return ky1.KeyValue(); }
211|     void SetKeyValue1(const T1& key1)
212|         { ky1.SetKeyValue(key1); }
213|     Key<T2>& Key2()
214|         { return ky2; }
```

```
215|     T2& KeyValue2()
216|         { return ky2.KeyValue(); }
217|     const T2& KeyValue2() const
218|         { return ky2.KeyValue(); }
219|     void SetKeyValue2(const T2& key2)
220|         { ky2.SetKeyValue(key2); }
221| };
222|
223| template <class T1, class T2>
224| CatKey<T1,T2>::CatKey(const T1& key1, const T2& key2) :
225|                 ky1(key1),ky2(key2)
226| {
227|     keylength = ky1.GetKeyLength() + ky2.GetKeyLength();
228| }
229|
230|
231| template <class T1, class T2>
232| int CatKey<T1,T2>::operator>(const PdyKey& key) const
233| {
234|     const CatKey<T1,T2> *ckp =
235|         static_cast<const CatKey<T1,T2>*>(&key);
236|     if (ky1 > ckp->ky1)
237|         return 1;
238|     if (ky1 == ckp->ky1 && ky2 > ckp->ky2)
239|         return 1;
240|     return 0;
241| }
242|
243| template <class T1, class T2>
244| int CatKey<T1,T2>::operator==(const PdyKey& key) const
245| {
246|     const CatKey<T1,T2> *ckp =
247|         static_cast<const CatKey<T1,T2>*>(&key);
248|     return ky1 == ckp->ky1 && ky2 == ckp->ky2;
249| }
250|
251| template <class T1, class T2>
252| void CatKey<T1,T2>::CopyKeyData(const PdyKey *key)
```

```
253|  {
254|      const CatKey<T1,T2> *ckp =
255|          static_cast<const CatKey<T1,T2>*>(key);
256|      ky1 = ckp->ky1;
257|      ky2 = ckp->ky2;
258|  }
259|
260|  template <class T1, class T2>
261|  PdyKey& CatKey<T1,T2>::operator=(const PdyKey& key)
262|  {
263|      if (this != &key)    {
264|          PdyKey::operator=(key);
265|          CopyKeyData(&key);
266|      }
267|      return *this;
268|  }
269|
270|  template <class T1, class T2>
271|  PdyKey *CatKey<T1,T2>::MakeKey() const
272|  {
273|      CatKey<T1,T2> *newkey = new CatKey<T1,T2>(T1(0),T2(0));
274|      newkey->ky1.SetKeyLength(ky1.GetKeyLength());
275|      newkey->ky2.SetKeyLength(ky2.GetKeyLength());
276|      newkey->SetKeyLength(keylength);
277|      return newkey;
278|  }
279|
280|  #endif
```

Listing C.12 KEY.CPP

```
1|  // ------------ key.cpp
2|
3|  #include "parody.h"
4|
5|  // ==========================================
6|  // base PdyKey class member functions
7|  // ==========================================
```

```
 8|
 9| PdyKey::PdyKey(NodeNbr fa)
10| {
11|     fileaddr = fa;
12|     lowernode = 0;
13|     indexno = 0;
14|     relatedclass = 0;
15|     if (Persistent::objconstructed != 0)    {
16|         // --- register the key with the object being built
17|         Persistent::objconstructed->RegisterKey(this);
18|         // --- assign index number based on position in object
19|         indexno = Persistent::objconstructed->indexcount++;
20|     }
21| }
22|
23| // ------ overloaded =
24| PdyKey& PdyKey::operator=(const PdyKey& key)
25| {
26|     if (this != &key)   {
27|         fileaddr = key.fileaddr;
28|         lowernode = key.lowernode;
29|         indexno = key.indexno;
30|         keylength = key.keylength;
31|         relatedclass = key.relatedclass;
32|     }
33|     return *this;
34| }
```

LISTING C.13 BTREE.H

```
1| // ------------- btree.h
2|
3| #ifndef BTREE_H
4| #define BTREE_H
5|
6| #include <fstream.h>
7| #include <string.h>
8| #include "linklist.h"
```

```
 9| #include "node.h"
10|
11| class PdyKey;
12| class TNode;
13| class Class;
14|
15| const int classnamesize = 32;
16|
17| // ==========================
18| // IndexFile class
19| // ==========================
20| class IndexFile : public NodeFile   {
21| public:
22|     IndexFile(const string& name) : NodeFile(name+".ndx")
23|         { /* ... */ }
24| };
25|
26| // -------- b-tree header record
27| class TreeHeader {
28|     friend class PdyBtree;
29|     friend class IndexFile;
30|     NodeNbr rootnode;    // node number of the root
31|     KeyLength keylength; // length of a key in this b-tree
32|     TreeHeader()
33|         { rootnode = 0; keylength = 0; }
34| };
35|
36| // --------- b-tree index
37| class PdyBtree   {
38|     TreeHeader header;    // btree header
39|     TNode *trnode;        // -> current node value
40|     PdyKey *nullkey;      // for building empty derived key
41|     IndexFile& index;     // index file this tree lives in
42|     IndexNo indexno;      // 0=primary key, > 0=secondary key
43|     Class *classindexed;  // -> class structure of indexed class
44|     NodeNbr currnode;     // current node number
45|     NodeNbr oldcurrnode;  // for repositioning
46|     short oldcurrkey;     // "          "
```

```
47|     streampos HdrPos()
48|         { return classindexed->headeraddr +
49|             indexno * sizeof(TreeHeader); }
50|     void ReadHeader()
51|         { index.ReadData(&header,sizeof(TreeHeader),HdrPos());}
52|     void WriteHeader()
53|         { index.WriteData(&header,sizeof(TreeHeader),HdrPos());}
54|     void SaveKeyPosition();
55| public:
56|     PdyBtree(IndexFile& ndx, Class *cls, PdyKey *ky)
57|                         throw (BadKeylength);
58|     ~PdyBtree();
59|     void Insert(PdyKey *keypointer);
60|     void Delete(PdyKey *keypointer);
61|     bool Find(PdyKey *keypointer);
62|     PdyKey *Current();
63|     PdyKey *First();
64|     PdyKey *Last();
65|     PdyKey *Next();
66|     PdyKey *Previous();
67|     IndexFile& GetIndexFile() const
68|         { return index; }
69|     PdyKey *NullKey() const
70|         { return nullkey; }
71|     PdyKey *MakeKeyBuffer() const;
72|     NodeNbr Root() const
73|         { return header.rootnode; }
74|     NodeNbr GetKeyLength() const
75|         { return header.keylength; }
76|     IndexNo Indexno() const
77|         { return indexno; }
78|     const Class *ClassIndexed() const
79|         { return classindexed; }
80|     void SetClassIndexed(Class *cid)
81|         { classindexed = cid; }
82| };
83|
84| // ------------ b-tree TNode class
```

```
 85| class TNode : Node  {
 86|     friend class PdyBtree;
 87|     struct TNodeHeader  {
 88|         bool isleaf;            // true if node is a leaf
 89|         NodeNbr parent;         // parent to this node
 90|         NodeNbr leftsibling;    // left sibling node
 91|         NodeNbr rightsibling;   // right sibling node
 92|         short int keycount;     // number of keys in this node
 93|         NodeNbr lowernode;      // lower node associated with
 94|                                 // keys < keys in this node
 95|         TNodeHeader()
 96|             { isleaf = false; parent = leftsibling =
 97|                  rightsibling =  keycount = lowernode = 0; }
 98|     } header;
 99|     PdyKey *currkey;            // current key
100|     PdyBtree *btree;            // btree that owns this node
101|     LinkedList<PdyKey> keys;    // the keys in this node
102|
103|     TNode(PdyBtree *bt, NodeNbr node);
104|     bool SearchNode(PdyKey *keyvalue);
105|     void Insert(PdyKey *keyvalue);
106|     short int m();
107|     void WriteBtreeKey(PdyKey *thiskey);
108|     void Adopt(NodeNbr node);
109|     void Adoption();
110|     bool isLeaf() const
111|         { return header.isleaf; }
112|     NodeNbr Parent() const
113|         { return header.parent; }
114|     NodeNbr LeftSibling() const
115|         { return header.leftsibling; }
116|     NodeNbr RightSibling() const
117|         { return header.rightsibling; }
118|     short int KeyCount() const
119|         { return header.keycount; }
120|     NodeNbr LowerNode() const
121|         { return header.lowernode; }
122|     bool Redistribute(NodeNbr sib);
```

```
123|     bool Implode(TNode& right);
124|     short int NodeHeaderSize() const
125|         { return sizeof(TNodeHeader)+Node::NodeHeaderSize(); }
126|     TNode& operator=(TNode& tnode);
127| public:          // due to a bug in Borland C++ 4.0
128|     ~TNode();
129| };
130|
131| #endif
```

Listing C.14 BTREE.CPP

```
 1| // --------------- btree.cpp
 2|
 3| #include <string.h>
 4| #include "parody.h"
 5|
 6| // ---------- constructor to open a btree
 7| PdyBtree::PdyBtree(IndexFile& ndx, Class *cls, PdyKey *ky)
 8|                     throw (BadKeylength)
 9|                     : index(ndx)
10| {
11|     nullkey = ky->MakeKey();
12|     nullkey->PdyKey::operator=(*ky);
13|     trnode = 0;
14|     classindexed = cls;
15|     currnode = 0;
16|
17|     indexno = ky->indexno;
18|
19|     // ------- read the btree header
20|     ReadHeader();
21|
22|     if (header.keylength == 0)
23|         header.keylength = ky->keylength;
24|     else if (ky->keylength != 0 &&
25|                 header.keylength != ky->keylength)
26|         throw BadKeylength();
```

```
27|  }
28|
29|  // ---------- destructor for a btree
30|  PdyBtree::~PdyBtree()
31|  {
32|      // ------- write the btree header
33|      WriteHeader();
34|      delete trnode;
35|      delete nullkey;
36|  }
37|
38|  // ----- make a key buffer
39|  PdyKey *PdyBtree::MakeKeyBuffer() const
40|  {
41|      PdyKey *thiskey = nullkey->MakeKey();
42|      thiskey->indexno = indexno;
43|      return thiskey;
44|  }
45|
46|  // --------------- insert a key into a btree
47|  void PdyBtree::Insert(PdyKey *keypointer)
48|  {
49|      // ---- don't insert duplicate keys
50|      if (!Find(keypointer))  {
51|
52|          PdyKey *newkey = keypointer->MakeKey();
53|          *newkey = *keypointer;
54|
55|          NodeNbr rootnode = 0, leftnode = 0, rightnode = 0;
56|          bool RootisLeaf = true;
57|
58|          bool done = false;
59|          // -------- insert key into btree
60|          while (currnode)    {
61|              int em = trnode->m();
62|              trnode->Insert(newkey);
63|                                      // first insertion is into leaf
64|                                      // if split, later insertions
```

```
65|                              // are into parents (non-leaves)
66|              if (!trnode->header.isleaf)
67|                  trnode->currkey->lowernode = rightnode;
68|
69|              done = trnode->header.keycount <= em;
70|              if (!done)
71|                  // ---- node is full,
72|                  //      try to redistribute keys among siblings
73|                  done = trnode->Redistribute(
74|                          trnode->header.leftsibling);
75|              if (!done)
76|                  done = trnode->Redistribute(
77|                          trnode->header.rightsibling);
78|
79|              if (done)
80|                  break;
81|              // ---- cannot redistribute filled node, split it
82|              RootisLeaf = false;
83|
84|              rightnode = index.NewNode();
85|              leftnode = currnode;
86|
87|              TNode right(this, rightnode);
88|              right.SetNodeNbr(rightnode);
89|              right.MarkNodeChanged();
90|
91|              // --- establish sibling and parent relationships
92|              //      between current node and new right sibling
93|              right.header.rightsibling =
94|                      trnode->header.rightsibling;
95|              trnode->header.rightsibling = rightnode;
96|              right.header.leftsibling = currnode;
97|              right.header.parent = trnode->header.parent;
98|
99|              // ----- if the current node is a leaf,
100|             //        so is the new sibling
101|             right.header.isleaf = trnode->header.isleaf;
102|
```

```
103|        // ----- compute new key counts for the two nodes
104|        trnode->header.keycount = (em + 1) / 2;
105|        right.header.keycount = em-trnode->header.keycount;
106|
107|        // ------ locate the middle key in the current node
108|        PdyKey *middlekey =
109|            trnode->keys.FindEntry(trnode->header.keycount);
110|
111|        // ---- set the pointer to keys less than
112|        //      those in new node
113|        if (!right.header.isleaf)
114|            right.header.lowernode = middlekey->lowernode;
115|
116|        // ----- point to the keys to move (1 past middle)
117|        PdyKey *movekey = trnode->keys.NextEntry(middlekey);
118|
119|        // ----- middle key inserts into parent
120|        trnode->keys.RemoveEntry(middlekey);
121|        *newkey = *middlekey;
122|        delete middlekey;
123|
124|        // ---- move keys from current to new right node
125|        for (int i = 0; i < right.header.keycount; i++) {
126|            PdyKey *nkey = trnode->keys.NextEntry(movekey);
127|            trnode->keys.RemoveEntry(movekey);
128|            right.keys.AppendEntry(movekey);
129|            movekey = nkey;
130|        }
131|
132|        // ---- prepare to insert key
133|        //      into parent of split nodes
134|        currnode = trnode->header.parent;
135|        if (!currnode) {
136|            // ---- no parent node, splitting the root node
137|            rootnode = index.NewNode();
138|            right.header.parent = rootnode;
139|            trnode->header.parent = rootnode;
140|        }
```

```
141|
142|            // --- the former right sibling of the current node
143|            //     is now the right sibling of the split node
144|            //     and must record the new node as left sibling
145|
146|            if (right.header.rightsibling)  {
147|                TNode farright(this, right.header.rightsibling);
148|                farright.header.leftsibling = rightnode;
149|                farright.MarkNodeChanged();
150|            }
151|
152|            // --- children of the new split node point to
153|            //     the current split node as parent. They must
154|            //      be adopted by the new split node
155|
156|            if (!right.header.isleaf)
157|                right.Adoption();
158|
159|            // ----- if splitting other than root, read parent
160|            //       position currkey to key where split node
161|            //       key will be inserted
162|
163|            if (currnode)   {
164|                delete trnode;  // writes the split node to disk
165|                // --- get the parent of the split nodes
166|                trnode = new TNode(this, currnode);
167|                // -- position currkey where new key will insert
168|                trnode->SearchNode(newkey);
169|            }
170|        }
171|
172|        if (!done)  {
173|            // ------ new root node ------ */
174|            delete trnode;
175|            if (rootnode == 0)
176|                rootnode = index.NewNode();
177|            trnode = new TNode(this, rootnode);
178|            trnode->header.isleaf = RootisLeaf;
```

```
179|                    currnode = header.rootnode = rootnode;
180|                    trnode->SetNodeNbr(rootnode);
181|                    trnode->Insert(newkey);
182|                    trnode->header.parent = 0;
183|                    trnode->header.keycount = 1;
184|                    if (!RootisLeaf)    {
185|                        trnode->header.lowernode = leftnode;
186|                        trnode->currkey->lowernode = rightnode;
187|                    }
188|                    trnode->MarkNodeChanged();
189|                }
190|            delete newkey;
191|        }
192|     delete trnode;
193|     trnode = 0;
194| }
195|
196| void PdyBtree::SaveKeyPosition()
197| {
198|     if (trnode->header.isleaf)  {
199|         oldcurrnode = 0;
200|         oldcurrkey =  0;
201|     }
202|     else    {
203|         oldcurrnode = currnode;
204|         oldcurrkey = trnode->keys.FindEntry(trnode->currkey);
205|     }
206| }
207|
208| // --------------- find a key in a btree
209| bool PdyBtree::Find(PdyKey *keypointer)
210| {
211|     oldcurrnode = 0;
212|     oldcurrkey =  0;
213|
214|     currnode = header.rootnode;
215|     while (currnode)    {
216|
```

```
217|          delete trnode;
218|          trnode = new TNode(this, currnode);
219|
220|          if (trnode->SearchNode(keypointer)) {
221|              // ---- search key is equal to a key in the node
222|              keypointer->fileaddr = trnode->currkey->fileaddr;
223|              oldcurrnode = 0;
224|              oldcurrkey =  0;
225|              return true;
226|          }
227|
228|          if (trnode->currkey == trnode->keys.FirstEntry())   {
229|              // ---- search key is < lowest key in node
230|              SaveKeyPosition();
231|              if (trnode->header.isleaf)
232|                  break;
233|              currnode = trnode->header.lowernode;
234|          }
235|          else if (trnode->currkey)   {
236|              // --- search key is < current key in node
237|              SaveKeyPosition();
238|              if (trnode->header.isleaf)
239|                  break;
240|              currnode =
241|                  trnode->keys.PrevEntry(trnode->currkey)->
242|                                              lowernode;
243|          }
244|          else   {
245|              // --- search key > highest key in node
246|              if (trnode->header.isleaf)
247|                  break;
248|              currnode = trnode->keys.LastEntry()->lowernode;
249|          }
250|      }
251|      return false;
252| }
253|
254| // --------------- delete a key from a btree
```

```
255|  void PdyBtree::Delete(PdyKey *keypointer)
256|  {
257|      if (Find(keypointer))   {
258|          if (!trnode->header.isleaf) {
259|
260|              // --- if not found in leaf node, go down to leaf
261|              TNode *leaf =
262|                  new TNode(this, trnode->currkey->lowernode);
263|              while (!leaf->header.isleaf)    {
264|                  NodeNbr lf = leaf->header.lowernode;
265|                  delete leaf;
266|                  leaf = new TNode(this, lf);
267|              }
268|
269|              // ---- Move the left-most key from the leaf
270|              //       to where deleted key was in higher node
271|              PdyKey *movekey = leaf->keys.FirstEntry();
272|              leaf->keys.RemoveEntry(movekey);
273|              leaf->header.keycount--;
274|              leaf->MarkNodeChanged();
275|
276|              trnode->keys.InsertEntry(movekey, trnode->currkey);
277|
278|              movekey->lowernode = trnode->currkey->lowernode;
279|
280|              trnode->keys.RemoveEntry(trnode->currkey);
281|              delete trnode->currkey;
282|              trnode->MarkNodeChanged();
283|              delete trnode;
284|
285|              trnode = leaf;
286|              trnode->currkey = trnode->keys.FirstEntry();
287|              currnode = trnode->GetNodeNbr();
288|          }
289|          else    {
290|              // ---- delete the key from the node
291|              trnode->keys.RemoveEntry(trnode->currkey);
292|              delete trnode->currkey;
```

```
293|                trnode->header.keycount--;
294|                trnode->MarkNodeChanged();
295|                if (trnode->header.keycount == 0)
296|                    header.rootnode = 0;
297|            }
298|            // ---- if the node shrinks to half capacity,
299|            //      try to combine it with a sibling node
300|            while (trnode->header.keycount > 0 &&
301|                        trnode->header.keycount <= trnode->m()/2) {
302|                if (trnode->header.rightsibling)    {
303|                    TNode *right =
304|                        new TNode(this,trnode->header.rightsibling);
305|                    if (trnode->Implode(*right))    {
306|                        delete right;
307|                        NodeNbr parent = trnode->header.parent;
308|                        if (parent == 0)    {
309|                            header.rootnode = trnode->GetNodeNbr();
310|                            break;
311|                        }
312|                        delete trnode;
313|                        trnode = new TNode(this, parent);
314|                        continue;
315|                    }
316|                    delete right;
317|                }
318|                if (trnode->header.leftsibling) {
319|                    TNode *left =
320|                        new TNode(this, trnode->header.leftsibling);
321|                    if (left->Implode(*trnode)) {
322|                        delete trnode;
323|                        NodeNbr parent = left->header.parent;
324|                        if (parent == 0)    {
325|                            header.rootnode = left->GetNodeNbr();
326|                            trnode = left;
327|                            break;
328|                        }
329|                        delete left;
330|                        trnode = new TNode(this, parent);
```

```
331|                    continue;
332|                }
333|              delete left;
334|            }
335|
336|          // --- could not combine with either sibling,
337|          //     try to redistribute
338|          if (!trnode->Redistribute(
339|                    trnode->header.leftsibling))
340|              trnode->Redistribute(
341|                    trnode->header.rightsibling);
342|          break;
343|        }
344|    }
345|    delete trnode;
346|    trnode = 0;
347| }
348|
349| // ------ return the address of the current key
350| PdyKey *PdyBtree::Current()
351| {
352|    if (trnode == 0)
353|        return 0;
354|    if (oldcurrnode != 0)    {
355|        currnode = oldcurrnode;
356|        delete trnode;
357|        trnode = new TNode(this, currnode);
358|        trnode->currkey = trnode->keys.FindEntry(oldcurrkey);
359|        oldcurrnode = 0;
360|        oldcurrkey =  0;
361|    }
362|    return trnode->currkey;
363| }
364|
365| // ------ return the address of the first key
366| PdyKey *PdyBtree::First()
367| {
368|    currnode = header.rootnode;
```

```
369|     if (currnode)   {
370|         delete trnode;
371|         trnode = new TNode(this, currnode);
372|         while (!trnode->header.isleaf)  {
373|             currnode = trnode->header.lowernode;
374|             delete trnode;
375|             trnode = new TNode(this, currnode);
376|         }
377|         trnode->currkey = trnode->keys.FirstEntry();
378|     }
379|     return Current();
380| }
381|
382| // ------ return the address of the last key
383| PdyKey *PdyBtree::Last()
384| {
385|     currnode = header.rootnode;
386|     if (currnode)   {
387|         delete trnode;
388|         trnode = new TNode(this, currnode);
389|         while (!trnode->header.isleaf)  {
390|             currnode = trnode->keys.LastEntry()->lowernode;
391|             delete trnode;
392|             trnode = new TNode(this, currnode);
393|         }
394|         trnode->currkey = trnode->keys.LastEntry();
395|     }
396|     return Current();
397| }
398|
399| // ------ return the address of the next key
400| PdyKey *PdyBtree::Next()
401| {
402|     if (trnode == 0 || trnode->currkey == 0)
403|         return First();
404|     if (!trnode->header.isleaf) {
405|         // --- current key is not in a leaf
406|         currnode = trnode->currkey->lowernode;
```

```
407|          delete trnode;
408|          trnode = new TNode(this, currnode);
409|          // ----- go down to the leaf
410|          while (!trnode->header.isleaf)  {
411|              currnode = trnode->header.lowernode;
412|              delete trnode;
413|              trnode = new TNode(this, currnode);
414|          }
415|          // ---- use the first key in the leaf as the next one
416|          trnode->currkey = trnode->keys.FirstEntry();
417|      }
418|    else    {
419|        // ------ current key is in a leaf
420|        PdyKey *thiskey = nullkey->MakeKey();
421|        *thiskey = *(trnode->currkey);
422|
423|        // ----- point to the next key in the leaf
424|        trnode->currkey =
425|            trnode->keys.NextEntry(trnode->currkey);
426|        while (trnode->currkey == 0 &&
427|                        currnode != header.rootnode)    {
428|            // --- current key was the last one in the leaf
429|            TNode pnode(this, trnode->Parent());
430|            pnode.SearchNode(thiskey);
431|            currnode = pnode.GetNodeNbr();
432|            *trnode = pnode;
433|        }
434|        delete thiskey;
435|    }
436|    return Current();
437| }
438|
439| // ------ return the address of the previous key
440| PdyKey *PdyBtree::Previous()
441| {
442|    if (trnode == 0 || trnode->currkey == 0)
443|        return Last();
444|    if (!trnode->header.isleaf) {
```

```
445|          // --- current key is not in a leaf
446|          PdyKey *ky = trnode->keys.PrevEntry(trnode->currkey);
447|          if (ky != 0)
448|              currnode = ky->lowernode;
449|          else
450|              currnode = trnode->header.lowernode;
451|          delete trnode;
452|          trnode = new TNode(this, currnode);
453|          // ----- go down to the leaf
454|          while (!trnode->header.isleaf)  {
455|              currnode = trnode->keys.LastEntry()->lowernode;
456|              delete trnode;
457|              trnode = new TNode(this, currnode);
458|          }
459|          // ---- use the last key in the leaf as the next one
460|          trnode->currkey = trnode->keys.LastEntry();
461|      }
462|  else    {
463|          // ------ current key is in a leaf
464|          PdyKey *thiskey = nullkey->MakeKey();
465|          *thiskey = *(trnode->currkey);
466|
467|          // ----- point to the previous key in the leaf
468|          trnode->currkey =
469|              trnode->keys.PrevEntry(trnode->currkey);
470|          while (trnode->currkey == 0 &&
471|                      currnode != header.rootnode)    {
472|              // --- current key was the first one in the leaf
473|              TNode pnode(this, trnode->Parent());
474|              pnode.SearchNode(thiskey);
475|
476|              if (pnode.currkey == 0)
477|                  pnode.currkey = pnode.keys.LastEntry();
478|              else
479|                  pnode.currkey =
480|                   . pnode.keys.PrevEntry(pnode.currkey);
481|              currnode = pnode.GetNodeNbr();
482|              *trnode = pnode;
```

```
483|          }
484|          delete thiskey;
485|      }
486|      return Current();
487| }
```

LISTING C.15 NODE.H

```
 1| // ------------ node.h
 2|
 3| #ifndef NODE_H
 4| #define NODE_H
 5|
 6| typedef unsigned short int NodeNbr;
 7| const short int nodelength = 128;
 8| const short int nodedatalength = nodelength - sizeof(NodeNbr);
 9|
10| // ----- exceptions to be thrown
11| class BadFileOpen{};
12| class FileReadError{};
13| class FileWriteError{};
14|
15| // ===========================
16| // Node File Header Record
17| // ===========================
18| class FileHeader    {
19|     NodeNbr deletednode;            // first deleted node
20|     NodeNbr highestnode;            // highest assigned node
21|     friend class NodeFile;
22|     FileHeader() { deletednode = highestnode = 0; }
23| };
24|
25| // ===========================
26| // Node File Header Class
27| // ===========================
28| class NodeFile  {
29|     FileHeader header;
30|     FileHeader origheader;
```

```
31|     fstream nfile;
32|     bool newfile;          // true if building new node file
33| public:
34|     NodeFile(const string& filename) throw (BadFileOpen);
35|     virtual ~NodeFile();
36|     void SetDeletedNode(NodeNbr node)
37|         { header.deletednode = node; }
38|     NodeNbr DeletedNode() const
39|         { return header.deletednode; }
40|     void SetHighestNode(NodeNbr node)
41|         { header.highestnode = node; }
42|     NodeNbr HighestNode() const
43|         { return header.highestnode; }
44|     NodeNbr NewNode();
45|     void ReadData(void *buf,
46|             unsigned short siz, long wh = -1)
47|                 throw (FileReadError);
48|     void WriteData(const void *buf,
49|             unsigned short siz, long wh = -1)
50|                 throw (FileWriteError);
51|     void Seek(streampos offset, ios::seek_dir dir = ios::beg)
52|         { nfile.seekg(offset,dir); nfile.seekp(offset,dir); }
53|     streampos FilePosition()
54|         { return nfile.tellg(); }
55|     bool NewFile() const
56|         { return newfile; }
57|     void ResetNewFile()
58|         { newfile = false; }
59| };
60|
61| // ============================
62| // Node Record
63| // ============================
64| class Node  {
65|     NodeNbr nextnode;
66|     void CloseNode();
67| protected:
68|     NodeFile *owner;
```

```
69|     NodeNbr nodenbr;     // current node number
70|     bool nodechanged;    // true if the node changed
71|     bool deletenode;     // true if the node is being deleted
72| public:
73|     Node(NodeFile *hd = 0, NodeNbr node = 0);
74|     virtual ~Node();
75|     Node& operator=(Node& node);
76|     void SetNextNode(NodeNbr node)
77|         { nextnode = node; MarkNodeChanged(); }
78|     NodeNbr NextNode() const
79|         { return nextnode; }
80|     void SetNodeNbr(NodeNbr node)
81|         { nodenbr = node; }
82|     NodeNbr GetNodeNbr() const
83|         { return nodenbr; }
84|     void MarkNodeDeleted()
85|         { deletenode = true; }
86|     void MarkNodeChanged()
87|         { nodechanged = true; }
88|     bool NodeChanged() const
89|         { return nodechanged; }
90|     long NodeAddress();
91|     virtual short int NodeHeaderSize() const
92|         { return sizeof(NodeNbr); }
93| };
94|
95| #endif
```

LISTING C.16 NODE.CPP

```
1| // ----------- node.cpp
2|
3| // ================================================
4| // Parody Node and NodeFile class member functions
5| // ================================================
6|
7| #include <io.h>
8|
```

```
 9| #include "parody.h"
10|
11| // -------- construct a node file
12| NodeFile::NodeFile(const string& filename) throw (BadFileOpen)
13| {
14|     newfile = access(filename.c_str(), 0) != 0;
15|     // ---- open the file
16|     nfile.open(filename.c_str(),
17|             ios::in | ios::out | ios::binary);
18|     if (nfile.fail())
19|         throw BadFileOpen();
20|     if (!newfile)
21|         // ---- an existing file, read the header
22|         ReadData(&header, sizeof header);
23|     else
24|         // ---- creating the file, write the empty header
25|         WriteData(&header, sizeof header);
26|     origheader = header;
27| }
28|
29| NodeFile::~NodeFile()
30| {
31|     if (header.deletednode != origheader.deletednode ||
32|             header.highestnode != origheader.highestnode)    {
33|         // ---- the file header has changed
34|         WriteData(&header, sizeof header, 0);
35|     }
36|     nfile.close();
37| }
38|
39| void NodeFile::ReadData(void *buf,
40|             unsigned short siz, long wh) throw (FileReadError)
41| {
42|     if (wh != -1)
43|         nfile.seekg(wh);
44|     nfile.read(reinterpret_cast<char*>(buf), siz);
45|     if (nfile.fail() || nfile.eof())    {
46|         nfile.clear();
```

```
47|            throw FileReadError();
48|      }
49|      nfile.seekp(nfile.tellg());
50| }
51|
52| void NodeFile::WriteData(const void *buf,
53|             unsigned short siz, long wh) throw (FileWriteError)
54| {
55|     if (wh != -1)
56|         nfile.seekp(wh);
57|     nfile.write(reinterpret_cast<const char*>(buf), siz);
58|     if (nfile.fail())   {
59|         nfile.clear();
60|         throw FileWriteError();
61|     }
62|     nfile.seekg(nfile.tellp());
63| }
64|
65| // ------- appropriate a new node
66| NodeNbr NodeFile::NewNode()
67| {
68|     NodeNbr newnode;
69|     if (header.deletednode) {
70|         newnode = header.deletednode;
71|         Node node(this, newnode);
72|         header.deletednode = node.NextNode();
73|         node.SetNextNode(0);
74|     }
75|     else
76|         newnode = ++header.highestnode;
77|     return newnode;
78| }
79|
80| // ----------- construct a new node
81| Node::Node(NodeFile *hd, NodeNbr node)
82| {
83|     nextnode = 0;
84|     nodechanged = deletenode = false;
```

```
 85|     nodenbr = node;
 86|     owner = hd;
 87|     if (nodenbr)    {
 88|         long nad = NodeAddress();
 89|         // ------- read the header
 90|         try {
 91|             owner->ReadData(&nextnode, sizeof nextnode, nad);
 92|         }
 93|         catch (FileReadError)   {
 94|             // ----- appending a new node
 95|             owner->WriteData(&nextnode, sizeof nextnode, nad);
 96|         }
 97|     }
 98| }
 99|
100| // ----- close a node
101| void Node::CloseNode()
102| {
103|     if (owner && nodenbr && (nodechanged || deletenode))    {
104|         if (deletenode) {
105|             nextnode = owner->DeletedNode();
106|             owner->SetDeletedNode(nodenbr);
107|         }
108|         long nad = NodeAddress();
109|         // ------- write the header
110|         owner->WriteData(&nextnode, sizeof nextnode, nad);
111|         if (deletenode) {
112|             // ------ zero fill the deleted node
113|             char fill[nodedatalength];
114|             memset(fill, 0, nodedatalength);
115|             fill[0] = -1;   // mark the node deleted
116|             owner->WriteData(fill, nodedatalength);
117|         }
118|     }
119| }
120|
121| // ------- assignment operator
122| Node& Node::operator=(Node& node)
```

```
123|  {
124|      CloseNode();
125|      nextnode = node.nextnode;
126|      owner = node.owner;
127|      nodenbr = node.nodenbr;
128|      nodechanged = node.nodechanged;
129|      deletenode = node.deletenode;
130|      return *this;
131|  }
132|
133|  // ------- destroy the node
134|  Node::~Node()
135|  {
136|      CloseNode();
137|  }
138|
139|  // ---------- compute the disk address of a node
140|  long Node::NodeAddress()
141|  {
142|      long adr = nodenbr-1;
143|      adr *= nodelength;
144|      adr += sizeof(FileHeader);
145|      return adr;
146|  }
```

LISTING C.17 TNODE.CPP

```
 1|  // ------------- tnode.cpp
 2|
 3|  // ==============================
 4|  // B-tree Tnode class
 5|  // ==============================
 6|
 7|  #include "parody.h"
 8|
 9|  TNode::TNode(PdyBtree *bt, NodeNbr nd) :
10|                      Node(&(bt->GetIndexFile()), nd)
11|  {
```

```
12|      btree = bt;
13|      currkey = 0;
14|      IndexFile& nx = btree->GetIndexFile();
15|      long nad = NodeAddress() + Node::NodeHeaderSize();
16|      // ------- read the header
17|      try {
18|          nx.ReadData(&header, sizeof(TNodeHeader), nad);
19|      }
20|      catch (FileReadError)   {
21|          // ----- appending a new node
22|          nx.WriteData(&header, sizeof(TNodeHeader), nad);
23|          return;
24|      }
25|      // ---- reading an existing node, read the keys
26|      for (int i = 0; i < header.keycount; i++)   {
27|          // ---- get memory for and read a key
28|          PdyKey *thiskey = btree->MakeKeyBuffer();
29|          thiskey->ReadKey(nx);
30|
31|          // ---- read the key's file address
32|          NodeNbr fa;
33|          nx.ReadData(&fa, sizeof(NodeNbr));
34|          thiskey->fileaddr = fa;
35|
36|          if (!header.isleaf) {
37|              NodeNbr lnode;
38|              nx.ReadData(&lnode, sizeof(NodeNbr));
39|              thiskey->lowernode = lnode;
40|          }
41|          keys.AppendEntry(thiskey);
42|      }
43| }
44|
45| // -------- write a key to the node's disk record
46| void TNode::WriteBtreeKey(PdyKey *thiskey)
47| {
48|      IndexFile& nx = btree->GetIndexFile();
49|      // -------- write the key value
```

```
50|     thiskey->WriteKey(nx);
51|     // ---- write the key's file address
52|     NodeNbr fa = thiskey->fileaddr;
53|     nx.WriteData(&fa, sizeof(NodeNbr));
54|     if (!header.isleaf) {
55|         // --- write the lower node pointer for non-leaf keys
56|         NodeNbr lnode = thiskey->lowernode;
57|         nx.WriteData(&lnode, sizeof(NodeNbr));
58|     }
59| }
60|
61| TNode::~TNode()
62| {
63|     if (header.keycount == 0)
64|         // ---- this node is to be deleted
65|         deletenode = true;
66|     else    {
67|         IndexFile& nx = btree->GetIndexFile();
68|         if (nodechanged)    {
69|             long nad = NodeAddress() + Node::NodeHeaderSize();
70|             // ------- write the node header
71|             nx.WriteData(&header, sizeof(TNodeHeader), nad);
72|         }
73|         // ------- write the keys
74|         PdyKey *thiskey = keys.FirstEntry();
75|         while (thiskey != 0)    {
76|             if (nodechanged)
77|                 WriteBtreeKey(thiskey);
78|             delete thiskey;
79|             thiskey = keys.NextEntry();
80|         }
81|         if (nodechanged)    {
82|             // ------ pad the node
83|             short int keyspace = header.keycount *
84|                     (btree->GetKeyLength() + sizeof(NodeNbr) +
85|                     (header.isleaf ? 0 : sizeof(NodeNbr)));
86|             int residual = nodedatalength -
87|                     keyspace - sizeof(TNodeHeader);
```

```
 88|              char *fill = new char[residual];
 89|              memset(fill, 0, residual);
 90|              nx.WriteData(fill, residual);
 91|              delete fill;
 92|          }
 93|      }
 94| }
 95|
 96| // ------- assignment operator
 97| TNode& TNode::operator=(TNode& tnode)
 98| {
 99|     PdyKey *thiskey = keys.FirstEntry();
100|     // ---- if receiver has any keys, delete them
101|     while (header.keycount > 0) {
102|         delete thiskey;
103|         --header.keycount;
104|         thiskey = keys.NextEntry();
105|     }
106|     keys.ClearList();
107|     Node::operator=(tnode);
108|     header = tnode.header;
109|     currkey = 0;
110|     // ------- copy the keys
111|     thiskey = tnode.keys.FirstEntry();
112|     while (thiskey != 0)    {
113|         PdyKey *newkey = btree->MakeKeyBuffer();
114|         *newkey = *thiskey;
115|         keys.AppendEntry(newkey);
116|         if (thiskey == tnode.currkey)
117|             currkey = newkey;
118|         thiskey = tnode.keys.NextEntry();
119|     }
120|     return *this;
121| }
122|
123| // -------- compute m value of node
124| short int TNode::m()
125| {
```

```
126|     int keyspace = nodelength - NodeHeaderSize();
127|     int keylen = btree->GetKeyLength();
128|     if (!header.isleaf)
129|         keylen += sizeof(NodeNbr);
130|     return keyspace / keylen;
131| }
132|
133| // ---------- search a node for a match on a key
134| bool TNode::SearchNode(PdyKey *keyvalue)
135| {
136|     currkey = keys.FirstEntry();
137|     while (currkey != 0)     {
138|         if (*currkey > *keyvalue)
139|             break;
140|         if (*currkey == *keyvalue)  {
141|             if (keyvalue->indexno == 0)
142|                 return true;
143|             if (currkey->fileaddr == keyvalue->fileaddr)
144|                 return true;
145|             if (keyvalue->fileaddr == 0)
146|                 return true;
147|             if (currkey->fileaddr > keyvalue->fileaddr)
148|                 break;
149|         }
150|         currkey = keys.NextEntry();
151|     }
152|     return false;
153| }
154|
155| void TNode::Insert(PdyKey *keyvalue)
156| {
157|     // -------- insert the new key
158|     PdyKey *ky = keyvalue->MakeKey();
159|     *ky = *keyvalue;
160|     if (currkey == 0)
161|         keys.AppendEntry(ky);
162|     else
163|         keys.InsertEntry(ky, currkey);
```

```
164|     header.keycount++;
165|     nodechanged = true;
166|     currkey = ky;
167| }
168|
169| // ---- a node "adopts" all its children by telling
170| //      them to point to it as their parent
171| void TNode::Adoption()
172| {
173|     Adopt(header.lowernode);
174|     PdyKey *thiskey = keys.FirstEntry();
175|     for (int i = 0; i < header.keycount; i++)   {
176|         Adopt(thiskey->lowernode);
177|         thiskey = keys.NextEntry();
178|     }
179| }
180|
181| // --- adopt a child node
182| void TNode::Adopt(NodeNbr node)
183| {
184|     if (node)   {
185|         TNode nd(btree, node);
186|         nd.header.parent = nodenbr;
187|         nd.nodechanged = true;
188|     }
189| }
190|
191| // ---- redistribute keys among two sibling nodes
192| bool TNode::Redistribute(NodeNbr sib)
193| {
194|     if (sib == 0)
195|         return false;
196|     TNode sibling(btree, sib);
197|
198|     if (sibling.header.parent != header.parent)
199|         return false;
200|
201|     int totkeys = header.keycount + sibling.header.keycount;
```

```
202|    if (totkeys >= m() * 2)
203|        return false;
204|
205|    // ---- assign left and right associations
206|    TNode *left, *right;
207|    if (sib == header.leftsibling)  {
208|        right = this;
209|        left = &sibling;
210|    }
211|    else    {
212|        right = &sibling;
213|        left = this;
214|    }
215|    // ------- compute number of keys to be in left node
216|    int leftct =
217|        (left->header.keycount + right->header.keycount) / 2;
218|    // ------- if no redistribution would occur
219|    if (leftct == left->header.keycount)
220|        return false;
221|    // ------- compute number of keys to be in right node
222|    int rightct =
223|        (left->header.keycount+right->header.keycount)-leftct;
224|    // ------- get the parent
225|    TNode parent(btree, left->header.parent);
226|    // --- position parent's currkey
227|    //     to one that points to siblings
228|    parent.SearchNode(left->keys.FirstEntry());
229|    // ----- will move keys from left to right or right to
230|    //       left depending on which node has the greater
231|    //       number of keys to start with.
232|    if (left->header.keycount < right->header.keycount) {
233|        // ----- moving keys from right to left
234|        int mvkeys = right->header.keycount - rightct - 1;
235|        // ----- move key from parent to end of left node
236|        left->currkey = parent.currkey;
237|        parent.currkey = parent.keys.NextEntry(parent.currkey);
238|        // ---- remove parent key from its list
239|        parent.keys.RemoveEntry(left->currkey);
```

```
240|          // ---- put it in left node's list
241|          left->keys.AppendEntry(left->currkey);
242|
243|          if (!left->header.isleaf)
244|              left->currkey->lowernode = right->header.lowernode;
245|          // --- point to the keys to move
246|          //     (at front of right node)
247|          PdyKey *movekey = right->keys.FirstEntry();
248|          // ---- move keys from right to left node
249|          for (int i = 0; i < mvkeys; i++)    {
250|              PdyKey *nkey = right->keys.NextEntry(movekey);
251|              right->keys.RemoveEntry(movekey);
252|              left->keys.AppendEntry(movekey);
253|              movekey = nkey;
254|          }
255|          // --- move separating key from right node to parent
256|          right->keys.RemoveEntry(movekey);
257|          parent.keys.InsertEntry(movekey, parent.currkey);
258|          if (!right->header.isleaf)
259|              right->header.lowernode = movekey->lowernode;
260|          movekey->lowernode = right->nodenbr;
261|          right->header.keycount = rightct;
262|          left->header.keycount  = leftct;
263|          if (!left->header.isleaf)
264|              left->Adoption();
265|      }
266|  else    {
267|          // -------- moving from left to right
268|          int mvkeys = left->header.keycount - leftct - 1;
269|          // ----- move key from parent to right node
270|          right->currkey = parent.currkey;
271|          parent.currkey = parent.keys.NextEntry(parent.currkey);
272|          // --- remove parent key from its list
273|          parent.keys.RemoveEntry(right->currkey);
274|          // ---- put it in right node's list
275|          right->keys.InsertEntry(right->currkey,
276|                              right->keys.FirstEntry());
277|          if (!right->header.isleaf)
278|              right->currkey->lowernode=right->header.lowernode;
```

```
279|            // ----- locate the first key to move in the left node
280|            PdyKey *movekey = left->keys.FindEntry(leftct);
281|            // ---- remember the key after the one being moved up
282|            PdyKey *nkey = left->keys.NextEntry(movekey);
283|            // ----- move key from left node up to parent
284|            left->keys.RemoveEntry(movekey);
285|            parent.keys.InsertEntry(movekey, parent.currkey);
286|
287|            right->header.lowernode = movekey->lowernode;
288|            movekey->lowernode = right->nodenbr;
289|            movekey = nkey;
290|            // --- move keys from the left node to the right node
291|            PdyKey *inskey = right->keys.FirstEntry();
292|            for (int i = 0; i < mvkeys; i++)    {
293|                PdyKey *nkey = left->keys.NextEntry(movekey);
294|                left->keys.RemoveEntry(movekey);
295|                right->keys.InsertEntry(movekey, inskey);
296|                movekey = nkey;
297|            }
298|            right->header.keycount = rightct;
299|            left->header.keycount  = leftct;
300|            if (!right->header.isleaf)
301|                right->Adoption();
302|        }
303|    nodechanged =
304|    sibling.nodechanged =
305|    parent.nodechanged = true;
306|    return true;
307| }
308|
309| // ------ implode the keys of two sibling nodes
310| bool TNode::Implode(TNode& right)
311| {
312|     int totkeys = right.header.keycount+header.keycount;
313|     if (totkeys >= m() ||
314|             right.header.parent != header.parent)
315|         return false;
316|     nodechanged = right.nodechanged = true;
317|     header.rightsibling = right.header.rightsibling;
```

```
318|       header.keycount += right.header.keycount+1;
319|       right.header.keycount = 0;
320|       // ---- get the parent of the imploding nodes
321|       TNode parent(btree, header.parent);
322|       parent.nodechanged = true;
323|       // ---- position parent's currkey to
324|       //      key that points to siblings
325|       parent.SearchNode(keys.FirstEntry());
326|       // ---- move the parent's key to the left sibling
327|       parent.keys.RemoveEntry(currkey);
328|       keys.AppendEntry(parent.currkey);
329|       parent.currkey->lowernode = right.header.lowernode;
330|       parent.header.keycount--;
331|       if (parent.header.keycount == 0)
332|           // -- combined the last two leaf nodes into a new root
333|           header.parent = 0;
334|       // -- move the keys from the right sibling into the left
335|       PdyKey *movekey = right.keys.FirstEntry();
336|       while (movekey != 0)     {
337|           PdyKey *nkey = right.keys.NextEntry(movekey);
338|           right.keys.RemoveEntry(movekey);
339|           keys.AppendEntry(movekey);
340|           movekey = nkey;
341|       }
342|       if (header.rightsibling)    {
343|           // - point right sibling of old right to imploded node
344|           TNode farright(btree, header.rightsibling);
345|           farright.header.leftsibling = GetNodeNbr();
346|           farright.nodechanged = true;
347|       }
348|     Adoption();
349|     return true;
350| }
```

LISTING C.18 PAYROLL.H

```
1|  // ---- payroll.h
2|
```

```
 3| #ifndef PAYROLL_H
 4| #define PAYROLL_H
 5|
 6| #include "parody.h"
 7| #include "gui.h"
 8|
 9| class SSN {
10|     long ssn;
11| public:
12|     SSN(long s=0) : ssn(s)
13|         { /* ... */ }
14|     friend ostream& operator<<(ostream&os, const SSN& sn);
15| };
16|
17| const short NameLength = 15;
18|
19| struct PayrollRcd   {
20|     SSN ssn;                  // Social Security Number
21|     char name[NameLength+1]; // Employee name
22|     Date pmtdate;             // Date paid
23|     Money wage;               // Hourly wage
24|     short reghours;           // regular hours worked
25|     short othours;            // overtime hours worked
26|     static void Header(ostream& os = cout);
27|     friend ostream& operator<<(ostream&os,const PayrollRcd&pr);
28| };
29|
30| #endif
```

Listing C.19 PAYROLL.CPP

```
 1| // --- payroll.cpp
 2|
 3| #include <iostream.h>
 4| #include <string.h>
 5| #include "payroll.h"
 6|
 7| GUI *gui;
```

```
 8|
 9| void PayrollRcd::Header(ostream& os)
10| {
11|     os <<
12|         "SSN          Name              Date     Wage   Reg  OT";
13|     os << endl;
14|     os <<
15|         "----------- ---------------- -------- ------- --- ---";
16|     os << endl;
17| }
18|
19| ostream& operator<<(ostream&os, const PayrollRcd& pr)
20| {
21|     os << pr.ssn;
22|     os << ' ';
23|     os.width(NameLength);
24|     os.setf(ios::left);
25|     os << pr.name;
26|     os << ' ';
27|     os << pr.pmtdate;
28|     os << ' ';
29|     os << pr.wage;
30|     os << "  ";
31|     os.width(2);
32|     os.setf(ios::right);
33|     os << pr.reghours;
34|     os << "  ";
35|     os.width(2);
36|     os << pr.othours;
37|     os << endl;
38|     return os;
39| }
40|
41| ostream& operator<<(ostream&os, const SSN& sn)
42| {
43|     os << sn.ssn/1000000 << '-' <<
44|         (sn.ssn%1000000)/10000 << '-' << sn.ssn%10000;
45|     return os;
```

```
46|  }
47|
48|  void AddRecord();
49|  void ListRecords();
50|
51|  int main()
52|  {
53|      gui = new GUI;
54|      Parody *payroll = new Parody("PAYROLL");
55|
56|      ScreenMenu("Payroll",
57|                      "Add record",   AddRecord,
58|                      "List records", ListRecords,
59|                      NULL).Execute();
60|
61|      gui->ClearScreen();
62|      delete payroll;
63|      delete gui;
64|      return 0;
65|  }
66|
67|  void AddRecord()
68|  {
69|      PayrollRcd pr;
70|      long ssn;
71|      gui->UserInput(&ssn,         "SSN (nnnnnnnnn)");
72|      pr.ssn = ssn;
73|      string name;
74|      gui->UserInput(&name,        "Name              ", NameLength);
75|      strncpy(pr.name, name.c_str(), NameLength);
76|      pr.name[NameLength] = '\0';
77|      gui->UserInput(&pr.pmtdate, "Date  ");
78|      gui->UserInput(&pr.wage,    "Wage            ");
79|      gui->UserInput(&pr.reghours, "Regular Hours  ");
80|      gui->UserInput(&pr.othours,  "Overtime Hours ");
81|      PayrollRcd::Header();
82|      cout << pr;
83|      if (gui->YesNo("Add record"))   {
```

```
84|              PersistentObject<PayrollRcd> ppr(pr);
85|              ppr.AddObject();
86|      }
87| }
88|
89| void ListRecords()
90| {
91|      PayrollRcd::Header();
92|      PersistentObject<PayrollRcd> ppr;
93|      ppr.FirstObject();
94|      while (ppr.ObjectExists())  {
95|          cout << ppr.Obj;
96|          ppr.NextObject();
97|      }
98|      gui->AnyKey();
99| }
```

LISTING C.20 LIFE.CPP

```
 1| // --------------- life.cpp
 2|
 3| // ==========================================
 4| // The Game of Life - a simulation
 5| // ==========================================
 6|
 7| #include <iostream.h>
 8| #include <strstrea.h>
 9| #include <iomanip.h>
10| #include <ctype.h>
11| #include "parody.h"
12| #include "gui.h"
13|
14| // ------- dimensions of the Life world
15| const short HT = SCREENHEIGHT-1;
16| const short WD = SCREENWIDTH;
17|
18| const short keylen = 6; // length of the name string key
19| const char Pop = 2;     // the populated display character
```

```
20|
21| // ----- collection of neighboring cells
22| class Life : public Persistent {
23|     Key<string> name;
24|     unsigned char world[WD][HT];
25|     short generation;
26|     bool alive;
27|     short popcount;
28|     static short Rules[2][9];
29|     short CountNeighbors(short x, short y) const;
30|     void Read();
31|     void Write();
32| public:
33|     Life(const string& nm = string('\0', keylen));
34|     ~Life()
35|         { SaveObject(); }
36|     void Generation();
37|     bool isAlive() const
38|         { return alive; }
39|     void Populate(short x, short y);
40|     void DePopulate(short x, short y);
41|     bool isPopulated(short x, short y) const
42|         { return world[x][y]; }
43|     void SetName(const string& nm)
44|         { name.SetKeyValue(nm); }
45|     string Name()
46|         { return name.KeyValue(); }
47| };
48|
49| GUI *gui;
50|
51| // ------ read the persistent Life object
52| void Life::Read()
53| {
54|     string nm;
55|     ReadObject(nm);
56|     name.SetKeyValue(nm);
57|     short ct, x, y;
```

```
58|      ReadObject(ct);
59|      while (ct--)    {
60|          ReadObject(x);
61|          ReadObject(y);
62|          Populate(x,y);
63|      }
64| }
65|
66| // ------ write the persistent Life object
67| void Life::Write()
68| {
69|      WriteObject(name.KeyValue());
70|      WriteObject(popcount);
71|      for (short x = 0; x < WD; x++)  {
72|          for (short y = 0; y < HT; y++)  {
73|              if (world[x][y])    {
74|                  WriteObject(x);
75|                  WriteObject(y);
76|              }
77|          }
78|      }
79| }
80|
81| // ------ rules for cell survival
82| short Life::Rules[2][9] = {
83|      // --- cell is unpopulated
84|      {0,0,0,2,0,0,0,0,0},
85|      // --- cell is populated
86|      {0,0,2,2,0,0,0,0,0}
87| };
88|
89| Life::Life(const string& nm) : name(nm)
90| {
91|      for (short x = 0; x < WD; x++)
92|          for (short y = 0; y < HT; y++)
93|              world[x][y] = 0;
94|      alive = false;
95|      generation = 0;
```

```
 96|     popcount = 0;
 97|     LoadObject();
 98| }
 99|
100| // ---------- populate a cell
101| void Life::Populate(short x, short y)
102| {
103|     if (!world[x][y])
104|         popcount++;
105|     world[x][y] = 1;
106|     alive = true;
107| }
108|
109| // ---------- depopulate a cell
110| void Life::DePopulate(short x, short y)
111| {
112|     if (world[x][y])
113|         --popcount;
114|     world[x][y] = 0;
115| }
116|
117| // ------- count a cell's neighbors
118| short Life::CountNeighbors(short x, short y) const
119| {
120|     short x1, y1, ct = 0;
121|     // ---- count 3 rows
122|     for (y1 = y-1; y1 < y+2; y1++)
123|         // ---- count 3 columns
124|         for (x1 = x-1; x1 < x+2; x1++)
125|             // --- don't count self
126|             if (!(y1 == y && x1 == x))  {
127|                 // --- wrap around margins
128|                 int x2 = x1, y2 = y1;
129|                 if (x2 == -1)
130|                     x2 = WD-1;
131|                 else if (x2 == WD)
132|                     x2 = 0;
133|                 if (y2 == -1)
```

```
134|                         y2 = HT-1;
135|                     else if (y2 == HT)
136|                         y2 = 0;
137|                     // --- count populated neighbor cells
138|                     if ((world[x2][y2]) & 1)
139|                         ct++;
140|                 }
141|     return ct;
142| }
143|
144| // -------- evolve one generation
145| void Life::Generation()
146| {
147|     register unsigned char *cell;
148|     short x, y;
149|     gui->SetCursor(0, HT);
150|     char st[81];
151|     strstream stat(st, 80, ios::out);
152|     stat << "Generation: " << generation++ << '\0';
153|     gui->StatusLine(stat.str());
154|     for (cell = world[0], x = 0; x < WD; x++)
155|         for (y = 0; y < HT; y++, cell++)
156|             *cell |= Rules[*cell][CountNeighbors(x, y)];
157|     alive = false;
158|     popcount = 0;
159|     for (cell = world[0], x = 0; x < WD; x++)   {
160|         for (y = 0; y < HT; y++, cell++)     {
161|             switch (*cell)  {
162|                 case 1:
163|                     gui->WriteChar(' ', x, y);
164|                     *cell = 0;
165|                     break;
166|                 case 2:
167|                     gui->WriteChar(Pop, x, y);
168|                 case 3:
169|                     if (*cell == 2)
170|                         alive = true;
171|                     *cell = 1;
```

```
172|                          popcount++;
173|                       break;
174|                  default:
175|                       break;
176|              }
177|           }
178|        }
179| }
180|
181| void ReadLife(const string& nm);
182| void BuildLife();
183| void ChangeLife();
184| void DeleteLife();
185| void ListLives();
186| void DisplayLife();
187| void RunLife();
188| void StepLife();
189| void LoadLife();
190| void SaveLife();
191|
192| // --- always -> current Life object
193| Life *lf;
194|
195| int main(int argc, char *argv[])
196| {
197|     Parody life("LIFE");
198|     gui = new GUI;
199|     if (argc > 1)   {
200|        gui->ClearScreen();
201|        ReadLife(argv[1]);
202|     }
203|     ScreenMenu( "The Game of Life",
204|                 "New",     BuildLife,
205|                 "Change",  ChangeLife,
206|                 "Delete",  DeleteLife,
207|                 "List",    ListLives,
208|                 "Display", DisplayLife,
209|                 "Run",     RunLife,
```

```
210|                        "Step",    StepLife,
211|                        "Load",    LoadLife,
212|                        "Save",    SaveLife,
213|                        NULL).Execute();
214|     gui->ClearScreen();
215|     delete gui;
216|     delete lf;
217|     return 0;
218| }
219|
220| // ------ create a new world
221| void BuildLife()
222| {
223|     delete lf;
224|     lf = new Life;
225|     ChangeLife();
226| }
227|
228| // ----- display the world
229| static void ShowWorld()
230| {
231|     if (lf != 0)
232|         for (short y = 0; y < HT; y++)
233|             for (short x = 0; x < WD; x++)
234|                 if (lf->isPopulated(x, y))
235|                     gui->WriteChar(Pop, x, y);
236| }
237|
238| // ------ change an existing world
239| void ChangeLife()
240| {
241|     short x = 0, y = 0;
242|     unsigned char lastc = 0;
243|     unsigned char c = 0;
244|     ShowWorld();
245|     gui->StatusLine
246|         ("up, down, ->, <-, Spacebar/Enter, Esc");
247|     while (c != ESC)    {
```

```
248|        gui->SetCursor(40, HT);
249|        cout << "x:" << setw(3) << x;
250|        cout << " y:" << setw(3) << y;
251|        cout.flush();
252|        gui->SetCursor(x, y);
253|        c = gui->GetKBChar();
254|        switch (tolower(c)) {
255|            case ' ':
256|            case '\r':
257|                // --- toggle a population
258|                if (!lf->isPopulated(x,y)) {
259|                    lf->Populate(x,y);
260|                    gui->WriteChar(Pop, x, y);
261|                }
262|                else   {
263|                    lf->DePopulate(x,y);
264|                    gui->WriteChar(' ', x, y);
265|                }
266|                gui->PutBack(lastc);
267|                break;
268|            case UPARROW:
269|                // --- up cursor
270|                if (y-- == 0)
271|                    y = HT-1;
272|                lastc = c;
273|                break;
274|            case DOWNARROW:
275|                // --- down cursor
276|                if (++y == HT)
277|                    y = 0;
278|                lastc = c;
279|                break;
280|            case LEFTARROW:
281|                // --- left cursor
282|                if (x-- == 0)
283|                    x = WD-1;
284|                lastc = c;
285|                break;
```

```
286|            case RIGHTARROW:
287|                // --- right cursor
288|                if (++x == WD)
289|                    x = 0;
290|                lastc = c;
291|                break;
292|            default:
293|                break;
294|        }
295|    }
296| }
297|
298| // ------- delete the current life object
299| void DeleteLife()
300| {
301|    if (lf != 0 && lf->ObjectExists()) {
302|        cout << "Current life object: "
303|            << lf->Name() << endl;
304|        if (gui->YesNo("Delete"))   {
305|            lf->DeleteObject();
306|            delete lf;
307|            lf = 0;
308|        }
309|    }
310| }
311|
312| // ---- display names of life worlds
313| void ListLives()
314| {
315|    delete lf;
316|    lf = 0;
317|    cout << "Game of Life Objects" << endl;
318|    cout << "--------------------" << endl;
319|    Life lif;
320|    lif.FirstObject();
321|    while (lif.ObjectExists()) {
322|        cout << "   " << lif.Name() << endl;
323|        lif.NextObject();
```

```
324|     }
325|     gui->AnyKey();
326| }
327|
328| // ----- display the world and wait
329| void DisplayLife()
330| {
331|     ShowWorld();
332|     gui->AnyKey();
333| }
334|
335| // ------ nonstop evolution
336| void RunLife()
337| {
338|     if (lf != 0)    {
339|         ShowWorld();
340|         while (lf->isAlive())    {
341|             if (gui->KBCharWaiting())    {
342|                 char c = gui->GetKBChar();
343|                 if (c == ESC)
344|                     break;
345|             }
346|             lf->Generation();
347|         }
348|     }
349| }
350|
351| // --------- single-step evolution
352| void StepLife()
353| {
354|     if (lf != 0)    {
355|         ShowWorld();
356|         gui->StatusLine("S-tep or Esc");
357|         short c;
358|         while ((c = gui->GetKBChar()) != ESC)
359|             if (tolower(c) == 's')
360|                 lf->Generation();
361|     }
```

```
362|  }
363|
364|  // -------- retrieve a persistent Life object
365|  void ReadLife(const string& nm)
366|  {
367|      delete lf;
368|      string name(nm);
369|      name.resize(keylen);
370|      lf = new Life(name);
371|      if (!lf->ObjectExists())
372|          gui->Error("Invalid name");
373|      else
374|          DisplayLife();
375|  }
376|
377|  const char *nameprompt = "Enter Life world name";
378|
379|  // --- retrieve persistent Life object from user input
380|  void LoadLife()
381|  {
382|      string nm;
383|      gui->UserInput(&nm, nameprompt, keylen);
384|      ReadLife(nm);
385|  }
386|
387|  // -------- store a persistent Life object
388|  void SaveLife()
389|  {
390|      if (lf != 0)    {
391|          string svnm = lf->Name();
392|          if (lf->ObjectExists())
393|              lf->ChangeObject();
394|          else    {
395|              string nm(svnm);
396|              gui->UserInput(&nm, nameprompt, keylen);
397|              lf->SetName(nm);
398|              if (lf->AddObject())
399|                  svnm = nm;
400|              else    {
```

```
401|                    lf->SetName(svnm);
402|                    gui->Error("Name already used");
403|                    return;
404|               }
405|
406|          }
407|          // --- force output now
408|          lf->SaveObject();
409|          gui->AnyKey();
410|     }
411| }
```

LISTING C.21 PERSONEL.H

```
 1| // ------------ personel.h
 2|
 3| #ifndef PERSONEL_H
 4| #define PERSONEL_H
 5|
 6| typedef short int EmployeeNumber;
 7| typedef short int DepartmentNumber;
 8| typedef short int ProjectNumber;
 9|
10| #include "parody.h"
11| #include "gui.h"
12| #include "dept.h"
13| #include "employee.h"
14| #include "project.h"
15| #include "assign.h"
16| #include "manager.h"
17|
18| extern GUI *gui;
19|
20| #endif
```

LISTING C.22 PERSONEL.CPP

```
 1| // ------------ personel.cpp
 2|
```

```
 3| // ---------------------------------------------------------
 4| // A Personnel Application
 5| // using PARODY,
 6| // the Persistent, (Almost) Relational Object Database
 7| // management system
 8| // ---------------------------------------------------------
 9|
10| #include "personel.h"
11|
12| // ----------- Employee prototypes
13| void QueryEmployees();
14| void AddEmployee();
15| void ChangeEmployee();
16| void DeleteEmployee();
17| void ListEmployees();
18| void ListEmployeeProjects();
19|
20| // ----------- Department prototypes
21| void QueryDepartments();
22| void AddDepartment();
23| void ChangeDepartment();
24| void DeleteDepartment();
25| void ListDepartments();
26| void ListDepartmentEmployees();
27| void ListAllDepartments();
28| void ListOneDepartment();
29|
30| // ---------- Project prototypes
31| void QueryProjects();
32| void AddProject();
33| void ChangeProject();
34| void DeleteProject();
35| void ListProjects();
36| void ListProjectEmployees();
37|
38| // ---------- Assignment prototypes
39| void QueryAssignments();
40| void AddAssignment();
```

```
41|   void ChangeAssignment();
42|   void DeleteAssignment();
43|   void ListAssignments();
44|   void PostAssignments();
45|
46|   // ---------- Manager prototypes
47|   void QueryManagers();
48|   void AddManager();
49|   void ListManagers();
50|
51|   // ====================================
52|   // Personnel Database
53|   // The Employee, Department, Project, and Assignment
54|   // classes depend on this personnel object.
55|   // ====================================
56|
57|   GUI *gui;
58|
59|   #include <malloc.h>
60|
61|   int main()
62|   {
63|       gui = new GUI;
64|       Parody *personnel = new Parody("PERSONEL");
65|       // ---- empty objects to declare relationships
66|       {
67|           Employee empl;
68|           Department dept;
69|           Project proj;
70|           Assignment assgn;
71|           Manager mgr;
72|       }
73|
74|       ScreenMenu( "Personnel Input",
75|                   "Employees",   QueryEmployees,
76|                   "Departments", QueryDepartments,
77|                   "Projects",    QueryProjects,
78|                   "Assignments", QueryAssignments,
```

```
79|                          "Managers",    QueryManagers,
80|                          NULL).Execute();
81|     gui->ClearScreen();
82|     delete personnel;
83|     delete gui;
84|     return 0;
85| }
86|
87| // -----------------------
88| // Employee processing
89| // -----------------------
90| void QueryEmployees()
91| {
92|     ScreenMenu( "Employees",
93|                     "Add",      AddEmployee,
94|                     "Change",   ChangeEmployee,
95|                     "Delete",   DeleteEmployee,
96|                     "List",     ListEmployees,
97|                     "Projects", ListEmployeeProjects,
98|                     NULL).Execute();
99| }
100|
101| // ----------- add employee objects
102| void AddEmployee()
103| {
104|     Employee *employee;
105|     while ((employee = Employee::Get()) != 0)    {
106|         if (employee->ObjectExists())    {
107|             Employee::Header();
108|             cout << *employee;
109|             gui->Error("Employee already on file");
110|         }
111|         else    {
112|             employee->Input();
113|             if (!employee->AddObject())
114|                 gui->Error("Add disallowed");
115|         }
116|         delete employee;
```

```
117|     }
118| }
119|
120| // ----------- change an existing employee object
121| void ChangeEmployee()
122| {
123|     Employee *employee = Employee::GetExisting();
124|     if (employee != 0)   {
125|         employee->SelectChange();
126|         delete employee;
127|     }
128| }
129|
130| // ----------- delete an existing employee object
131| void DeleteEmployee()
132| {
133|     Employee *employee = Employee::GetExisting();
134|     if (employee != 0)   {
135|         if (gui->YesNo("Delete the employee record"))
136|             if (!employee->DeleteObject())
137|                 gui->Error("Delete disallowed");
138|         delete employee;
139|     }
140| }
141|
142| // -------- list all the employees
143| void ListEmployees()
144| {
145|     Employee empl;
146|     empl.FirstObject();
147|     Employee::Header();
148|     while (empl.ObjectExists())     {
149|         cout << empl;
150|         empl.NextObject();
151|     }
152|     gui->AnyKey();
153| }
154|
```

```
155|   // ------- list the projects an employee is assigned to
156|   void ListEmployeeProjects()
157|   {
158|       Employee *employee = Employee::GetExisting();
159|       if (employee != 0)   {
160|           Project::Header();
161|           Assignment assgn;
162|           assgn.SetEmplNo(employee->EmplNo());
163|           assgn.FindObject(&assgn.EmplNoKey());
164|           while (assgn.ObjectExists() &&
165|                       assgn.EmplNo() == employee->EmplNo())   {
166|               Project proj(assgn.ProjNo());
167|               if (proj.ObjectExists())
168|                   cout << proj;
169|               assgn.NextObject(&assgn.EmplNoKey());
170|           }
171|           delete employee;
172|       }
173|       gui->AnyKey();
174|   }
175|
176|   // -----------------------
177|   // Department processing
178|   // -----------------------
179|   void QueryDepartments()
180|   {
181|       ScreenMenu( "Departments",
182|                       "Add",       AddDepartment,
183|                       "Change",    ChangeDepartment,
184|                       "Delete",    DeleteDepartment,
185|                       "List",      ListDepartments,
186|                       "Employees", ListDepartmentEmployees,
187|                       NULL).Execute();
188|   }
189|
190|   // ---------- add department objects
191|   void AddDepartment()
192|   {
```

```
193|     Department *department;
194|     while ((department = Department::Get()) != 0)        {
195|         if (department->ObjectExists()) {
196|             Department::Header();
197|             cout << *department;
198|             gui->Error("Department already on file");
199|         }
200|         else    {
201|             department->Input();
202|             if (!department->AddObject())
203|                 gui->Error("Add disallowed");
204|         }
205|         delete department;
206|     }
207| }
208|
209| // ---------- change a department object
210| void ChangeDepartment()
211| {
212|     Department *department = Department::GetExisting();
213|     if (department != 0) {
214|         department->SelectChange();
215|         delete department;
216|     }
217| }
218|
219| // ---------- delete a department object
220| void DeleteDepartment()
221| {
222|     Department *department = Department::GetExisting();
223|     if (department != 0) {
224|         if (gui->YesNo("Delete the department record"))
225|             if (!department->DeleteObject())
226|                 gui->Error("Delete disallowed");
227|         delete department;
228|     }
229| }
230|
```

```
231|  // ---------- list the departments
232|  void ListDepartments()
233|  {
234|      Department dept;
235|      dept.FirstObject();
236|      Department::Header();
237|      while (dept.ObjectExists())      {
238|          cout << dept;
239|          dept.NextObject();
240|      }
241|      gui->AnyKey();
242|  }
243|
244|  // --------- list employees in departments
245|  void ListDepartmentEmployees()
246|  {
247|      ScreenMenu( "List Employees by Department",
248|                    "All departments", ListAllDepartments,
249|                    "One department",  ListOneDepartment,
250|                    NULL).Execute();
251|      gui->AnyKey();
252|  }
253|
254|  // ------- list employees in all departments
255|  void ListAllDepartments()
256|  {
257|      Employee empl;
258|      Employee::Header();
259|      empl.FirstObject(empl.DeptKey());
260|      while (empl.ObjectExists())      {
261|          cout << empl;
262|          empl.NextObject(empl.DeptKey());
263|      }
264|      gui->AnyKey();
265|  }
266|
267|  // ------- list employees in a selected department
268|  void ListOneDepartment()
```

```
269|  {
270|      Department *department;
271|      while ((department=Department::GetExisting()) != 0) {
272|          int deptno = department->DeptNo();
273|          Employee::Header();
274|          Employee empl;
275|          empl.SetDeptNo(deptno);
276|          empl.FindObject(empl.DeptKey());
277|          while (empl.ObjectExists() && empl.DeptNo()==deptno) {
278|              cout << empl;
279|              empl.NextObject(empl.DeptKey());
280|          }
281|          delete department;
282|      }
283|      gui->AnyKey();
284|  }
285|
286|  // -----------------------
287|  // Project processing
288|  // -----------------------
289|  void QueryProjects()
290|  {
291|      ScreenMenu( "Projects",
292|                      "Add",        AddProject,
293|                      "Change",     ChangeProject,
294|                      "Delete",     DeleteProject,
295|                      "List",       ListProjects,
296|                      "Employees",  ListProjectEmployees,
297|                      NULL).Execute();
298|  }
299|
300|  // ---------- a project objects
301|  void AddProject()
302|  {
303|      Project *project;
304|      while ((project = Project::Get()) != 0)        {
305|          if (project->ObjectExists())      {
306|              Project::Header();
```

```
307|            cout << *project;
308|            gui->Error("Project already on file");
309|        }
310|    else    {
311|            project->Input();
312|            if (!project->AddObject())
313|                gui->Error("Add disallowed");
314|        }
315|        delete project;
316|    }
317| }
318|
319| // -------- change a project object
320| void ChangeProject()
321| {
322|    Project *project = Project::GetExisting();
323|    if (project != 0)    {
324|        project->SelectChange();
325|        delete project;
326|    }
327| }
328|
329| // -------- delete a project object
330| void DeleteProject()
331| {
332|    Project *project = Project::GetExisting();
333|    if (project != 0)    {
334|        if (gui->YesNo("Delete the project record"))
335|            if (!project->DeleteObject())
336|                gui->Error("Delete disallowed");
337|        delete project;
338|    }
339| }
340|
341| // ------------- list the project objects
342| void ListProjects()
343| {
344|    Project proj;
```

```
345|    proj.FirstObject();
346|    Project::Header();
347|    while (proj.ObjectExists())    {
348|        cout << proj;
349|        proj.NextObject();
350|    }
351|    gui->AnyKey();
352| }
353|
354| // -------- list employees assigned to a project
355| void ListProjectEmployees()
356| {
357|    Project *project = Project::GetExisting();
358|    if (project != 0)    {
359|        Employee::Header();
360|        Assignment assgn;
361|        assgn.SetProjNo(project->ProjNo());
362|        assgn.FindObject(&assgn.ProjNoKey());
363|        while (assgn.ObjectExists() &&
364|                  assgn.ProjNo() == project->ProjNo())    {
365|            Employee empl(assgn.EmplNo());
366|            if (empl.ObjectExists())
367|                cout << empl;
368|            assgn.NextObject(&assgn.ProjNoKey());
369|        }
370|        delete project;
371|    }
372|    gui->AnyKey();
373| }
374|
375|
376| // ----------------------
377| // Assignments
378| // The Assignments class is a "connector" file
379| // ----------------------
380| void QueryAssignments()
381| {
382|    ScreenMenu( "Assignments",
```

```
383|                    "Add",         AddAssignment,
384|                    "Change",      ChangeAssignment,
385|                    "Delete",      DeleteAssignment,
386|                    "List",        ListAssignments,
387|                    "Post hours",  PostAssignments,
388|                    NULL).Execute();
389| }
390|
391| // ---------- add an assignment object
392| void AddAssignment()
393| {
394|     for (;;)         {
395|         Assignment *assignment = Assignment::Get();
396|         if (assignment == 0)
397|             break;
398|         if (assignment->ObjectExists()) {
399|             Assignment::Header();
400|             assignment->DetailDisplay();
401|             gui->Error("Assignment already on file");
402|         }
403|         else    {
404|             assignment->Input();
405|             assignment->AddObject();
406|         }
407|         delete assignment;
408|     }
409| }
410|
411| // ----------- change an assignment object
412| void ChangeAssignment()
413| {
414|     Assignment *assignment = Assignment::GetExisting();
415|     if (assignment != 0) {
416|         assignment->Input();
417|         delete assignment;
418|     }
419| }
420|
```

```
421|  // ---------- delete an assignment object
422|  void DeleteAssignment()
423|  {
424|      Assignment *assignment = Assignment::GetExisting();
425|      if (assignment != 0) {
426|          if (gui->YesNo("Delete the assignment"))
427|              assignment->DeleteObject();
428|          delete assignment;
429|      }
430|  }
431|
432|  // ----- post hours expended by the employee to the project
433|  void PostAssignments()
434|  {
435|      Assignment *assignment = Assignment::GetExisting();
436|      if (assignment != 0) {
437|          short int hours;
438|          gui->UserInput(&hours, "Hours expended");
439|          if (hours != 0) {
440|              assignment->AddHours(hours);
441|              Project project(assignment->ProjNo());
442|              if (project.ObjectExists())
443|                  project.AddHours(hours);
444|          }
445|          delete assignment;
446|      }
447|  }
448|
449|  // -------- list the assignment objects
450|  void ListAssignments()
451|  {
452|      Assignment assgn;
453|      assgn.FirstObject();
454|      Assignment::Header();
455|      while (assgn.ObjectExists())    {
456|          assgn.DetailDisplay();
457|          assgn.NextObject();
458|      }
```

```
459|     gui->AnyKey();
460| }
461|
462| // ----------------------
463| // Managers
464| // ----------------------
465|
466| void QueryManagers()
467| {
468|     ScreenMenu( "Manager Input",
469|                 "Add",  AddManager,
470|                 "List", ListManagers,
471|                 NULL).Execute();
472| }
473|
474| // ------- add manager objects
475| void AddManager()
476| {
477|     Manager *manager;
478|     while ((manager = Manager::Get()) != 0)    {
479|         if (manager->ObjectExists())
480|             gui->Error("Manager already on file");
481|         else    {
482|             manager->Input();
483|             if (!manager->AddObject())
484|                 gui->Error("Add disallowed");
485|         }
486|         delete manager;
487|     }
488| }
489|
490| // ------- list manager objects
491| void ListManagers()
492| {
493|     Manager mgr;
494|     mgr.FirstObject();
495|     Employee::Header();
496|     while (mgr.ObjectExists())    {
```

```
497|         cout << mgr;
498|         mgr.NextObject();
499|     }
500|     gui->AnyKey();
501| }
```

LISTING C.23 EMPLOYEE.H

```
 1| // -------------- employee.h
 2|
 3| #ifndef EMPLOYEE_H
 4| #define EMPLOYEE_H
 5|
 6| #include "parody.h"
 7| #include "dept.h"
 8|
 9| // ==================================
10| // Employee class
11| // ==================================
12| class Employee : public Persistent  {
13|     Key<EmployeeNumber> emplno;
14|     Key<DepartmentNumber> deptno;
15|     string name;
16| protected:
17|     virtual void Read();
18|     virtual void Write();
19| public:
20|     Employee(EmployeeNumber en = 0);
21|     virtual ~Employee();
22|     EmployeeNumber EmplNo() const
23|         { return emplno.KeyValue(); }
24|     DepartmentNumber DeptNo() const
25|         { return deptno.KeyValue(); }
26|     Key<DepartmentNumber> *DeptKey() { return &deptno; }
27|     const string& Name() const
28|         { return name; }
29|     void SetEmplNo(EmployeeNumber en);
30|     void SetName(const string& nm);
```

```
31|      void SetDeptNo(DepartmentNumber dn);
32|      // ----- user interface functions
33|      static void Header(ostream& os = cout);
34|      static Employee *Get();
35|      static Employee *GetExisting();
36|      void Input();
37|      void InputName();
38|      void InputDepartment();
39|      void TryChange();
40|      void SelectChange();
41|      friend ostream& operator<<(ostream&os, const Employee& em);
42| };
43|
44| inline void Employee::SetEmplNo(EmployeeNumber en)
45| {
46|      emplno.KeyValue() = en;
47| }
48|
49| inline void Employee::SetName(const string& nm)
50| {
51|      name = nm;
52|      ChangeObject();
53| }
54|
55| inline void Employee::SetDeptNo(DepartmentNumber dn)
56| {
57|      deptno.KeyValue() = dn;
58|      ChangeObject();
59| }
60|
61| #endif
```

Listing C.24 EMPLOYEE.CPP

```
1| // -------------- employee.cpp
2|
3| #include <iomanip.h>
4| #include "personel.h"
```

```
 5|
 6| Employee::Employee(EmployeeNumber en) : emplno(en), deptno(0)
 7| {
 8|     deptno.Relate(&typeid(Department));
 9|     // --- if class not derived from Employee
10|     if (en != -1)
11|         LoadObject();
12| }
13|
14| Employee::~Employee()
15| {
16|     // --- if class not derived from Employee
17|     if (emplno.KeyValue() != -1)
18|         SaveObject();
19| }
20|
21| // ------- read a persistent employee object
22| void Employee::Read()
23| {
24|     EmployeeNumber emno;
25|     DepartmentNumber dpno;
26|     ReadObject(emno);
27|     emplno.SetKeyValue(emno);
28|     ReadObject(name);
29|     ReadObject(dpno);
30|     deptno.SetKeyValue(dpno);
31| }
32|
33| // ------- write a persistent employee object
34| void Employee::Write()
35| {
36|     WriteObject(emplno.KeyValue());
37|     WriteObject(name);
38|     WriteObject(deptno.KeyValue());
39| }
40|
41| // ---------- display an employee object
42| ostream& operator<<(ostream&os, const Employee& em)
```

```
43|  {
44|      os.width(5);
45|      os << em.emplno.KeyValue();
46|      os.width(0);
47|      os << ' ';
48|      os.setf(ios::left, ios::adjustfield);
49|      os.width(15);
50|      os << em.name.substr(0, 15);
51|      os.width(0);
52|      os.setf(ios::right, ios::adjustfield);
53|      os << ' ';
54|      os.width(5);
55|      os << em.deptno.KeyValue() << endl;
56|      os.width(0);
57|      os.flush();
58|      return os;
59|  }
60|
61|  // ----- try to change an employee object
62|  void Employee::TryChange()
63|  {
64|      if (!ChangeObject())
65|          gui->Error("Change disallowed");
66|  }
67|
68|  // ------- input employee name from user
69|  void Employee::InputName()
70|  {
71|      gui->UserInput(&name, "Name", 25);
72|      if (ObjectExists())
73|          TryChange();
74|  }
75|
76|  // ------- input employee department from user
77|  void Employee::InputDepartment()
78|  {
79|      DepartmentNumber dept;
80|      gui->UserInput(&dept, "Department No");
```

```
 81|        deptno.SetKeyValue(dept);
 82|     if (ObjectExists())
 83|         TryChange();
 84| }
 85|
 86| // -------- employee input
 87| void Employee::Input()
 88| {
 89|     InputName();
 90|     InputDepartment();
 91| }
 92|
 93| static Employee *This;
 94|
 95| static void ChangeName()
 96| {
 97|     This->InputName();
 98| }
 99|
100| static void ChangeDept()
101| {
102|     This->InputDepartment();
103| }
104|
105| // ------- select an employee data member to change
106| void Employee::SelectChange()
107| {
108|     This = this;
109|     OneLineMenu("N-ame, D-epartment",
110|                   ChangeName, ChangeDept).Execute();
111| }
112|
113| // --------- get an existing employee object
114| Employee *Employee::GetExisting()
115| {
116|     Employee *employee = Get();
117|     if (employee != 0)  {
118|         if (employee->ObjectExists())  {
```

```
119|              Header();
120|              cout << *employee;
121|          }
122|          else    {
123|              gui->Error("No such employee on file");
124|              delete employee;
125|              employee = 0;
126|          }
127|      }
128|      return employee;
129| }
130|
131| // --------- get an employee object
132| Employee *Employee::Get()
133| {
134|      EmployeeNumber emplno;
135|      Employee *employee = 0;
136|      gui->UserInput(&emplno,
137|          "Enter employee number (0 to ignore)");
138|      if (emplno != 0)
139|          employee = new Employee(emplno);
140|      return employee;
141| }
142|
143| // ------ display employee object header
144| void Employee::Header(ostream& os)
145| {
146|      os << endl;
147|      os << "Empl# Employee        Dept#" << endl;
148|      os << "----- --------------- -----" << endl;
149|      os.flush();
150| }
151|
152|
```

LISTING C.25 DEPT.H

```
1| // ------------- dept.h
2|
```

```
 3| #ifndef DEPARTMENT_H
 4| #define DEPARTMENT_H
 5|
 6| #include "parody.h"
 7| #include "employee.h"
 8|
 9| // ======================================
10| // Department class
11| // ======================================
12| class Department : public Persistent    {
13|     Key<DepartmentNumber> deptno;
14|     string name;
15|     Key<EmployeeNumber> manager;
16|     void Read();
17|     void Write();
18| public:
19|     Department(DepartmentNumber dn = 0);
20|     ~Department()
21|         { SaveObject(); }
22|     const string& Name() const
23|         { return name; }
24|     DepartmentNumber DeptNo() const
25|         { return deptno.KeyValue(); }
26|     void SetName(string& nm);
27|     void SetManager(EmployeeNumber mgr);
28|     // ----- user interface functions
29|     void Input();
30|     void InputName();
31|     void InputManager();
32|     void TryChange();
33|     void SelectChange();
34|     static Department *Get();
35|     static Department *GetExisting();
36|     static void Header(ostream& os = cout);
37|     friend ostream& operator<<(ostream&os,const Department& dp);
38| };
39|
40| inline void Department::SetName(string& nm)
41| {
```

```
42|        name = nm;
43|        ChangeObject();
44| }
45|
46| inline void Department::SetManager(EmployeeNumber mgr)
47| {
48|        manager.KeyValue() = mgr;
49|        ChangeObject();
50| }
51|
52| #endif
```

LISTING C.26 DEPT.CPP

```
 1| // ------------- dept.cpp
 2|
 3| #include <iomanip.h>
 4| #include "personel.h"
 5|
 6| // ==================================
 7| // Department class
 8| // ==================================
 9| Department::Department(DepartmentNumber dn) :
10|                         deptno(dn), manager(0)
11| {
12|     manager.Relate(&typeid(Employee));
13|     LoadObject();
14| }
15|
16| // ------- read a persistent department object
17| void Department::Read()
18| {
19|     DepartmentNumber dpno;
20|     ReadObject(dpno);
21|     deptno.SetKeyValue(dpno);
22|     ReadObject(name);
23|     EmployeeNumber mgr;
24|     ReadObject(mgr);
```

```
25|     manager.SetKeyValue(mgr);
26| }
27|
28| // ------- write a persistent department object
29| void Department::Write()
30| {
31|     WriteObject(deptno.KeyValue());
32|     WriteObject(name);
33|     WriteObject(manager.KeyValue());
34| }
35|
36| // --------- display department object header
37| void Department::Header(ostream& os)
38| {
39|     os << endl;
40|     os << "Dept# Department      Mgr#" << endl;
41|     os << "----- -------------- -----" << endl;
42|     os.flush();
43| }
44|
45| // --------- display department object
46| ostream& operator<<(ostream&os,const Department& dp)
47| {
48|     os.width(5);
49|     os << dp.deptno.KeyValue();
50|     os.width(0);
51|     os << ' ';
52|     os.setf(ios::left, ios::adjustfield);
53|     os.width(15);
54|     os << dp.name.substr(0, 15);
55|     os.width(0);
56|     os.setf(ios::right, ios::adjustfield);
57|     os << ' ';
58|     os.width(5);
59|     os << dp.manager.KeyValue();
60|     os.width(0);
61|     os << endl;
62|     os.flush();
```

```
63|     return os;
64| }
65|
66| static Department *This;
67|
68| static void ChangeName()
69| {
70|     This->InputName();
71| }
72|
73| static void ChangeMgr()
74| {
75|     This->InputManager();
76| }
77|
78| // ------- select department data member to change
79| void Department::SelectChange()
80| {
81|     This = this;
82|     OneLineMenu("N-ame, M-anager",
83|                 ChangeName, ChangeMgr).Execute();
84| }
85|
86| // -------- read department name from user
87| void Department::InputName()
88| {
89|     gui->UserInput(&name, "Name", 25);
90|     if (ObjectExists())
91|         TryChange();
92| }
93|
94| // -------- read department manager from user
95| void Department::InputManager()
96| {
97|     cout << "Manager:" << endl;
98|     cout.flush();
99|     Employee *mgr = Employee::GetExisting();
100|     if (mgr != 0)   {
```

```
101|            SetManager(mgr->EmplNo());
102|            if (ObjectExists())
103|                TryChange();
104|            delete mgr;
105|        }
106| }
107|
108| // ------- try to change the department object
109| void Department::TryChange()
110| {
111|     if (!ChangeObject())
112|         gui->Error("Change disallowed");
113| }
114|
115| // -------- department object user input
116| void Department::Input()
117| {
118|     InputName();
119|     InputManager();
120| }
121|
122| // -------- get an existing department object
123| Department *Department::GetExisting()
124| {
125|     Department *department = Get();
126|     if (department != 0)    {
127|         if (department->ObjectExists()) {
128|             Header();
129|             cout << *department;
130|         }
131|         else    {
132|             gui->Error("No such department on file");
133|             delete department;
134|             department = 0;
135|         }
136|     }
137|     return department;
138| }
```

```
139|
140| // -------- get a department object
141| Department *Department::Get()
142| {
143|     DepartmentNumber deptno;
144|     Department *department = 0;
145|     gui->UserInput(&deptno,
146|         "Enter department number (0 to ignore)");
147|     if (deptno != 0)
148|         department = new Department(deptno);
149|     return department;
150| }
```

Listing C.27 PROJECT.H

```
 1| // ------------- project.h
 2|
 3| #ifndef PROJECT_H
 4| #define PROJECT_H
 5|
 6| #include "parody.h"
 7| #include "employee.h"
 8|
 9| // ====================================
10| // Project class
11| // ====================================
12| class Project : public Persistent   {
13|     Key<ProjectNumber> projno;
14|     string name;
15|     Key<EmployeeNumber> manager;
16|     short int hours_expended;
17|     void Read();
18|     void Write();
19| public:
20|     Project(ProjectNumber prno = 0);
21|     ~Project()
22|         { SaveObject(); }
23|     const string& Name() const
```

```
24|            { return name; }
25|        ProjectNumber ProjNo() const
26|            { return projno.KeyValue(); }
27|        short int Hours() const
28|            { return hours_expended;  }
29|        void SetName(string& nm);
30|        void SetManager(EmployeeNumber mgr);
31|        void SetHours(short int hrs);
32|        void AddHours(short int hrs);
33|        // ------- user interface functions
34|        void Input();
35|        void InputName();
36|        void InputManager();
37|        void InputHours();
38|        void TryChange();
39|        void SelectChange();
40|        static Project *Get();
41|        static Project *GetExisting();
42|        static void Header(ostream& os = cout);
43|        friend ostream& operator<<(ostream&os, const Project& pr);
44| };
45|
46| inline void Project::SetName(string& nm)
47| {
48|     name = nm;
49|     ChangeObject();
50| }
51|
52| inline void Project::SetManager(EmployeeNumber mgr)
53| {
54|     manager.KeyValue() = mgr;
55|     ChangeObject();
56| }
57|
58| inline void Project::SetHours(short int hrs)
59| {
60|     hours_expended = hrs;
61|     ChangeObject();
```

```
62| }
63|
64| inline void Project::AddHours(short int hrs)
65| {
66|     hours_expended += hrs;
67|     ChangeObject();
68| }
69|
70| #endif
```

LISTING C.28 PROJECT.CPP

```
 1| // ------------- project.cpp
 2|
 3| #include <iomanip.h>
 4| #include "personel.h"
 5|
 6| // ===================================
 7| // Project class
 8| // ===================================
 9|
10| Project::Project(ProjectNumber prno) : projno(prno), manager(0)
11| {
12|     manager.Relate(&typeid(Employee));
13|     hours_expended = 0;
14|     LoadObject();
15| }
16|
17| // -------- read a persistent project object
18| void Project::Read()
19| {
20|     ProjectNumber prno;
21|     ReadObject(prno);
22|     projno.SetKeyValue(prno);
23|     ReadObject(name);
24|     EmployeeNumber mgr;
25|     ReadObject(mgr);
26|     manager.SetKeyValue(mgr);
```

```
27|        ReadObject(hours_expended);
28| }
29|
30| // -------- write a persistent project object
31| void Project::Write()
32| {
33|        WriteObject(projno.KeyValue());
34|        WriteObject(name);
35|        WriteObject(manager.KeyValue());
36|        WriteObject(hours_expended);
37| }
38|
39| // -------- display a project object header
40| void Project::Header(ostream& os)
41| {
42|        os << endl;
43|        os << "Proj# Project         Mgr#  Hours" << endl;
44|        os << "----- --------------- ----- -----" << endl;
45|        os.flush();
46| }
47|
48| // -------- display a project object
49| ostream& operator<<(ostream&os, const Project& pr)
50| {
51|        os.width(5);
52|        os << pr.projno.KeyValue();
53|        os.width(0);
54|        os << ' ';
55|        os.setf(ios::left, ios::adjustfield);
56|        os.width(15);
57|        os << pr.name.substr(0, 15);
58|        os.setf(ios::right, ios::adjustfield);
59|        os.width(0);
60|        os << ' ';
61|        os.width(5);
62|        os << pr.manager.KeyValue();
63|        os.width(0);
64|        os << ' ';
```

```
65|     os.width(5);
66|     os << pr.hours_expended;
67|     os.width(0);
68|     os << endl;
69|     os.flush();
70|     return os;
71| }
72|
73| static Project *This;
74|
75| static void ChangeName()
76| {
77|     This->InputName();
78| }
79|
80| static void ChangeMgr()
81| {
82|     This->InputManager();
83| }
84|
85| static void ChangeHours()
86| {
87|     This->InputHours();
88| }
89|
90| // ----- select a project data member to change
91| void Project::SelectChange()
92| {
93|     This = this;
94|     OneLineMenu("N-ame, M-anager, Hours",
95|             ChangeName, ChangeMgr, ChangeHours).Execute();
96| }
97|
98| // -------- project object input
99| void Project::Input()
100| {
101|     InputName();
102|     InputManager();
```

```
103|     InputHours();
104| }
105|
106| // ----- get the project number from the user
107| void Project::InputName()
108| {
109|     gui->UserInput(&name, "Name", 25);
110|     if (ObjectExists())
111|         TryChange();
112| }
113|
114| // ----- get the project manager from the user
115| void Project::InputManager()
116| {
117|     cout << "Manager: ";
118|     cout.flush();
119|     Employee *employee = Employee::GetExisting();
120|     if (employee != 0) {
121|         SetManager(employee->EmplNo());
122|         delete employee;
123|         if (ObjectExists())
124|             TryChange();
125|     }
126| }
127|
128| // ----- get the project hours expended from the user
129| void Project::InputHours()
130| {
131|     gui->UserInput(&hours_expended, "Hours expended");
132|     if (ObjectExists())
133|         TryChange();
134| }
135|
136| // ------ try to change the project object
137| void Project::TryChange()
138| {
139|     if (!ChangeObject())
140|         gui->Error("Change disallowed");
```

```
141|  }
142|
143|  // --------- get an existing project object
144|  Project *Project::GetExisting()
145|  {
146|      Project *project;
147|      if ((project = Get()) != 0) {
148|          if (project->ObjectExists())     {
149|              Header();
150|              cout << *project;
151|          }
152|          else     {
153|              gui->Error("No such project on file");
154|              delete project;
155|              project = 0;
156|          }
157|      }
158|      return project;
159|  }
160|
161|  // --------- get a project object
162|  Project *Project::Get()
163|  {
164|      ProjectNumber projno;
165|      Project *project = 0;
166|      gui->UserInput(&projno,
167|          "Enter project number (0 to ignore)");
168|      if (projno != 0)
169|          project = new Project(projno);
170|      return project;
171|  }
```

LISTING C.29 ASSIGN.H

```
1|  // ------- assign.h
2|
3|  #ifndef ASSIGN_H
4|  #define ASSIGN_H
```

```
 5|
 6| // ======================================
 7| // Assignment class
 8| // employee/project assignment
 9| // ======================================
10| class Assignment : public Persistent     {
11|     CatKey<EmployeeNumber,DepartmentNumber> assignment;
12|     short int hours_expended;
13|     void Read();
14|     void Write();
15| public:
16|     Assignment(EmployeeNumber en = 0, DepartmentNumber pn = 0);
17|     ~Assignment()
18|         { SaveObject(); }
19|     Key<EmployeeNumber>& EmplNoKey()
20|         { return assignment.Key1(); }
21|     Key<ProjectNumber>& ProjNoKey()
22|         { return assignment.Key2(); }
23|     EmployeeNumber& EmplNo()
24|         { return assignment.KeyValue1(); }
25|     ProjectNumber& ProjNo()
26|         { return assignment.KeyValue2(); }
27|     void SetEmplNo(EmployeeNumber en)
28|         { assignment.SetKeyValue1(en); }
29|     void SetProjNo(ProjectNumber pn)
30|         { assignment.SetKeyValue2(pn); }
31|     short int Hours() const
32|         { return hours_expended; }
33|     void SetHours(short int hrs);
34|     void AddHours(short int hrs);
35|     // ----- user interface functions
36|     void DetailDisplay(ostream& os = cout);
37|     void Input();
38|     static Assignment *Get();
39|     static Assignment *GetExisting();
40|     static void Header(ostream& os = cout);
41|     friend ostream& operator<<(ostream&os,const Assignment& as);
42| };
```

```
43|
44| inline void Assignment::SetHours(short int hrs)
45| {
46|     hours_expended = hrs;
47|     ChangeObject();
48| }
49| inline void Assignment::AddHours(short int hrs)
50| {
51|     hours_expended += hrs;
52|     ChangeObject();
53| }
54|
55| #endif
```

LISTING C.30 ASSIGN.CPP

```
 1| // ---------- assign.cpp
 2|
 3| #include <iomanip.h>
 4| #include "personel.h"
 5|
 6| // ------- construct from employee number, project number
 7| Assignment::Assignment(EmployeeNumber en, ProjectNumber pn) :
 8|                         assignment(en, pn)
 9| {
10|     EmplNoKey().Relate(&typeid(Employee));
11|     ProjNoKey().Relate(&typeid(Project));
12|     hours_expended = 0;
13|     LoadObject();
14| }
15|
16| // --------- read the persistent assignment object
17| void Assignment::Read()
18| {
19|     ReadObject(EmplNo());
20|     ReadObject(ProjNo());
21|     ReadObject(hours_expended);
22| }
```

```
23|
24| // --------- write the persistent assignment object
25| void Assignment::Write()
26| {
27|     WriteObject(EmplNo());
28|     WriteObject(ProjNo());
29|     WriteObject(hours_expended);
30| }
31|
32| // -------- display an assignment object header
33| void Assignment::Header(ostream& os)
34| {
35|     os << endl;
36|     os << "Empl# Employee         Proj# "
37|         "Project         Hours" << endl;
38|     os << "----- --------------- ----- "
39|         "--------------- -----" << endl;
40|     os.flush();
41| }
42|
43| // -------- display an assignment object
44| ostream& operator<<(ostream&os,const Assignment& as)
45| {
46|     os <<   "Empl #: "
47|         << setw(5)
48|         << (const_cast<Assignment&>(as)).EmplNo()
49|         << setw(0);
50|     os << " Proj #: "
51|         << setw(5)
52|         << (const_cast<Assignment&>(as)).ProjNo()
53|         << setw(0);
54|     os << " Hours: "
55|         << setw(5)
56|         << as.hours_expended
57|         << setw(0)
58|         << endl;
59|     os.flush();
60|     return os;
```

```
61|  }
62|
63|  // -------- display an assignment object's details
64|  void Assignment::DetailDisplay(ostream& os)
65|  {
66|      Employee empl(EmplNo());
67|      Project proj(ProjNo());
68|
69|      os << setw(5) << empl.EmplNo();
70|      os << setw(0);
71|      os << ' ';
72|      os.setf(ios::left, ios::adjustfield);
73|      os << setw(15) << empl.Name().substr(0, 15);
74|      os.setf(ios::right, ios::adjustfield);
75|      os << setw(0);
76|      os << ' ';
77|      os << setw(5) << proj.ProjNo();
78|      os << setw(0);
79|      os << ' ';
80|      os.setf(ios::left, ios::adjustfield);
81|      os << setw(15) << proj.Name().substr(0, 15);
82|      os.setf(ios::right, ios::adjustfield);
83|      os << setw(0);
84|      os << ' ';
85|      os << setw(5) << hours_expended << endl;
86|      os << setw(0);
87|      os.flush();
88|  }
89|
90|  // --- get an existing assignment object
91|  Assignment *Assignment::GetExisting()
92|  {
93|      Assignment *assignment;
94|      if ((assignment = Get()) != 0)  {
95|          if (assignment->ObjectExists()) {
96|              Header();
97|              assignment->DetailDisplay();
98|          }
```

```
 99|        else    {
100|            gui->Error("No such assignment on file");
101|            delete assignment;
102|            assignment = 0;
103|        }
104|    }
105|    return assignment;
106| }
107|
108| // --- get an assignment object
109| Assignment *Assignment::Get()
110| {
111|    Assignment *assignment = 0;
112|    Employee *employee = Employee::GetExisting();
113|    if (employee != 0)  {
114|        Project *project = Project::GetExisting();
115|        if (project != 0)   {
116|            assignment = new Assignment(employee->EmplNo(),
117|                        project->ProjNo());
118|            delete project;
119|        }
120|        delete employee;
121|    }
122|    return assignment;
123| }
124|
125| // -------- assignment object input
126| void Assignment::Input()
127| {
128|    gui->UserInput(&hours_expended, "Hours expended");
129|    if (ObjectExists())
130|        ChangeObject();
131| }
```

Listing C.31 MANAGER.H

```
 1| // -------------- manager.h
 2|
```

```
 3| #ifndef MANAGER_H
 4| #define MANAGER_H
 5|
 6| #include "parody.h"
 7| #include "employee.h"
 8|
 9| // =====================================
10| // Manager class
11| // =====================================
12| class Manager : public Employee {
13|     Money bonus;
14|     void Read();
15|     void Write();
16| public:
17|     Manager(EmployeeNumber en = 0);
18|     ~Manager();
19|     // ----- user interface functions
20|     static Manager *Get();
21|     void Input();
22|     friend ostream& operator<<(ostream&os, const Manager& mgr);
23| };
24|
25| #endif
```

LISTING C.32 MANAGER.CPP

```
 1| // ---- manager.cpp
 2|
 3| #include "personel.h"
 4|
 5| Manager::Manager(EmployeeNumber en) : Employee(-1)
 6| {
 7|     SetEmplNo(en);
 8|     LoadObject();
 9| }
10|
11| Manager::~Manager()
12| {
```

```
13|      SaveObject();
14|      SetEmplNo(-1);
15| }
16|
17| void Manager::Read()
18| {
19|      Employee::Read();
20|      ReadObject(bonus);
21| }
22|
23| void Manager::Write()
24| {
25|      Employee::Write();
26|      WriteObject(bonus);
27| }
28|
29| // --------- get an employee object
30| Manager *Manager::Get()
31| {
32|      EmployeeNumber emplno;
33|      Manager *manager = 0;
34|      gui->UserInput(&emplno,
35|          "Enter manager's employee number (0 to ignore)");
36|      if (emplno != 0)
37|          manager = new Manager(emplno);
38|      return manager;
39| }
40|
41| void Manager::Input()
42| {
43|      Employee::Input();
44|      gui->UserInput(&bonus, "Bonus");
45| }
46|
47| // ---------- display a manager object
48| ostream& operator<<(ostream&os, const Manager& mgr)
49| {
50|      os << static_cast<const Employee&>(mgr)
```

```
51|           << " --- Bonus: " << mgr.bonus << endl;
52|      os.flush();
53|      return os;
54| }
```

Listing C.33 PROJVIEW.CPP

```
 1| // ----- projview.cpp
 2|
 3| // -------------------------------------------------------
 4| // View two projects stored in the PERSONEL database
 5| // -------------------------------------------------------
 6|
 7| #include "personel.h"
 8|
 9| GUI *gui;
10|
11| int main()
12| {
13|      gui = new GUI;
14|      Parody *personnel = new Parody("PERSONEL");
15|
16|      Project *proj1, *proj2;
17|
18|      try
19|      {
20|          proj1 = Project::Get();
21|          proj2 = Project::Get();
22|      }
23|      catch(Persistent *obj)
24|      {
25|          gui->Error("You are viewing the same project twice");
26|          proj2 = static_cast<Project*>(obj);
27|      }
28|
29|      Project::Header();
30|      if (proj1->ObjectExists())
31|          cout << *proj1;
```

```
32|     if (proj2->ObjectExists())
33|         cout << *proj2;
34|
35|     Persistent::Destroy(proj1);
36|     Persistent::Destroy(proj2);
37|
38|     gui->AnyKey();
39|
40|     delete personnel;
41|     delete gui;
42|
43|     return 0;
44| }
```

Listing C.34 INDEX.CPP

```
 1| // ---------- index.cpp
 2|
 3| // =====================================
 4| // A program to rebuild the indexes
 5| // for a specific PARODY database
 6| // =====================================
 7| #include <stdio.h>
 8| #include "personel.h"    // application-specific header
 9|
10| #define dbname "PERSONEL"
11| GUI *gui;
12|
13| void BuildIndex()
14| {
15|     remove(dbname ".ndx");  // delete old index file
16|     Parody *personnel = new Parody(dbname);
17|     ObjectHeader objhdr;
18|
19|     // ---- empty objects to declare relationships
20|     {
21|         Employee empl;
22|         Department dept;
```

```
23|            Project proj;
24|            Assignment assgn;
25|    }
26|
27|    const ClassID EMPLOYEE =
28|        personnel->GetClassID(typeid(Employee).name());
29|    const ClassID DEPARTMENT =
30|        personnel->GetClassID(typeid(Department).name());
31|    const ClassID PROJECT =
32|        personnel->GetClassID(typeid(Project).name());
33|    const ClassID ASSIGNMENT =
34|        personnel->GetClassID(typeid(Assignment).name());
35|
36|    NodeNbr nd = 1;
37|    NodeNbr end = personnel->datafile.HighestNode();
38|    // ------- scan Parody nodes
39|    while (nd <= end)   {
40|        // --- read the object header for this node
41|        personnel->GetObjectHeader(nd, objhdr);
42|        // --- object relative node# 0 is 1st node of object
43|        if (objhdr.ndnbr == 0) {
44|            // --- tell Parody to rebuild indexes this object
45|            personnel->RebuildIndexes(nd);
46|            // ----- rebuild depending on class type
47|            if (objhdr.classid == EMPLOYEE) {
48|                Employee empl;
49|                cout << "Empl: " << empl;
50|            }
51|            else if (objhdr.classid == DEPARTMENT)  {
52|                Department dept;
53|                cout << "Dept: " << dept;
54|            }
55|            else if (objhdr.classid == PROJECT) {
56|                Project proj;
57|                cout << "Proj: " << proj;
58|            }
59|            else if (objhdr.classid == ASSIGNMENT)  {
60|                Assignment assgn;
```

```
61|                    cout << "Asgn: " << assgn;
62|                }
63|            }
64|            nd++;
65|        }
66|        delete personnel;
67| }
68|
69| int main()
70| {
71|     BuildIndex();
72|     return 0;
73| }
```

LISTING C.35 FAMILY.H

```
1| // ---- family.h
2|
3| #include "parody.h"
4| #include "date.h"
5|
6| enum Sex { unknown, male, female };
7| const int namelen = 18;
8|
9| class FamilyMember : public Persistent  {
10|     Key<string> name;
11|     Sex sex;
12|     Date birthdate;
13|     Date deathdate;
14|     Reference<FamilyMember> mother;
15|     Reference<FamilyMember> father;
16|     void Read();
17|     void Write();
18| public:
19|     FamilyMember(const string& nm = string('\0', namelen));
20|     FamilyMember(ObjAddr oa) : name("")
21|         { LoadObject(oa); }
22|     ~FamilyMember()
```

```
23|          { SaveObject(); }
24|      string& Name()
25|          { return name.KeyValue(); }
26|      void SetName(const string& nm)
27|          { name.SetKeyValue(nm); }
28|      Sex GetSex()
29|          { return sex; }
30|      void SetSex(Sex sx);
31|      bool isMale()
32|          { return sex == male; }
33|      bool isFemale()
34|          { return sex == female; }
35|      const Date& BirthDate() const
36|          { return birthdate; }
37|      const Date& DeathDate() const
38|          { return deathdate; }
39|      void SetBirthDate(const Date& dt)
40|          { birthdate = dt; }
41|      void SetDeathDate(const Date& dt)
42|          { deathdate = dt; }
43|      void SetMother(FamilyMember *mth)
44|          { if (mth->sex == female) mother = *mth; }
45|      void SetFather(FamilyMember *fth)
46|          { if (fth->sex == male) father = *fth; }
47|      static void Header(ostream& os = cout);
48|      friend ostream&operator<<(ostream&os,FamilyMember&f);
49| };
```

LISTING C.36 FAMILY.CPP

```
1| // ------ family.cpp
2|
3| #include "family.h"
4|
5| // -------------------------------------
6| // FamilyMember class member functions
7| // -------------------------------------
8|
9| FamilyMember::FamilyMember(const string& nm) : name(nm)
```

```
10|  {
11|      sex = static_cast<Sex>(0);
12|      LoadObject();
13|  }
14|
15|  void FamilyMember::Read()
16|  {
17|      string nm;
18|      ReadObject(nm);
19|      name.SetKeyValue(nm);
20|      ReadObject(sex);
21|      ReadObject(birthdate);
22|      ReadObject(deathdate);
23|      mother.ReadObject();
24|      father.ReadObject();
25|  }
26|
27|  void FamilyMember::Write()
28|  {
29|      WriteObject(name.KeyValue());
30|      WriteObject(sex);
31|      WriteObject(birthdate);
32|      WriteObject(deathdate);
33|      mother.WriteObject();
34|      father.WriteObject();
35|  }
36|
37|  void FamilyMember::Header(ostream& os)
38|  {
39|      os << "Name             Sex  Born     Died      "
40|          "Mother            Father" << endl;
41|      os << "----------------- --- -------- -------- "
42|          "----------------- -----------------" << endl;
43|  }
44|
45|  static void DisplayName(ostream& os, FamilyMember *mbr)
46|  {
47|      os.width(namelen+1);
48|      os.setf(ios::left);
```

```
49|      if (mbr == 0)
50|          os << " ";
51|      else
52|          os << mbr->Name();
53| }
54|
55| ostream& operator<<(ostream& os,FamilyMember& fm)
56| {
57|      os.width(namelen);
58|      os.setf(ios::left);
59|      os << fm.Name();
60|      os << ' ';
61|      if (fm.isMale())
62|          cout << 'M';
63|      else if (fm.isFemale())
64|          cout << 'F';
65|      else
66|          cout << ' ';
67|      os << "   ";
68|      os << fm.birthdate;
69|      os << ' ';
70|      os << fm.deathdate;
71|      os << ' ';
72|      DisplayName(os, fm.mother.obj);
73|      DisplayName(os, fm.father.obj);
74|      os << endl;
75|      return os;
76| }
77|
78| void FamilyMember::SetSex(Sex sx)
79| {
80|      if (sx == unknown || sx == male || sx == female)
81|          sex = sx;
82| }
```

LISTING C.37 FAMTREE.CPP

```
1| // ----- famtree.cpp
2|
```

```
 3| #include "family.h"
 4| #include "gui.h"
 5|
 6| Parody *ftree;
 7| GUI *gui;
 8| static FamilyMember *fm;
 9| static FamilyMember *fml;
10| static short linect = 0;
11| static short selected;
12| static bool quitting;
13|
14| static void AddRecord();
15| static void ListRecords();
16| static void ViewRecord();
17| static void ChangeSex();
18| static void ChangeBirthDate();
19| static void ChangeDeathDate();
20| static void ChangeRcd();
21| static void DeleteRcd();
22| static void ChangeName();
23| static void ChangeParent();
24| static void ChangeDates();
25| static void ChangeMother();
26| static void ChangeFather();
27| static void Marriages();
28| static void SelectMember();
29| static FamilyMember *GetListedMember(Sex sx = unknown);
30|
31| int main()
32| {
33|     gui = new GUI;
34|     ftree = new Parody("FAMILY");
35|
36|     ScreenMenu("Family Tree",
37|             "Add family members",   AddRecord,
38|             "List family members",  ListRecords,
39|             "View a family member", ViewRecord,
40|             NULL).Execute();
41|     gui->ClearScreen();
```

```
42|     delete ftree;
43|     delete gui;
44|     return 0;
45| }
46|
47| static void More()
48| {
49|     // --- intentionally empty
50| }
51|
52| static void Quit()
53| {
54|     quitting = true;
55| }
56|
57| static void ReadName(string& nm)
58| {
59|     gui->UserInput(&nm, "Name", 80);
60|     nm.resize(namelen);
61| }
62|
63| static FamilyMember *GetExistingMember()
64| {
65|     FamilyMember *fmbr;
66|     string name;
67|     ReadName(name);
68|     try {
69|         fmbr = new FamilyMember(name);
70|         if (!fmbr->ObjectExists())  {
71|             Persistent::Destroy(fmbr);
72|             fmbr = 0;
73|         }
74|     }
75|     catch (Persistent *obj) {
76|         fmbr = static_cast<FamilyMember*>(obj);
77|     }
78|     return fmbr;
79| }
```

```
 80|
 81| static void AddRecord()
 82| {
 83|     string name;
 84|     ReadName(name);
 85|     fm = new FamilyMember(name);
 86|     if (fm->ObjectExists())
 87|         gui->Error("Name is already used");
 88|     else    {
 89|         ChangeSex();
 90|         ChangeBirthDate();
 91|         ChangeDeathDate();
 92|         FamilyMember::Header();
 93|         cout << *fm;
 94|         if (gui->YesNo("Add record"))
 95|             if (!fm->AddObject())
 96|                 gui->Error("Cannot add");
 97|     }
 98|     Persistent::Destroy(fm);
 99|     fm = 0;
100| }
101|
102| static void ListRecords()
103| {
104|     FamilyMember::Header();
105|     FamilyMember fm;
106|     fm.FirstObject();
107|     while (fm.ObjectExists())   {
108|         cout << fm;
109|         fm.NextObject();
110|     }
111|     gui->AnyKey();
112| }
113|
114| static void ViewRecord()
115| {
116|     if ((fm = GetExistingMember()) == 0)
117|         fm = GetListedMember();
```

```
118|     if (fm != 0)     {
119|         FamilyMember::Header();
120|         cout << *fm;
121|         OneLineMenu("C-hange, D-elete, Q-uit",
122|             ChangeRcd, DeleteRcd, Quit).Execute();
123|         Persistent::Destroy(fm);
124|         fm = 0;
125|     }
126| }
127|
128| static void ChangeRcd()
129| {
130|     OneLineMenu("N-ame, S-ex, D-ates, P-arent, Q-uit",
131|                     ChangeName,
132|                     ChangeSex,
133|                     ChangeDates,
134|                     ChangeParent,
135|                     Quit).Execute();
136|     if (!fm->ChangeObject())
137|         gui->Error("Cannot change");
138|     else    {
139|         FamilyMember::Header();
140|         cout << *fm;
141|         gui->AnyKey();
142|     }
143| }
144|
145| static void ChangeName()
146| {
147|     string name;
148|     ReadName(name);
149|     fm->SetName(name);
150| }
151|
152| static void ChangeSex()
153| {
154|     char sex = 0;
155|     while (sex != 'm' && sex != 'f')     {
```

```
156|          gui->UserInput(&sex, "Sex");
157|          if (sex == ESC)
158|              return;
159|          cout << '\b' << sex;
160|      }
161|      fm->SetSex(sex == 'm' ? male : female);
162| }
163|
164| static void ChangeDates()
165| {
166|      OneLineMenu("B-irth, D-eath, Q-uit",
167|          ChangeBirthDate,ChangeDeathDate,Quit).Execute();
168| }
169|
170| static void ChangeBirthDate()
171| {
172|      Date dt;
173|      gui->UserInput(&dt, "Date of birth");
174|      fm->SetBirthDate(dt);
175| }
176|
177| static void ChangeDeathDate()
178| {
179|      Date dt;
180|      gui->UserInput(&dt, "Date of death");
181|      fm->SetDeathDate(dt);
182| }
183|
184| static void ChangeParent()
185| {
186|      OneLineMenu("M-other, F-ather, Q-uit",
187|          ChangeMother,ChangeFather,Quit).Execute();
188| }
189|
190| static void SelectMember()
191| {
192|      short seln;
193|      gui->UserInput(&seln, "Enter member #");
```

```
194|    if (seln < 1 || seln > linect)
195|        gui->Error("Invalid selection");
196|    else    {
197|        while (seln++ < linect+1)   {
198|            try {
199|                fml->PreviousObject();
200|            }
201|            catch (Persistent* obj) {
202|                Persistent::Destroy(obj);
203|                fml->PreviousObject();
204|            }
205|        }
206|        selected = true;
207|    }
208| }
209|
210| static FamilyMember *GetListedMember(Sex sx)
211| {
212|    gui->ClearScreen();
213|    fml = new FamilyMember;
214|    try {
215|        fml->CurrentObject();
216|    }
217|    catch (Persistent* obj) {
218|        Persistent::Destroy(obj);
219|        fml->NextObject();
220|    }
221|
222|    linect = 0;
223|    selected = 0;
224|    quitting = false;
225|    while (fml->ObjectExists()) {
226|        if (sx == unknown || sx == fml->GetSex())   {
227|            cout.width(5);
228|            cout << ++linect << ": " << fml->Name() << endl;
229|        }
230|        try {
231|            fml->NextObject();
```

```
232|            }
233|         catch (Persistent* obj) {
234|             Persistent::Destroy(obj);
235|             fml->NextObject();
236|         }
237|         if (linect == SCREENHEIGHT-3 || !fml->ObjectExists()) {
238|             OneLineMenu("M-ore, S-elect, Q-uit",
239|                 More,SelectMember,Quit).Execute();
240|             if (quitting || selected != 0)
241|                 break;
242|         }
243|     }
244|     if (!selected)  {
245|         Persistent::Destroy(fml);
246|         fml = 0;
247|     }
248|     return fml;
249| }
250|
251| static void ChangeMother()
252| {
253|     FamilyMember *mth = 0;
254|     if ((mth = GetExistingMember()) == 0)
255|         mth = GetListedMember();
256|     if (mth != 0)   {
257|         if (mth == fm)
258|             gui->Error("Cannot be one's own mother");
259|         else if (mth->GetSex() != female)
260|             gui->Error("Mother must be female");
261|         else
262|             fm->SetMother(mth);
263|         Persistent::Destroy(mth);
264|     }
265| }
266|
267| static void ChangeFather()
268| {
269|     FamilyMember *fth = 0;
```

```
270|    if ((fth = GetExistingMember()) == 0)
271|        fth = GetListedMember();
272|    if (fth != 0)    {
273|        if (fth == fm)
274|            gui->Error("Cannot be one's own father");
275|        else if (fth->GetSex() != male)
276|            gui->Error("Father must be male");
277|        else
278|            fm->SetFather(fth);
279|        Persistent::Destroy(fth);
280|    }
281| }
282|
283| static void DeleteRcd()
284| {
285|    if (gui->YesNo("Delete family member"))
286|        if (!fm->DeleteObject())
287|            gui->Error("Cannot delete");
288| }
```

Glossary

This glossary defines terms that have specific meaning in the realms of C++, object-oriented programming, and database management. To help you separate the meanings, the definitions are prefixed with (OOP) for object-oriented programming terms, (C++) for terms that apply specifically to the C++ language, and (DB) for terms related to databases and database management.

abstract base class—(OOP) A class definition that will always be a base class for other classes to be derived from. No specific objects of the base class will be declared by the program. A C++ abstract base class is one that has a pure virtual function, a protected constructor, or a protected destructor.

abstract data type—(OOP) Also called "ADT." A user-defined data type built as a C++ class. The details of implementation are not necessarily a part of the ADT. See also "primitive data type" and "concrete data type."

abstraction—(OOP) Defining an abstract data type by designing a class.

anonymous object—(C++) An internal, temporary object created by the compiler.

argument—(C++) The value passed to a function. Its type must match that of the function's corresponding parameter as declared in the function's prototype. See also "parameter."

base class—(OOP) A class from which other classes derive characteristics. All the characteristics of the base class are inherited by the derived class. Also called "superclass."

catalog—(DB) The file of database format and rules statements that constitute the definition of the database schema.

child record—(DB) A record in a database that is related to higher records in the database. The higher records are *parent* records.

class—(OOP) A user-defined data type that may consist of data members and member functions.

class hierarchy—(OOP) A system of base and derived classes.

column—(DB) A data element field in a relational database table of rows and columns. A column represents all the instances of the same data element in the file/table.

concrete data type—A user-defined or library data type complete with interface and implementation. The CDT is meant to be instantiated as an object and is not intended solely to be derived from.

constructor—(C++) The function executed by the compiler when the program declares an instance of a class. See also "destructor."

data definition language—(DB) The language that describes the schema for a database.

data element—(DB) A single entity of data, usually one item of a data type. Collections of data elements form files in a database.

data manipulation language—(DB) The language that application programs use to store, retrieve, and maintain data in a database. Sometimes referred to by the less-specific term "application program interface."

data member—(C++) A data component of a class. It may be any valid data type, including class objects and references.

database—(DB) A collection of data files loosely integrated to support a common application.

database management system—(DB) General-purpose systems software that manages the storage and retrieval of data in a database.

declaration—(C++) As opposed to "definition." A declaration is the statement that defines the format of a type. A declaration reserves no memory.

definition—(C++) As opposed to "declaration." A definition is the statement that declares the existence of an object. A definition reserves memory.

derived class—(OOP) A class that inherits some of its characteristics from a base class. Also called a "subclass."

destructor—(C++) The function executed by the compiler when a declared instance of a class goes out of scope. See also "constructor."

domain—(DB) A column in a relational database that adheres to specified rules in the schema with respect to content and format. Similar to a "data element" except that the catalog rules restrict the allowable data values.

encapsulation—(OOP) The activity of defining a class with its data members and member functions encapsulated into the definition. Encapsulation implies an implementation, which is hidden from the class user, and an interface, which is visible to the class user.

extraction operator—(C++) The overloaded >> operator that reads (extracts) values from an input stream. See also "insertion operator."

file—(DB) A collection of records of a common format in a database.

free store—(C++) The C++ heap. A dynamic memory pool that programs use to allocate and release temporary memory buffers.

friend—(C++) A function that has access to the private members of a class but that is not a member function of that class. The class definition declares the function to be a friend.

hierarchical data model—(DB) A database of parent and child files. Each record in a parent file may have multiple child records. Each record in a child file may have only one parent record. A child file may be parent to lower child files, forming a multiple-level hierarchy. See also "network data model" and "relational data model."

hierarchy—(OOP) See "class hierarchy."

inheritance—(OOP) The ability for one class to inherit the characteristics of another. The inherited class is said to be derived from the base class. Also called "subclassing."

implementation—(OOP) The private members of a class. The implementation defines the details of how the class implements the behavior of the abstract base type. See also "interface."

index—(DB) The file that associates key data values with the records that they index.

inline function—(C++) A function that the compiler compiles as inline code every time the function is called.

insertion operator—(C++) The overloaded << operator that writes (inserts) values to an output stream. See also "extraction operator."

instantiate—(OOP) Declare an object of a data type, usually a class.

interface—(OOP) The public members of a class, which define the class user's interface to the class's data and its behavior. Usually implemented as member functions. See also "implementation."

intrinsic data type—(OOP) See "primitive data type."

join—(DB) A relational database operator that creates a new table by logically joining two other tables on the basis of common values in a common column.

key—(DB) A data element used to index a record in a database.

linkage specification—(C++) Notation that tells the C++ compiler that a function was or is to be compiled with the linkage conventions of another language.

manipulator—(C++) A value that a program sends to a stream to tell the stream to modify one of its modes.

member—(C++) A component of a class, either a data member or a member function.

member function—(C++) A function component of a class, also called a "method." A member function may be virtual.

message—(OOP) A message is the invocation of a class's member function in the name of a declared object of the class. The message is said to be sent to the object to tell it to perform its function. The message includes the function call and the arguments that accompany it.

method—(OOP) A method in C++ is a member function of a class. Programs send messages to objects by invoking methods.

multiple inheritance—(OOP) The ability for a derived class to inherit the characteristics of more than one base class.

network data model—(DB) A database of parent and child files. Each record in a parent file may have multiple child records. Each record in a child file may have multiple parent records. A child file may be a parent to lower child files, forming a multiple-level network. See also "hierarchical data model" and "relational data model."

object—(OOP) A declared instance of a data type including standard C++ data types as well as objects of classes.

object database—(OOP) A collection of persistent objects.

overloaded function—(C++) A function that has the same name as one or more other functions but that has a different parameter list. The compiler selects which function to call based on the data types and number of arguments in the call.

overloaded operator—(C++) A function that executes when a C++ operator is seen in a defined context with respect to a class object.

overriding function—(C++) A function in a derived class that has the same name, return type, and parameter list as a function in the base class. The compiler calls the overriding function when the program calls that function in the name of an object of the derived class. If the function in the base class is "virtual," the compiler calls the derived class's function even when the call is through a pointer or reference to the base class. See also "pure virtual function."

parameter—(C++) The declaration of a data item that a function expects to be passed to it. This declaration includes the item's type and name and appears in the function's declaration block at the beginning of the function. When the parameter appears in the function's prototype, the parameter's name may be omitted. See "argument" and "prototype."

parameter list—(C++) The list of parameter types and names in a function declaration block. Also the same list, which may exclude the names, in a function prototype.

parent record—(DB) A record in a database that is related to lower records in the database. The lower records are "child" records.

persistence—(OOP) The ability of an object to succeed its creator and to subsequently exist in a space other than the space in which it was created.

persistent object—(OOP) An object that exhibits persistence.

polymorphism—(OOP) The ability for methods in a class hierarchy to exhibit different behavior for the same message depending on the type of the object for which the method is invoked and without regard to the class type of the reference to the object.

primary key—(DB) The key data value that uniquely identifies a record in a database file. See also "secondary key."

primitive data type—(OOP) A data type known to the compiler. Primitive data types in C++ are *char, int, float, double,* and *pointer.* The integer types may be further qualified as long, short, and unsigned. All types may be organized into arrays of like types and structures and unions of varying types. Also called "intrinsic data types."

private class members—(C++) Members of a class for which access is granted only to the class's member functions and to friend functions of the class.

project—(DB) A relational database operator that creates a different view of a table from a subset of its columns. See also "select" and "join."

protected class members—(C++) Members of a class that are private except to member functions of derived classes.

prototype—(C++) The definition of a function's name, return type, and parameter list.

public class members—(C++) Members of a class to which access is granted to all functions within the scope of an object of the class.

pure virtual function—(C++) A virtual function in a base class that must have a matching function in a derived class. A program may not declare an instance of a class that has a pure virtual function. A program may not declare an instance of a derived class if that derived class has not provided an overriding function for each pure virtual function in the base.

query—(DB) A process that creates a new view of the contents of a relational database by applying and combining the select, project, and join operators. The new view is presented as another table.

record—(DB) An aggregate of data elements that form to support one functional aspect of a database's application. A collection of records of common format forms a file.

reference—(C++) A variable name that is an alias for another variable.

relation—(DB) A relational database term that is often interchanged with *file* and *table*, although *relation* does not imply any physical implementation.

relational data model—(DB) A representation of data as tables of rows and columns. Any relationships between tables are formed by common values in common columns. See also "hierarchical data model" and "network data model."

repeating group—(DB) An array with fixed or variable dimension of similar data elements in a database record. Not permitted in a relational database.

row—(DB) Relational database term that is analogous to *record* in traditional databases.

schema—(DB) The formal definition of the format of a database. The schema defines the files, their format, and their relationships.

secondary key—(DB) A key data value that indexes a file on other than its primary key. The value of a secondary key does not have to be unique. Multiple records can have the same value. When a secondary key is the primary key of another file, the two files have a many-to-one relationship.

select—(DB) A relational database operator that selects rows from a table based on the criteria of a query. See also "project" and "join."

stream—(C++) A category of character-oriented data files or devices where the data characters exist in an input or output stream.

subclass—(OOP) See "derived class."

subclassing—(OOP) See "inheritance."

superclass—(OOP) See "base class."

table—(DB) In a relational database, a file of rows and columns.

this—(C++) A pointer that exists in all nonstatic member functions. The pointer is a pointer to an object of the class. It points to the object for which the function is being executed.

tuple—(DB) A relational database term that refers to a particular row in a table of rows and columns. Analogous to "record" in traditional databases and "object" in object databases.

type—(OOP) The type of a program constant or variable, which can be of a primitive or an abstract data type.

type conversion—(C++) The conversion of one type to another. The compiler has built-in type conversions, and a class may define its own conversions for converting from an object of the class to another type and from another type to an object of the class.

type-safe linkage—(C++) A technique that ensures that functions and function calls in separately compiled program modules use consistent parameter lists.

view—(DB) A user's perception of the data in a database, which may or may not coincide with the actual data representation. A view is prepared for the user by a program, typically a query program.

virtual function—(C++) A member function in a class from which other classes may be derived. If the derived class has a function with the same name and parameter list, the derived class's function is always executed for objects of the derived class. See also "pure virtual function" and "overriding function."

Index

M

make 189

makefile 187, 188, 191

MakeKey 114

Manager class 178

manager.cpp 175, 178

manager.h 175, 178

manipulator 392

many-to-many relationship 35, 95, 97

MAXCOMMANDS 196

McCreight, E. 218

member 393

member function 20, 393

memory model 189

menus 163, 166

message 13, 17, 393

method 13, 17, 98, 393

Microsoft C++ 7

MODEL macro 189

Money class 158, 161, 204

money.cpp 158, 161

money.h 158, 161

Month 199

MS-DOS 6, 106

multiple inheritance 2, 13, 22, 393

MustDestroy exception 212

N

navigating the database 73, 142, 180

navigational access 58, 142

network 2

network data model 32, 393

NextEntry 203

NextObject 74, 144, 146, 149, 180, 181, 208

NoDatabase exception 212

Node class 104, 214

node header block 220

node threads 216

node.h 196, 214

NodeFile class 104

nodelength 196

NodeNbr 196, 214, 220

nodes 214

nodes, allocating 215

nodes, deleting 215

Disk Instructions

Installing PARODY II and the Example Programs
To install:

1. Log onto the source diskette drive (a: or b:)
2. Enter this command at the DOS or OS/2 command line:

```
install c:\parody2
```

Where c: is the destination drive and \parody2 is the subdirectory.